Praise for *Healthcare Disrupted*

"A confluence of scientific, economic, social, and technological forces is compelling changes throughout the healthcare industry. *Healthcare Disrupted* offers an in-depth examination of the current state of this industry and of strategies that will emerge to maximize value for providers, payers, industry, and—most importantly—patients. I particularly appreciated the descriptions of the four business models likely to emerge: Lean Innovators, Around-the-Patient Innovators, Value Innovators, and New Health Digitals. *Healthcare Disrupted* is an inspirational call-to-action for everyone associated with healthcare, especially the innovators who will develop the next generation of therapeutics, diagnostics, and devices."

—Bob Horvitz, Ph.D., David H. Koch Professor of Biology, MIT; Nobel Prize in Physiology or Medicine

"During a time of tremendous change and uncertainty, *Healthcare Disrupted* gives executives a framework and language to determine how they will evolve their products, services, and strategies to flourish in a increasingly value-based healthcare system. Using a powerful mix of real world examples and unanswered questions, Elton and O'Riordan lead you to see that 'no action' is not an option—and push you to answer the most important question: 'What is your role in this digitally driven change and how can your firm can gain competitive advantage and lead?'"

—David Epstein, Division Head, Novartis Pharmaceuticals

"In the rough and tumble shakeout of the healthcare industry, the search for new business models and an understanding of emerging models is critical for patient outcomes to catch up with scientific progress. Elton and O'Riordan in their new book bring some great new insights into this arena that have broad implications for thinking about healthcare globally."

—Trevor Mundel, M.D. and Ph.D., President of Global Health at the Bill & Melinda Gates Foundation

"In a time of dizzying change across all fronts: from biology, to delivery, to the use of big data, *Health Disrupted* captures the impact of these forces and thoughtfully develops new approaches to value creation in the healthcare industry. A must-read for those who strive to capitalize on change and reinvent the industry."

—Deborah Dunsire, M.D., President and CEO,
FORUM Pharmaceuticals

"While no one can definitively say how healthcare will look 10 years from now, Elton and O'Riordan go a long way to provide insights into the changes underway and the likely innovations that will characterize the future of healthcare. A good read for anyone worried about tomorrow's healthcare and what can be done now to prepare for that future."

—Cuong Do, Executive Vice President,
Global Strategy, Samsung

This book comes at a perfect time, as science and technology have never been so rich to address the disrupted healthcare environment. Anyone active in healthcare, any patient, and any future patient (that means all of us!) should read this book and reflect on how they contribute to build a system aligned on delivering superior value to patients by innovation, incentives, systems, and communications.

—Roch Doliveux, Honorary CEO, UCB

"*Healthcare Disrupted* reveals how seismic shifts in healthcare delivery will significantly improve patient and economic outcomes. It gives companies options for how to adapt and stay relevant in the new age of digital medicine and outlines four new business models that can drive growth and performance. This is a ground-breaking book."

—Clive A. Meanwell, M.D. and Ph.D., CEO, The Medicines Company

HEALTHCARE
DISRUPTED

Next Generation Business Models and Strategies

JEFF ELTON and ANNE O'RIORDAN

WILEY

Cover image: © Oleksiy Maksymenko/Getty Images
Cover design: Wiley

Published by John Wiley & Sons, Inc., Hoboken, New Jersey.
Published simultaneously in Canada.

For general information about our other products and services, please contact our Customer Care Department within the United States at (800) 762–2974, outside the United States at (317) 572–3993 or fax (317) 572–4002.

Wiley publishes in a variety of print and electronic formats and by print-on-demand. Some material included with standard print versions of this book may not be included in e-books or in print-on-demand. If this book refers to media such as a CD or DVD that is not included in the version you purchased, you may download this material at http://booksupport.wiley.com. For more information about Wiley products, visit www.wiley.com.

Library of Congress Cataloging-in-Publication Data:

Names: Elton, Jeff, author. | O'Riordan, Anne, author.
Title: Healthcare disrupted: next generation business models and strategies / Jeff Elton and Anne O'Riordan.
  Description: Hoboken, New Jersey: John Wiley & Sons, Inc. [2016], | Includes index.
  Identifiers: LCCN 2015041521 (print) | LCCN 2015042198 (ebook) |
  ISBN 9781119171881 (cloth: alk. paper) | ISBN 9781119171898 (epdf) |
  ISBN 9781119171904 (epub)
  Subjects: | MESH: Health Care Sector--trends. | Medical Informatics--trends.
| Models, Economic. | Organizational Innovation. | Quality Improvement--trends.
  Classification: LCC RA971.3 (print) | LCC RA971.3 (ebook) | NLM W 74.1 | DDC
362.1068–dc23
LC record available at http://lccn.loc.gov/2015041521

Printed in the United States of America

10 9 8 7 6 5 4 3 2 1

Contents

Preface

There are more than 7 billion people in the world, and the population is aging in almost every major region. Healthcare costs in most countries are rising faster than gross domestic product (GDP). Prevailing approaches to healthcare reward volume (of sales, of procedures, of patients treated) over positive outcomes or positive changes to health system performance. At the same time, awareness of the importance of health to national economic productivity and long-run performance around the world has never been so acute. Governments, institutions, companies, and individuals are feeling pressure to redress the balance of health, responsibility, and outcomes and to ensure that all constituents play a productive part.

And we have a tremendously exciting opportunity.

In the coming 3, 5, or 10 years, we can dramatically improve patient care around the world. Through profound commitments to collaboration and disruption along nontraditional lines, we can improve the standard of care on a global scale. New targeted therapeutics, smart diagnostics, advanced informatics, and digital technologies promise to redefine healthcare as less reactive and dependent on traditional facilities and acute interventions, and rather as proactive management of health. Rapidly developing economies and countries will meet critical healthcare needs more efficiently and effectively. More people will stay healthy for longer periods of time, avoiding hospital stays and readmissions at a much greater rate. Well-developed healthcare systems will definitively move toward the practice of precision medicine, where the focus is truly on the patient, and where a variety of forms of information and evidence are brought to bear in real time to tailor treatment approaches. These systems will also raise expectations—and standards—around the world of what healthcare can and should be.

Seismic shifts in the healthcare industry have already begun. For the first time, we are seeing large-scale collaboration across industry boundaries. Providers, pharmaceutical companies, medical device organizations, payers, nurses, caregivers, health care personnel (HCP), patients, citizens, wellness companies, and technology disrupters are joining forces in new and innovative ways—all centered around driving the health and wellness outcomes that are critical for long-term economic sustainability. And positive catalysts abound, including advances in science, the evolution and availability of genomic, health, and lifestyle data, and the abundance of technology solutions coming to the market every day to help us monitor, measure, and adjust our habits to improve our health and the outcomes of treatment.

In fact, a confluence of forces—economic, social, and technological— are compelling changes to everyone's "job" in healthcare in the years to come: individuals, health providers, health insurers, policy makers, regulators, therapeutics innovators, app developers, digital infrastructure providers, and more, with no exceptions.

The question is: What "whole" will we make of all of these changes? Right now, we are seeing the outlines of new, very performance- and value-focused business and operating models form. These emerging models are more than promising; healthcare with higher value and impact is at stake—healthcare that can better contribute to the quality of patients' lives, and the productivity of companies and countries. But their success—analogous to thriving and leading through the digital disruptions that have reshaped far-flung industries such as media, entertainment, financial services, insurance, photography, telecommunications, transportation, and lodging—isn't guaranteed.

To harness their potential, executives, boards, and industry leaders will need to understand the implied redefinitions of markets, the evolution of services-centric approaches, and the parameters of new outcomes- and value-centric performance models, as well as the fundamental impacts of these models on their organizations.

We wrote this book to recognize and acknowledge this catalytic moment, and to predict and discuss the potential business models that can and should evolve. We realize that no models have yet been carved in stone—and for many, the delineation lines drawn in the new business models will not be as clear and succinct as those we lay out in the coming chapters. But with a more comprehensive grasp of the fast-changing context in which they work, and the capabilities they need to excel, we believe that readers will be able to develop strong, forward-thinking, and flexible strategies for their organizations that will enable them to transform (or invent) themselves effectively. We believe they will be able to become leaders of a new era in healthcare, and vastly improve an ecosystem that is only just beginning to take shape. In doing so, they will set the new foundations of healthcare; as these foundations solidify, they will become the vanguard on which all other aspects of the industry will build.

Our primary focus throughout this book is the evolution necessary in the pharmaceutical, biopharmaceutical, device, and diagnostics fields and the new digital healthcare disruptors that are propelling change and paving the way for entirely new operating models. We recognize that all other players—providers, payers, HCPs, and other healthcare-related institutions throughout the world—also need to change. Through the lens of the organizations featured in this book, other stakeholders in the world of healthcare will also be able to see their own roles and choices more clearly.

In other words, we purposefully include a broad view: In the first part of the book, Chapters 1 and 2, we describe the tsunami of change going on in the sector as a whole and outline the most important strategic questions facing all types of participants in the sector. In Part II, we describe four distinct business models that are coming into focus in the pharmaceutical, biopharmaceutical, medical device, and digital health technologies fields—the result of legacy companies' transformative efforts, start-up ventures, and also the expansion of established, successful businesses from other fields that now see healthcare as a very attractive new market. In the final chapters, we provide a new framework for industry partnerships and collaboration, the new requirements of value-centric solutions, and how to build the talent and performance systems for these new outcomes and value-focused organizations. We close with a view to the future, reconsidering the basis for how valuations have shifted from disruption in other industries and summarizing the fundamental questions any leadership team, board, or analyst of markets needs to be asking.

We can achieve a best-case scenario for healthcare in the future. But only if all of the healthcare industry's stakeholders—including patients—understand the forces that are driving healthcare's changing ecosystem, and the strategic challenges, opportunities, and business models that are emerging as a result.

And only if we are able to work together proactively to create the future.

Acknowledgments

Discussing the topic of healthcare disruption in any meaningful, purposeful way requires significant input from a multiplicity of sources—on the industry, on the structure and organization of companies, and on the scale and influence of change, from the macroeconomic through the social, scientific, and technological, to the core of how a patient reacts, interacts, and operates with the entire system. It is a task that cannot be addressed without a significant wealth of experience and help. Our research and work have hugely benefited from a global network of colleagues dedicated to the healthcare industry. It has been challenged, informed, and enriched by our clients, by our experienced research team, and by industry thought leaders, and further shaped by our own interactions with the healthcare system as patients, parents, and caretakers.

We are privileged to have such an incredible global network of people, experiences, and capabilities to draw upon to complete this work. There are also some key people without whom this book would not have been possible.

We wish to thank our Accenture global project team, led by Katherine (Kate) Gordon Murphy, including Jennifer Garland, Phil Davis, Nick Vigil, and Andrea Alary. Kate in particular has worked tirelessly to advance the research for this book, and the company's work in advanced patient pathways strategies, real-world clinical analytics, and advanced patient care management services.

Our Accenture colleagues in this area are pioneers who truly place the patient at the center of all they do. While the list is long, we would like to give a special acknowledgment and thanks to Sander van Noordende, James Crowley, Andrea Brueckner, Thomas Schwenger, Arjun Bedi, Narendra Mulani, Jeffrey Russell, Ken Munie, Jasper Putlitz, M.D., Shawn Roman, Tony Romito, Gayle Sirard, Arda Ural, Ph.D., Jan Ising, Josh Miller, David Champeaux, M.D., Michael Lamoureux, Ben Gross, Ph.D., Cecil Lynch, M.D., Dennis Urbaniak, Eva Wiedenhoeft, Alison Goodrich, Craig Oates, and Mark Fisher. Their collective experience represents over 500 years of work dedicated to health and life sciences clients around the globe—helping them to rethink, reshape, and restructure their companies to deliver better patient and economic outcomes. Their insights and experiences have been invaluable to the concepts, observations, and hypotheses expressed in this book.

Accenture's CEO advisory committee was a testing ground for many of the ideas contained herein and for that we give special thanks to Fred Hassan, Deborah Dunsire, M.D., and Clive Meanwell, Ph.D. and M.D. In addition, Roch Doliveux, former CEO of UCB S.A., made significant contributions to the overarching concept of patient-centricity.

In any topic as broad and technical as "Healthcare Disrupted," it is always a challenge to communicate the key concepts successfully to a diverse audience. Here we thank Regina Maruca and Jens Schadendorf. They brought experience and knowledge of the process of writing and publishing a book that was exceptional and deeply valued.

We would like to give our warmest thanks to our families. Jeff's wife, Anne, and children, Eva and Owen, were highly engaged and shared his passion throughout, actively supporting the many evenings, weekends, and vacations allocated to this project. Anne's husband, Bradley, and her boys, Alex and Stephen, provided both encouragement and enthusiasm on a topic that they know is dear to her heart.

Finally, we are enormously grateful to our publisher, John Wiley & Sons, and in particular to Richard Narramore, who approached this project with enthusiasm, commitment, and a clarity of purpose that was a persistent guide.

—Jeff Elton, Ph.D., *Boston, MA, USA*
Anne O'Riordan, *Hong Kong, PRC*

Introduction

There have been only a few times over the past 100 years when leading companies delivering fundamental products and services have been challenged just to survive. The challenges they've faced have usually involved one or a combination of major technological shifts, government or other regulatory changes, new economic models, and disruptive competition. Some have made it; some haven't. Only a few have managed to hold on to their leadership status.

Think of Kodak and Polaroid in photography and imaging, Digital Equipment and Data General in computing, Nokia and BlackBerry in mobile phones, and Blockbuster video stores for home entertainment, to name a few of the most visible. The one-two punch of digital photography and smartphones with advanced cameras turned wet-chemistry photography into a niche field. Personal computers that could access greater power through the combination of advanced graphical interfaces and Internet connectivity sidelined mid-range and mainframe computer companies. Google's Android and Apple's iOS mobile operating systems, integrated app stores, plus content partners' own ecosystems upended the order of things in mobile handsets. Deregulation, competition from cable infrastructure operators, and the rise in popularity of mobile devices and the Internet as a means of communication forced the transformation of local landline and long-distance services. And Netflix developed an Internet delivery model that, together with other types of delivery systems, hit video stores where it hurt; then streaming did most of them in.

Importantly, during these times, we also saw a personal computer company with modest market share, Apple, and an Internet search engine company, Google (now Alphabet), become the highest value enterprises in the world in terms of market capitalization. These companies took the throw-weight of all the aforementioned disruptions and collapsed distinctions between communications, entertainment, work, and commerce, providing ranges of solutions and convenience others did not foresee. Together they transformed the medium, mechanisms, and economics of personal relationships, where we worked, how we consumed entertainment, and the music industry. We welcomed the changes, and they emerged as winners.

Healthcare is on the brink of a similarly monumental change. "Brink" might not even be a strong enough word; the disruptions are already underway. We wrote this book after two years of research to capture this point in time and give executives across pharmaceutical, biopharmaceutical, medical device, medical diagnostics, and health services companies an opportunity to step back and see the big picture. We wrote it to help them understand the changes that are coming and position their companies to use those changes as building blocks for new and successful strategies. To that end, we frame key trends and offer options for new business models that can drive growth and performance. Ultimately, our goal is to advance a productive discussion about how all stakeholders in healthcare (the aforementioned types of companies, plus regulators, insurers, healthcare providers, and individuals) can take on new roles to drive better health for patients and add value to the healthcare system overall.

THEN, NOW, AND POTENTIAL

Consider some of the newfound abilities and possibilities that are changing our expectations—as policy makers, as executives, as individuals, and as populations—of what "care" can and should be, and how it should be financed.

We used to think of "evidence" of effectiveness as meaning the results of clinical trials and post-approval studies that took years to progress.[1] *Now, through digitally gathered real-world data, we can gain that evidence at population scale in hours, days, or weeks at most.*[2,3]

Pharmaceutical and device (life sciences) companies used to put their products out on the market and wonder why results in the actual clinical settings were different from what they expected. *Now, with the ability to track activities and outcomes in almost real time, they can identify the factors in people's lives that influence the effectiveness of treatment approaches and therapeutic products. They can see the extent to which extenuating circumstances (such as gaps in treatment, non-adherence to dietary and activity modifications) influence outcomes. As a result, they can contemplate new strategies that might include filling those gaps for patients.*

Providers used to see patients in offices or facilities designed for the purpose, and after an examination or a procedure, tell patients what to do, and then, barring emergency, wait until the next scheduled check-in to learn how their treatment plans were working out. *Now they can extend their involvement with patients beyond the office, hospital, or clinic, track progress in real time, and adjust treatments as necessary along the way.*[4]

From Inputs to Outcomes

Now, in other words, we're seeing an emerging rationale for moving from an input-based approach (inputs being patients seen, or drugs and devices sold) to an output-based approach (outputs being patients' best possible health outcomes) to healthcare. In the literature of economics, there is a strong distinction between payment that is based on input and payment based on output.[5] When payment is based on inputs, there is a built-in adverse incentive to "shirk," that is, to do as little as possible and receive the same compensation. When payment is based on outputs, the incentive is to optimize productivity and maximize "system" benefits.

In Europe, for example, we're seeing a move toward "value-based reimbursement," where the health authorities and providers are being asked to balance the needs of the system as a whole with the treatment they are providing to the individual. The idea is to assess the healthcare industry on its ability to provide the greatest possible benefit to a population against a set of resource constraints. Variants of that approach are going into place in the United States as part of the Affordable Care Act (ACA) and supporting legislation.

Meanwhile, in the same spirit, we're seeing payers moving into the direct provision of care, technology companies spinning out of provider systems, technology companies connecting remote clinical monitoring technologies together as a service, and medical device companies providing direct patient care management services. We're seeing health providers manage financial risk, make tradeoffs among the services they offer, and pursue payment through "alternative" or outcomes-based approaches. Each of these entities is working together with other partners to create, advance, or deliver their services. The relationships are extending back from early drug discovery, right through clinical development, to commercialization and patient end-use.

Power to the Patient

Unsurprisingly, the patient's power as a consumer is also evolving. One hundred years ago, healthcare was largely inaccessible to most people even in the wealthiest economies. Sixty years ago, we created mandates and public institutions that ensured some measure of access to the majority of people in the United States and Europe. Over the course of the past 50 to 60 years, healthcare unions, private employers, states, and countries have ensured increasing access. Regulations and programs for reimbursement, professional credentialing and guidelines, institutional licensure, and product approvals have focused on institutions and health professionals—ensuring access to a safe and efficacious service for citizens and employees as a "benefit." Now, we're entering a time when the priorities of the individual patient with a specific disease or health condition can drive a real determination of value in therapies (drugs and combinations thereof), interventions, and services. The patient is taking on more direct responsibility for outcomes, viewing them from a new vantage point as beneficiary *and* active customer. Healthcare is pivoting to the patient.

EMERGING MODELS

Is it any wonder that new business models with fundamentally different economics are forming and solidifying, setting precedents and standards for others to follow and try to surpass? Already we see this happening beyond isolated use cases. We are seeing a bifurcation of strategies and business models between those catering to the needs of the mass market and those focused on serving niche groups/disease areas. In addition we see disruptors—those companies leveraging new technologies and new science to cut across traditional industry processes to make a step change in how healthcare is delivered and patient outcomes are affected.

For example, we're seeing players that are driving value by bringing the good science developed over the past 20 years to the market in the most efficient way possible. These *Lean Innovators*, many built on the chassis of a generics company, are arriving with extremely efficient, world-class manufacturing and supply chains. They have an eye for acquisition and aspirations of rapid growth, and they will challenge incumbents and the cost structures, productivity, and operating models of the past.

We are also seeing *Around-the-Patient Innovators*—companies (or divisions) that are bringing the latest scientific insights and a focus on the most devastating of patient diseases to bear to advance new specialty therapeutics and complementary product and service offerings.

Embracing outcomes as their strategic center, *Value Innovators*, a third model, will define and differentiate themselves on integrated, digitally enabled services that include remote sensors, devices, and centrally located clinical staff. These organizations will focus on improving patient and clinical outcomes on a broad scale; and they will be willing to tie economics of their business to their ability to achieve patient outcomes and system efficiencies in how healthcare resources are deployed.

Finally, we're seeing the fast rise of *New Health Digitals*, companies that most likely grew and evolved outside of healthcare and life sciences, that see this sector as a natural sector for their relationships, partnerships, infrastructure, performance systems, and capabilities. We are only just beginning to gain a sense of these organizations' interests, models, and influence. But it is clear that their economics—driven by global scale, vast ecosystems of devices and applications, broad developer communities, and the cloud—will provide some solutions at orders of magnitude with less cost and greater capability.

Four models are clearly emerging, but likely we will see more. Even as we put the final touches on this manuscript, technological advances continue to astound us and foreshadow breakthrough opportunities in medicines, treatment, and business models. In August 2015, for example, the U.S. Food and Drug Administration (FDA) approved the first 3D-printed drug, Spiritam, developed by the U.S.-based pharmaceuticals company Aprecia. Used in treatments for people who suffer from epilepsy, Spiritam is made by layering powdered medicine with liquid to create a pill that dissolves almost instantly when taken with just a sip of water.

The initial hope is that by making the pill easier to swallow, more patients will be inclined to stay the course with their treatment. But the implications of the technology are potentially far greater. We can envision localized manufacturing "to order" in the dosage form best suited for an individual patient. We can envision therapeutic combinations required for the management of a specific patient's comorbidities coming together in a single dose to aid compliance and lower medication errors.[6,7,8] It would not be inconceivable to see an "Amazon-like" entity—streamlining ordering and manufacturing processes, and delivering within hours—disrupting traditional retail pharmacies, pharmaceutical generics, therapeutics distributors, and patient adherence services. Could an enterprise that doesn't actually own any assets be a future "Uber" of retail pharmacy and generics manufacturing? Yes, it could.

DISRUPTING AND RESHAPING RESPONSIBLY

We approached this book as professionals with a goal of supporting the healthcare industry's evolution toward a more effective state. But healthcare is very personal. And so throughout the process of writing this book, we've found ourselves reflecting on and talking about the implications of these changes for our families and ourselves—and for those populations with the highest unmet needs. We have come to the conclusion that executives in healthcare, life sciences, and new health-focused technology companies will need courage to shape the healthcare environment and transition successfully—courage that will take different forms as they explore business and operating models that go far beyond their companies' traditional products, technologies, or services.

They will need to work through questions of privacy and use of broad sources of data for the benefit of the patient—advancing a new level of trust and operating competence. They will need to resolve all dilemmas—ethical or financial—in favor of their responsibilities to patients. They will need to take the high road, versus a defensive posture, with regulators as rightfully representing the interest of patients in the way that only health providers previously could. Collaborations founded on trust and courage may even prove to be as important as having economic fundamentals and a "winning" business model.

Executives, managers, team leaders, and associates at all levels will also need courage to break down organizational barriers within their organizations and to act as integrators. They won't necessarily be shipping products, but rather they will be integral to producing product and service packages of value, and interacting directly with patients, health providers, and others. They will need courage to help patients connect the dots and resolve the gaps and deficiencies that limit outcomes. Managers, and those with expertise in one or another area, will have to think differently, broadening their horizons in order to work well with people and organizations that have never before been partners, with new immediate priorities.

There is a real opportunity here to shape the future, rather than be shaped by it. In order to take advantage of this opportunity, though, more than a few people will have to move fast and far out of their comfort zones. Building a strong foundation for a healthcare system that works as well as we can imagine will take more than safe strategies and test-the-water approaches.

This isn't about responding to a shifting environment by making incremental strategic changes. It isn't even about reacting to growth, cost pressures, and/or a significant change in competitive dynamics. This is about determining the role their organizations will play in a broadly defined industry that is rethinking how it creates and rewards value, and even what "value" means. It is about planting a flag and taking a stand when the stakes are high and the ground beneath your feet is moving so rapidly it seems out of focus.

THE TSUNAMI
OF CHANGE

Chapter 1

Why and How the Healthcare Industry Is Changing So Rapidly

The collective throw-weight of socio-economic and policy changes, technological advances, and structural shifts has primed the healthcare industry for upheaval and disruption—and presented an incredible opportunity to advance the standard of care worldwide.

Over the past several decades, as the healthcare industry (including providers, payers, life science companies, health services companies, and other ancillary businesses) has grown in size and complexity, choices regarding patient care have often become entangled in a myriad of objectives and controls. To survive and thrive, healthcare-related companies and organizations have focused increasingly on individual objectives—the products companies on product sales, the healthcare delivery organizations on providing services at the right price point, the payers on actuarial modeling. And somewhere in the mix, the common goal of achieving the best outcomes for the patient and overall value for the healthcare system was diminished.

But that's all changing. There have been periods throughout economic history where a confluence of policy, technological, and industry structural changes has created a foundation for upheaval and disruption—times where

3

opportunistic strategies have offered handsome near-term rewards, where new entrants have had the potential to be the better operators, and where consolidations and integrated approaches have created unprecedented opportunities. Healthcare is in one of those periods now. And in 10 to 15 years, it will function fundamentally differently than it currently does. Value, defined anew, will increasingly be the metric that matters as healthcare pivots back to the patient in extraordinarily new and different ways.

* * *

The world changed, and healthcare—broadly speaking—did not. Like all good catalytic circumstances, this one offers to healthcare the opportunity to leapfrog and make fundamental and sweeping changes that will sustain for years to come. As a result, many of us who work in, with, and around the industry now find ourselves simultaneously playing catch-up and looking forward with a new sense of responsibility to ensure that those without care can access it, to build strength into our national health systems, and to see that healthcare truly re-emerges as patient-responsive, responsible, and centric. We're directly confronting the companies and business models we've built or built upon, and we're defining what worked, what did not work, and what will work in the future. We are also comparing where healthcare stands relative to other industries that have transformed themselves in recent years.

But we're doing all of this under increasing pressure.

The global population is expected to increase by 1 billion by 2025. By then, more than 500 million people will be over the age of 50. Projections from a variety of sources (including the United Nations and the World Health Organization) report that by that same year, 70 percent of all illnesses will be chronic diseases. Overall we are living longer, living with an increasing amount of chronic and comorbid illnesses, and doing so regardless of what country or region of the world we are living in.

We're also spending more money. In developed countries such as the United States and Germany, where the aging workforce is a key driver of rising healthcare costs, spending on healthcare ranges from 11 to 18 percent of gross domestic product (GDP). In recently developed countries such as China and Brazil, it is between 5 and 10 percent. Overall healthcare spending will be doubling from an aggregate $8.4 trillion in 2015 to $18.3 trillion in 2030 with an estimated lost productivity from chronic diseases alone of $47 trillion over the same period. As Figure 1.1 shows, all of the world's major healthcare systems face enormous cost pressures and potential productivity losses.

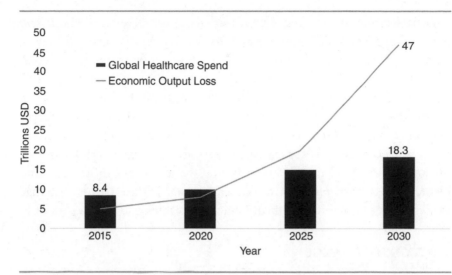

FIGURE 1.1   Global Healthcare Spend and Value of Lost Output Opportunities

Source: WHO Global Health Data Repository, *World Healthcare Outlook,* Economist Intelligence Unit; http://www.eiu.com/industry/Healthcare and http://apps.who.int/gho/data/node.main.

OPPORTUNITIES

We may be behind the curve and facing unprecedented challenges, but there are also considerable forces pushing us forward.

One piece of good news is that concurrent with (and perhaps as a result of) aging populations and the prevalence of chronic disease, many markets have seen a significant rise in "health consciousness," which is framing new opportunities for companies to develop (and do very well selling) entire lines of consumer goods and services that facilitate health and wellness.

These offerings increasingly leverage disruptive digital forces that are a key enabler of the changes we are witnessing. Some of them, for example, built into wearable technologies (e.g., watches and activity monitors) and even mobile phones offer customers unprecedented capability to track and store health data. And so the manufacturers of these devices and their digital ecosystems (e.g., app stores) are thus increasingly bringing the healthcare system right to patients—changing the nature of how the healthcare system understands and interacts with patients, and making healthcare look more and more like a consumer market.

Other digital data—from electronic medical records (EMRs) and personalized genomic information, to lifestyle and personal health data—along with the ability to analyze that data, represent another revolutionary force driving unprecedented insights and facilitating scientific breakthroughs in the development of new drugs and therapeutic services.

Healthcare is relatively nascent in its ability to use these data, whereas consumer markets, financial services, and other areas are highly advanced. But that imbalance itself is revealing pockets of opportunity. While external macroeconomic and demographic trends shape the healthcare environment, internal market forces are taking advantage of these trends to change every aspect of how the healthcare market operates and serves patients.

THE SIGNS OF CHANGE

Disruptive indicators lead the way in all major marketplace changes, and we're seeing them now in healthcare. For example:

An unprecedented number of mergers and acquisitions (M&A) have taken place recently in the pharmaceutical and medical device fields. In 2014 alone in those fields, there was $438 billion worth of M&A activity.[1] A similar trend is evident among payers. Traditional private health insurers are increasingly aware of their own modest scale; in the United States even the largest private health insurers cover only 10 to 15 percent of prospective individuals, a small proportion by any industrial standards. This awareness is driving meta-scale combinations, which will in turn accelerate the pace of healthcare innovation through applications of large-scale, real-world health claims data sets.[2,3]

New business models are emerging, and they're breaking old boundaries. Traditionally, there were three distinct types of healthcare players: health providers (delivering treatment and services), health manufacturers (pharmaceutical and medical device companies), and health payers (insurers). However, the traditional lines of distinction among different types of companies are blurring. Device companies are transforming into service entities, providing catheterization lab management services and focusing on the remote management of specific patient populations. Pharmaceutical companies are focusing on service. Providers are extending services beyond their traditional regimens into home care and post-discharge monitoring. Additionally, we're seeing new types of *collaborative pairings*—medical device companies with pharmaceutical firms, digital technology companies with pharmaceutical firms, payers with providers, payers with digital technology companies, and so forth, for example, Novartis co-investing with Qualcomm, or Humana's acquisition of Concentra.[4]

New players are making noise and resetting expectations of what's possible. Chief among these are influential consumer digital technology companies that bring new capabilities to the table and offer new forms of partnership. Apple Inc., for example, has launched an app that provides a network for the sharing of health information between its vast consumer base and researchers interested in large-scale data sets.[5] Additionally, Google Inc.'s partnership with AbbVie Inc. promises to yield $1.5 billion in research activity around developing solutions for age-related illnesses.[6]

And all of these changes are taking place against a backdrop of full-fledged industry reform.

A CLOSER LOOK AT HEALTHCARE REFORM

Admittedly, we're taking a rapid tour through the foundations of disruption in the healthcare industry. However, current reform efforts warrant a slight slowdown and a closer look.

Reform, in this context, refers to a broad set of sweeping changes that are needed to solve problems that cannot be solved by tuning or tweaking existing policies and incentives. Industry reform generally occurs in areas where there is significant government oversight and where that oversight forms the "rules of engagement" for industry players. While undoubtedly a simplification, two examples demonstrate the point: Campaign finance rules and banking have each been reformed—the first to limit and enable sources of influence and the second to create agencies and new rules to limit broad risks to the national economy and to protect the financial interests of individuals.[7,8]

The fundamental problem compelling reform efforts in healthcare was (and still is) that the value created—for patients, for providers, for payers—did not (and still does not) align with spending levels. The industry has for years increased expenditures without improving returns to health—paying for procedures done, but not for what those procedures are supposed to accomplish.

In the United States, the Netherlands, Germany, and many other locations, this approach is known as *fee-for-service*, and it utilizes tables of codes, procedures, and treatment groupings to determine how much is paid for what is done. Healthcare providers are thus given incentives to do "more" in the most acute setting and with the most skilled clinical personnel, in order to "code" as highly as they can in order to optimize revenues. And manufacturers selling therapeutics, devices, and diagnostics are motivated to encourage key decision makers at provider and payer organizations to get their products and services used or prescribed as often as possible.

With these incentives, and without an efficient market for value in terms of outcomes, healthcare costs over the past decade and more rose faster than general inflation.[9] It's true that the fee-for-service approach originated during a period when we needed more healthcare capacity—more facilities, more physicians, and more allied healthcare professionals, all of whom were tasked with providing healthcare to a growing private workforce of increasingly skilled workers. However, once a capacity threshold had been reached and the value of pure supply had diminished, the industry missed a chance to transition to an output-based system.[10,11]

Failed Healthcare Fixes

Not that no one tried. There have in fact been valiant attempts to reform key aspects of the fee-for-service, pay for input model. The 1980s, for example, witnessed the development of implemented diagnosis-related groups (DRGs), which classified hospital procedures into tightly related sets of activities that could be assigned a single price or payment. The idea was that the costs of treatment for a particular diagnosis would follow standards derived from historical aggregate analyses. If a drug or treatment was not related to the specific procedure or group under consideration, it would be challenged when submitted for reimbursement, potentially not reimbursed, or reimbursed at a lower level. DRGs did slow the cost trend and lowered some costs of patients' initial visits, but they also created adverse incentives that compelled providers to discharge patients too quickly; they had no quality criteria assigned to the care delivered; and they allowed hospitals and physicians to be paid for additional outpatient visits and readmissions associated with the original DRG-defined care provided. And so, unintentionally, DRGs resulted in increasing numbers of patients being readmitted or having extensive follow-up care.

In the United States, the 1990s saw another attempt: capitation. Since fee-for-service provided incentives to do more, capitation capped the amount reimbursed for specific procedures, like coronary artery bypass graft or the normal delivery of a newborn. But clinical care ended up being more complicated than the system could support. Comparable populations in different regions could have different acuities and therefore different risks. The system encouraged focusing on specific procedures for higher volumes, market share, and positive margins, often limiting reimbursement for, and de-emphasizing, routine or preventative care. The model also saw different private insurers implementing their own capitation approaches that often expected providers to differentiate their care based on who was paying—something that not only proved difficult to do but also was inadvisable for the sake of quality and consistency.

Other attempts to introduce cost containment and discretionary measures also failed. Some countries chose to implement policies that restricted access, creating queues or waiting periods to constrain demand.[12] Some created councils or committees to approve or deny access to expensive procedures or medicines.[13] Some limited the approval or commercial availability of therapeutics, technologies, or procedures they did not want to, or had no ability to, pay for. Some set limits on their healthcare spend to a percentage of GDP and then put mechanisms into place to force tradeoffs.[14] Others created technology assessment groups to place a value on new therapeutics, diagnostics, and interventional devices as the basis for their availability and reimbursement.[15] Nevertheless, most of these approaches ultimately failed, serving only to control the rate of increase in aggregate spending, but not to improve overall productivity, efficiency, or population outcomes.[16]

REAL REFORM: WHY THIS TIME WILL BE DIFFERENT

The weight of the fee-for-service model has become too much to bear, and everyone knows it. We have seen increasing, broad awareness of the fact that the model is deeply flawed and we now know that no mere modification will yield a different outcome. But we have also seen technology advance to open up other possible solutions.

Consider: In order to make payments on the basis of inputs (treatments offered, procedures performed, actions taken), a healthcare system—a provider treating a patient and seeking reimbursement from an insurer—needed only to have administrative support for scheduling and coding, and an accounting capability to track the costs and charges incurred for specific patients and specific procedures.

For payment based on outputs or patient value (best possible health achieved) and system value (effective treatments at efficient costs), that system would have needed to be able to measure clinical outcomes realized—and that capability, until recently, was not part of most hospital, health, or enterprise-resource-planning systems.

Now, it is. Now, it is possible to collect data on the clinical activities of healthcare, the health status of a patient pretreatment, and the change in health status after treatment. These data, captured through EMRs, are enabling reform efforts to create standards for how care is administered and outcomes captured. In addition, using publicly available data, analysts, academics, and other parties can calculate the health status of a patient population and assess the health risks of the individuals within it.[17] And so for the first time, it is possible to set the foundations for a healthcare market focused on output and value.

Global Healthcare Reforms Ensure the Move from Volume to Value

Reform efforts are taking these advances as motivation and as fuel.

In the United States, for example, several new initiatives have been implemented as part of healthcare reform. These include: financial incentives to health providers to achieve meaningful use (a certain standard of improvement in quality, safety, and efficiency and efficacy of care) of EMR technology under the HITECH Act[18]; Patient Centered Medical Homes (PCMHs) and accountable care organizations (ACOs) that provide integrated models of care within specific regions and for specific populations of patients; Shared Savings programs created as part of the Affordable Care Act (ACA); quality reporting on care providers and physicians; and the Center for Medicare and Medicaid innovation to pilot different quality and outcomes reimbursement models within regions and targeted populations of patients. Many of these programs assume an increasing level of private sector engagement and co-investment in order to move toward an outcomes- and value-based system.[19,20]

Figures 1.2 and 1.3 illustrate how these programs will progress, strongly de-emphasizing the Fee-for-Service (FFS)–based models in favor

	Category 1: Fee for Service—No Link to Quality	Category 2: Fee for Service—Link to Quality	Category 3: Alternative Payment Models Built on Fee-for-Service Architecture	Category 4: Population-Based Payment
Description	*Payments are based on volume of services and not linked to quality or efficiency.*	*At least a portion of payments vary based or the quality or efficiency of healthcare delivery.*	*Some payment is linked to the effective management of a population or an episode of care. Payments still triggered by delivery of services, but opportunities for shared savings or two-sided risk.*	*Payment is not directly triggered by service delivery so volume is not linked to payment. Clinicians and organizations are paid and responsible for the care of a beneficiary for a long period (e.g. ≥ 1 year.)*
Medicare FFS	• Limited in Medicare fee for service • Majority of Medicare payments now are linked to quality	• Hospital value-based purchasing • Physician value-based modifier • Readmission/hospital acquired condition reduction program	• Accountable care organizations • Medical homes • Bundled payments • Comprehensive primary care initiative • Comprehensive ESRD • Medicare – Medicaid financial alignment initiative fee-for-service model	• Eligible Pioneer accountable care organizations in 3–5 years

FIGURE 1.2 Payment Taxonomy Framework

Source: https://www.cms.gov/Newsroom/MediaReleaseDatabase/Fact-sheets/2015-Fact-sheets-items/2015-01-26-3.html.

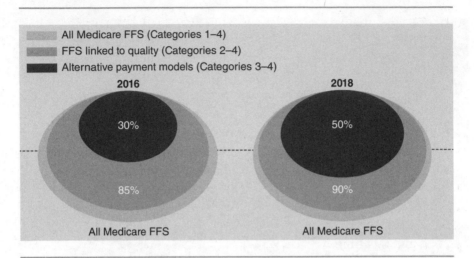

FIGURE 1.3   Target Percentage of Medicare FFS Payments Linked to Quality and Alternative Payment Models in 2016 and 2018
Source: https://www.cms.gov/Newsroom/MediaReleaseDatabase/Fact-sheets/2015-Fact-sheets-items/2015-01-26-3.html.

of those that rely on alternative payments (payment linked to an outcome but still provided with provision of clinical services) and population-based assessments (linked to a real-world measurable population outcome).[21]

By 2018, in fact, these performance-based reimbursement mechanisms are anticipated to comprise 50 percent or more of payments made by Medicare. (Medicare accounts for 50 percent or more of the payments made in a variety of major chronic and acute chronic diseases, such as cardiovascular, neurodegenerative, and certain cancers.) This is why we strongly believe that the U.S. market will increasingly tilt toward a value basis for pricing therapeutics, devices, and care services.

This shift also opens up more opportunities for sharing risk and delivery models for advanced clinical services that involve remote management and monitoring of higher cost and higher risk patient populations. Also, many of these initiatives increasingly focus on patient involvement, engagement, and responsibilities. The Physician Quality Reporting System and Meaningful Use initiatives, for example, are penalty- and incentive-based programs that focus on adherence to required standards—emphasizing consistency of infrastructure and quality control.

But the real changes in the United States will occur through the broader implementation of the accountable care organizations (ACOs). At its essence, the ACO integrates acute or inpatient health providers with outpatient and physician office–based care under a common set of criteria for quality and cost defined for a population. Shared savings and shared benefits are realized by achieving or exceeding specific population health targets. By adding risk and care coordination as additional requirements for fund allocations, the ACOs are the bridge from the fee-for-service foundation of the old healthcare system to the value-based system of the future. The first 27 ACO Shared Savings Programs were launched in April 2012 and their initial progress to goals was reported in late 2014. While only a modest beginning, ACOs were shown to reduce Medicare expenditure within the first year of their operation.[22]

As Figure 1.4 shows, many U.S. institutions are using an approach to operationalizing value-based care that focuses on three distinct elements: Population Management, Affordability, and Patience Experience. In doing so, they are trying to shift their operating focus from volume to health at the population and personal level, and to system-wide efficiency.[23]

Dr. Vivek Murthy, MD, Surgeon General of the United States, has been candid about his hopes for reform: "My overarching goal is to get every individual, every institution and every sector . . . to ask themselves the question [of] what they can do to improve the health and the strength of our nation," he said in an interview with the *Washington Post*, published in April 2015. "The health challenges that we face right now are too big to be solved by the traditional health sector alone. . . ."

Murthy went on to note, "Many of the patients that I [have seen] come in with illnesses and conditions that were preventable. And that's not an experience that's unique to me. Doctors all across the country, nurses across the country, share similar stories of feeling a great deal of sadness when they see the pain and the suffering that patients and their families go through, and realize that if we had a system that could care for people better, that was actually more focused on prevention than our current system, that we may be able to prevent a lot of the illness, the suffering and the health care costs that we see in our current world."[24]

Population Management	Affordability	Patient Experience

• Focus on inclusive understanding of health; collaboration
• Beyond inpatient and acute care
  ○ Preventive care
  ○ Chronic care
• Population health and outcomes analysis
  ○ Utilization and medical cost predictive modeling
  ○ Condition identification and risk stratification
  ○ Outcomes performance measurement
  ○ Wellness and prevention
• Care transition/redesign
• Innovation/mobile health
  ○ Texts, Internet, Telehealth
	• Medical-population cost management
	  ○ Reduce PMPM
	  ○ Avoidable episodes of care
	  ○ Actuarial tools
	• Revenue/technology opportunities
	  ○ Quality, P4P
	  ○ HIT (EMR, other)
	  ○ Market share
	  ○ Patient base
	• Operational efficiency/cost
	• Admin costs
	• Manage risk-sharing agreements (ACO, PCMH, bundled payments)
	• Nontraditional revenue streams
	• Compliance and penalties
	• Utilization, Disease, Case Management
	• Complex Care Management
	• End of Life/Hospice
		• Quality
		• Home based or close to home services
		• Patient engagement
		  ○ Self-management
		• Patient satisfaction/retention
		• Patient-centered care
		• Care continuity
		• Patient adherence
		  ○ Medication
		  ○ Programs
		  ○ Support network
		• Self and home care
		• Patient access enhanced
		  ○ Multi-channel communications patient engagement, remote monitoring, and remote care coordination

FIGURE 1.4   Value-Based Care

Source: Derived from the Institute for Healthcare Improvement http://www.ihi.org/engage/initiatives/tripleaim/pages/default
.aspx.

Reform in Socialized Medicine Systems

Meanwhile, in socialized medicine systems throughout Europe, Japan, and China (post the 2009–2011 Healthcare Reform), where access to health systems for the broad population is a fundamental element of constitutional right, the push is to increase efficiency and effectiveness.

In Europe, for example, the clear trend is toward population- or value-based reimbursement. Europe has a high proportion of seniors relative to other geographies, with a quarter of its population expected to be over age 60 by 2020, with chronic diseases affecting a third of its population. Comparatively, constrained national budgets meant annual health spending actually decreased slightly (0.6 percent) between 2009 and 2012, and there will be an estimated shortage of 1 million healthcare workers by 2020. These opposing trends are compelling healthcare payers to find new approaches to continue to meet the healthcare needs of their citizens.

Their efforts had slow starts, as they wrestle with key issues such as data privacy, funding levels, and the balance between public and private care. And all of these initiatives have required multifaceted changes spanning technology, cultural, and care management processes.

Nonetheless, health authorities across different countries are now experimenting with several alternative models and relationships. These range from regional pilots to full-scale transformations of healthcare delivery models—such as creating virtual care centers that provide remote delivered services to patients with multiple conditions while maintaining them at home.

According to a 2013 European Commission survey, in fact, three countries (the Netherlands, Denmark, and the United Kingdom) have succeeded in digitizing over 80 percent of their patient health records and, while challenges continue to be addressed, that achievement has supported country-wide efforts to pilot models focused on patient outcomes and care coordination. Denmark has been a leader in the use of new digital approaches, including remote monitoring, video consults and remote conferencing (including translation), and photo exchange. In Denmark, for example, new models of diabetes care have used these systems to support incentivizing GPs to coordinate care or to bundle payments to "care groups."

The United Kingdom, meanwhile, has emphasized more stringent and transparent measurement of healthcare outcomes and linked these explicitly to assessing pilots in new delivery models (e.g., technologically enabled remote engagement and consults) deployed by NHS providers and private care providers as well. In the United Kingdom, 2012 legislation allows "any qualified provider" (NHS or private) to respond to tenders or be reimbursed by NHS-set tariff, with contracting generally focused on care in specific specialties (e.g., radiology/diagnostic imaging, orthopedics, ophthalmology). Large tenders included £800m for elder care and £1.2bn for cancer care. Of these NHS contracts about 6 percent of its budget went to private companies, which won about one third of recent tenders, a major emerging change in the structure of the U.K. healthcare delivery system.[25]

France has also been rapidly implementing major reforms. The French government views fragmented governance and misaligned policies as a root cause of the current inefficiencies and lack of a population-based healthcare focus there. To respond, the national health agency created Agence pour les Systèmes d'Information de Santé Partagés (ASIP) in 2009, an eHealth competence center,[26] and established tenders for five regional pilots (80m euros over three years) to develop multichannel centers to support chronically ill patients (200 to 1,000 in each region). Given the economic constraints, these tenders specifically sought new thinking on new economic models for care services that would allow them to access funding sources and partners outside the public budget.

There are also major new proposals for bundled payments for hospitals, based on the 2014 pilots in chronic renal insufficiency and radiotherapy cancer treatment. As we were writing these words, new disease management programs were being piloted on the national, regional, and local levels. These programs are driven by national reforms for digital health launching in five regions. New disease management programs will likely be developed at the regional level over the next five years.[27]

DRG reforms are debated in the 2015 draft of France's Social Security Financing Act. On September 24, 2015, the French Minister of Social Affairs, Health and Women's Rights Marisol Touraine and the Secretary of State for the Budget Christian Eckert presented a draft for France's 2016 Social Security Financing Act (Projet de Loi de Financement de la Sécurité Sociale; PLFSS) to outline a plan for the reduction of the Social Security General Scheme by EUR3 billion in 2016, increasing over time to EUR6 billion. As part of this, quality incentives are being proposed for 2016 in acute care hospitals, for nosocomial infections, re-hospitalizations, and in-hospital drug use. Now, guidelines for new Health Technology Assessment (HTA) requirements call for significant increases in comparative or cost effectiveness for reimbursement. While these initiatives continue to be controversial, they should establish a new baseline cost remedying the budget deficit attributable to shortfalls in healthcare funding.

In Spain, little is being done at the federal level, but each state is advancing its own solution to cost and capacity constraints and population health, increasingly emphasizing risk-sharing agreements that allow for non-compensation for ineffective interventions or treatments. Most solutions and new structures there are being implemented regionally.[28]

The Basque Country provides a good example of one micro-region's unique initiatives. This area has one of the highest proportions of elderly in Europe, and 80 percent of patient encounters with the public health system are related to chronic diseases. Unsustainable estimates of future health spending drove the Basque Country health department to seek a comprehensive change to its approach to population health management, ultimately launching 14 strategic initiatives to reshape its system to better support patients with chronic diseases. The effort is ongoing, but services provided by the O-sarean[29] Multichannel Health Service Centre since 2009 have begun to reverse the historical upward trends in healthcare spending in the area. These efforts are helping patients stay informed, and increasing homecare almost 50 percent through a revolutionary and well-received telemedicine program, ultimately leading to $55 million in savings through 52,000 fewer hospital stays in the region between 2009 and 2011.

Other areas continue to lay digital foundations to catalyze the evolution of their healthcare as well. Certain regions in Italy have been tendering for solutions ranging from population analytics to designing and delivering patient clinical treatment pathways with the goal of better managing both patient outcomes and the allocation of healthcare resources. The Trento province in particular has been a leader in eHealth solutions and is using its digital care platform, TreC (Cartella Clinica del Cittadino), to support pilots in remote monitoring and self-management of patients in oncology, diabetes, hypertension, and youth asthma.

In Sweden, where new medical technologies have to be funded out of existing hospital budgets, registries[30] serve as vehicles for value-based incentives,[31] and novel programs in value-based reimbursement are underway in major regions. For example, in Stockholm, the County

Council and the Karolinska Institute (a major academic and regional care center) are working together to align healthcare infrastructure, capacity, and payment models to advance the health of the population and to more efficiently allocate spending to the areas of greatest need.[32]

In some areas, such as in the United Kingdom and some Spanish regions, hospital systems with incentives to reduce unplanned readmissions have made strides in improving their effectiveness around patient discharge and remote monitoring. For example, La Fe Hospital in Valencia partnered with Accenture having been leading the way in a clinical trial to validate the potential impact to patient outcomes and budget savings of a multi-chronic disease patient care management program. The trial resulted in a 65 percent reduction in costs and 80 percent reduction in participants' annual days in the hospital. Other hospitals in France and Italy have sent out confidential tenders to develop better programs to manage chronically ill patients.

Germany, too, has been contemplating changes. The primary focus there has been on stemming the rising costs associated with immigration and an aging population. In 2010, the public health insurance system projected a deficit of €9 billion for the upcoming year. The CDU-FPD political coalition passed the GKV-Finanzierungsgesetz for insurance reform and the Arzneimittelmarktneuordnungsgesetz (AMNOG) for pharmaceutical reform, both of which went into effect in early 2011. The GKV-Finanzierungsgesetz leaves the insurance system generally intact, altering the financing ratios for public health insurance (Gesetzliche Krankenversicherung, GKV) and implementing measures incentivizing competition to hold down the costs of private insurance. Meanwhile, the AMNOG focuses on cost containment of pharmaceuticals by leveraging the purchasing and tendering scale of the Krankenkassen.

Different Stages of Evolution in Top Markets

Countries across the globe are at different stages of evolution in the movement from no coverage to universal coverage governed by traditional instruments such as drug approval, discounting, and cost control, toward integrated systems held accountable for outcomes.[33] These renovations of the healthcare payment system and a move toward outcomes-based reimbursement are propelling the industry forward and forcing a rethink of the core business models that serve this industry.

This time efforts can be, and are, aimed at addressing the underlying problem with the healthcare ecosystem overall. This time reform and disruption will work together to shift the basis for payment *from inputs to outcomes realized* and effect on the healthcare system. As socioeconomic pressures increase, as science continues to break new boundaries, and as the new breed of patient-consumers demands higher levels of integrated services and capabilities, the availability of data—genomic, lifestyle, medical, clinical, and scientific—coupled with the methods of using and analyzing that data will compel and enable us all to challenge the traditional norms, satiate needs, and address the rising cost-of-care crisis.

FROM REACTIVE TO PROACTIVE

The move to value- and outcomes-based compensation changes the way the healthcare system positions itself with respect to the patient. Whereas to a large extent, today's healthcare system is reactionary, giving us the health services that result from our persistence, our phone calls, our queuing, our waiting in waiting rooms, and our calls to healthcare insurers, tomorrow's system can be a force for health maintenance and health solutions.

ACO entities in the United States and new public policy in various European countries act as an essential support to the health of specific patient populations within defined services regions. This provides them with the financial means and incentive to focus on maintaining patient health. With the ubiquity of the electronic medical record and technologies, such as the Health Information Exchanges (HIEs) in many countries, there is now the ability to pull data together on individual patients, confederate those data together, develop a picture of a population of patients, and then identify the needs of the individual patient relative to the goals of the overall population.[34]

In the United States, for example, it is anticipated that close to 95 percent of all patients and patient encounters will be captured in the various physicians' offices, ambulatory facilities, and acute hospitals as part of mechanisms integrated into healthcare reform legislation, incentives, and penalties. To date, more than $20.9 billion in Medicare EHR Incentive Program payments have been made between May 2011 and July 2015, highlighting the influence and impact this is having on practices and available infrastructure.[35] Based on that assessment,

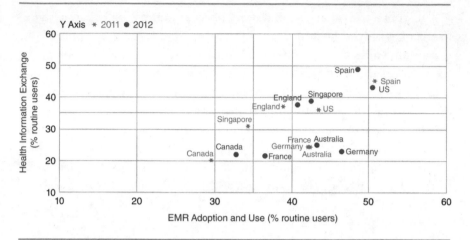

FIGURE 1.5 Countries Are Showing Increases in Connected Health Maturity across Both HIE and EMR

Source: Accenture Doctors Survey, "Connected Health Maturity Index: Total Doctors, 2011–2012." Accenture analysis from the Doctors Survey: https://www.accenture.com/us-en/~/media/Accenture/Conversion-Assets/DotCom/Documents/Global/PDF/Industries_11/Accenture-Doctors-Survey-US-Country-Profile-Report.pdf#zoom=50; and https://www.accenture.com/us-en/insight-digital-doctor-is-in.aspx.

messages and requests can be sent to that patient's personal care physician and medical practice with specific guidance. In turn, the patient can receive notifications about vaccinations, nutritional counseling, or a request for a formal assessment of the effectiveness of specific chronic disease management therapeutics. There are comparable scenarios for proactive management of more acute patients or patients who are more ill. (Figure 1.5 shows the impressive rate of increase in EMR usage even in 2012.)

Insurers are also becoming active in the area of prevention, doing their part to keep costs under control. Discovery Health, a South Africa–based health insurer, has deployed proactive "Vitality" programs across the United Kingdom, Africa, and Asia that offer loyalty rewards to citizens who eat healthy foods, exercise regularly, and provide links to their Fitbit™ data to demonstrate those healthy habits. The insurer offers lower premiums as incentives for demonstrated healthy behaviors; it also offers rewards on a weekly and monthly basis. While the ultimate goal is to reduce policy payouts, the result is a more health-conscious population focused on prevention rather than cure.

And critically, the pharmaceutical, biopharmaceutical, medical device, and medical diagnostics companies have an unprecedented opportunity to enable and effect change. In fact, these organizations may hold a critical link between what can be and what will be.

With the external environment changing at an accelerating pace, many organizations are seeing core elements of their operating models diminish in effectiveness, or even begin to act as barriers to strong performance. Nearly every major pharmaceutical, biopharmaceutical, medical device, and medical diagnostic company has the opportunity and responsibility to overhaul its strategy, defining its own future paths on multiple dimensions, and developing coherent responses to the powerful rising trends and focus on better patient and economic outcomes as the new currency.

Chapter 2

Strategic Choices No Healthcare Company Can Avoid

To thrive in the emerging healthcare ecosystem, senior leaders will need to: clarify their company's market positioning regarding patient outcomes and value to the healthcare system; define the differentiating capabilities necessary to deliver on those goals; and create a high-performance enterprise of partners, collaborators, and talent.

When the fundamentals of market structure shift irreversibly and unpredictably—as they are doing in healthcare—new strategic choices are essential. The move from volume to value is not just about reshaping reimbursement models, but also about changing the criteria on which many critical corporate decisions will be made. Value will increasingly be part of supporting a price as well as the basis for some payment models. Value is also increasingly a driver of change, not just for companies that make specialized products with potential for great impact, but also for manufacturers of "me too" products and other providers of healthcare services.

The strongest innovators will seek an early shift to the value model, while others may look at acquiring, consolidating, and opportunistically pricing therapeutics as these changes take place. The increasingly clear focus on value will also pave the way for new disruptors to enter the industry, particularly those in digital healthcare, a process that, as we've seen, has already begun. Strategic decisions will be about redefining business and operating models—and perhaps about managing multiple models across geographies, therapeutic areas, and patient populations.

* * *

Regardless of the type of company, the products and services it offers now, and the products and services it may envision offering, the key to success in this evolving healthcare ecosystem will be figuring out how to create value—value for the patients in terms of outcomes, and value for the players in the healthcare market in terms of sustainability and profitability. To do so, senior leaders will need to focus on three core elements of their business:

1. Clarifying their unique *market positioning* in light of the emerging healthcare ecosystem
2. Defining the *differentiating capabilities* necessary to hold that market position
3. Creating a *high-performance anatomy*—that is, an organization, measures, and structure—that is laser-focused on delivering that position

These elements form the basis of the Accenture High Performance Framework, which compels executives to ask themselves a series of questions, outlined in this chapter. Answering these questions in a way that will drive exceptional performance means making the kinds of strategic choices that bring clarity to the organization's purpose, direction, and day-to-day execution. Ultimately, these choices determine the business model (or models) that an organization deploys.

MARKET POSITIONING: "WHAT MARKET WILL MY ORGANIZATION SEEK TO SHAPE AND WHAT WILL IT TAKE TO INFLUENCE THAT MARKETPLACE?"

Historically we defined three types of market positions: leader, fast follower, or struggler. Leaders often had significant market share—the proportion of the total addressable patient population that could be prescribed their therapeutics. They also had the majority "share of voice" for their various marketing initiatives. Fast-follower positions, however, sometimes had an advantage over market leaders because they didn't have to develop a market for a new class of drug and bear all the associated investments. (In any case, fast followers were generally in positive slots. Worse case, they got to "draft" the leaders in developing the market with physicians, creating a basis of reimbursement with payers and gaining market recognition for the category with patients.) In the "volume period," more was better for most companies, save for the strugglers—those that were unable to gain or sustain traction, possibly due to internal management issues, fatal flaws in strategy, or uncompetitive products.

But in the demanding, increasingly value-centric world, the definition of markets and market position is evolving. A three-tier classification will no longer work. Instead, market positioning is looking more like staking a claim on a complex map, with new sources of differentiation and distinctiveness creating micromarkets of leading and fast-following opportunities across different populations, new approaches to delivering value, and new performance attributes enabling long-term success.

Determining optimal market positioning in this arena begins with considering, broadly, what value will mean in the context of an organization, its customers, and its ecosystem. In other words, senior management first needs to articulate a *Value Strategy*. From that strategy will arise several sets of operating choices. The first set focuses on new revenue models and payment mechanisms tuned to the increasingly challenging economics of healthcare. The second set defines key aspects of the new operating model, focusing on the capabilities, technologies, and services that complement the therapeutics or devices used to address a particular patient disease or condition, and also add value to health systems. The final set addresses more wholesale changes in the business model, evaluating a range of options from product-based to pure service and outcomes-based approaches, and creating an altogether new basis for collaboration and participation in patient care and health.

Market Position Part I: The Value Strategy

We can think of value in three dimensions: outcomes, healthcare system benefit, and trajectory. The Value Strategy should define specific sets of patients for whom the company will be delivering specific therapeutic and quality of life outcomes, the advantages being delivered relative to the standard of care, the differential advantage the company has in delivering this value, the critical characteristics of its operating model, and how it is paid commensurate with the value realized.

The Value Strategy should further define how outcomes delivered to patients equate with or may be translated to value realized by healthcare systems. Healthcare system benefits may come through reduced days in facilities, care delivered in remote versus acute settings, surgical interventions avoided, and longer time between acute interventions, to name only a few potential sources. While today it remains possible to receive reimbursement without specific evidence of health system benefit, we believe that this is only a temporary state. With many health systems (especially those that are single or highly consolidated payers) constraining their health resources to a percentage of GDP, it is only a matter of time before value, as a lens for market access, becomes the standard. More immediately, the Value Strategy will guide the structure of a critical supporting document—a value dossier.[1] The dossier should contain data and analyses that determine market access, population coverage, and specific reimbursement levels. It should outline the real-world data analyses, observational studies, and potentially pragmatic studies that will further substantiate value for patient populations.

Finally, the Value Strategy should have a clear view of the patient journey, its key positive influence and failure points, and how specific sets of services might augment the role of current healthcare providers in ensuring positive and meaningful clinical outcomes. It will also provide guidance on the language and norms most consistent with the outcomes that patients desire and the health system targets, setting a "north star" for internal and external communications and firmly situating the organization in its target market.

Market Position Part II: Forming New Partnerships

The scope of healthcare, health services, and the sets of activities that need to be choreographed to assist with achieving the highest value outcomes are enormous. We've talked about the direct spending on healthcare as an increasing percentage of the GDP of the most mature and modern economies. But as our research for this book has shown us, the activities that will ultimately be considered part of healthcare spending transcend what's already included. These need to be taken into consideration as well, as senior leaders articulate their market position. As an example, consider health-related services that extend outside of formal health facilities, including the digital aspects of medicine, such as home-based sensor monitoring; patient digital engagement focused on medical adherence; aligned nutrition, activity, and emotional status monitoring; and a variety of outbound clinical (e.g., telephone and telepresence nurse- and care-coaching services) and digital interactions (e.g., health avatars).

Delivering value in this new healthcare environment will almost certainly require a broad set of partnerships, relationships, and even joint-ventured initiatives. The breadth and scope of healthcare changes and range of different regional delivery systems all indicate that partnering models will be quite diverse. Elements to consider include:

1. Access to, and advanced intelligence into, *real-world data that provide insights* for digital medicine initiatives, value dossiers, value based pricing, and value-contracting. Collaborative and partnered approaches will predominate in data access and in global IT cloud services that can integrate and analyze the data from many disparate sources.[2]

2. Research, development, and commercialization of *digital medical technologies* and solutions. A variety of remote sensors and monitors will be appearing in patient homes and as wearables, and these will fuel demand for the integration and aggregation of their data into high-value solutions that complement the specific biological benefits of therapeutics and regulated devices (e.g., implantable pacemakers and defibrillators).[3] (You can picture patients saying, "I can have this data at my fingertips; why can't you use it?") Similarly, digital engagement and insight technologies (e.g., Apple HealthKit and ResearchKit; Google Health Watch) will be scaling and moving into standard practice.[4] Physicians and other allied healthcare professionals will also be working with decision support tools that help bring to bear evidence combined with the beneficial interpretation of individual patient health data, increasing physician precision, enhancing patient outcomes, and delivering greater value.[5]

3. Creation of a *regional infrastructure for delivery of value-based healthcare* solutions. It is often difficult for organizations to deploy tailored models and approaches for all of the individual geographies

that make up their target market. As a result, we anticipate seeing an array of new collaborations bringing an organization's matured capabilities and models from one geography to another.

4. New *value-chain–centric collaborations and combinations* to provide new entities and value delivery capabilities. Many of these could involve health provider and healthcare insurer, multiple healthcare providers, and combinations thereof with pharmaceutical or medical device companies.[6]

Realizing new insights, new approaches, and new sources of value within a meaningful time frame will require collaboration. Leaders of the future will translate their strategies into collaboration requirements, often having their current and prospective ecosystem of partners informing their overarching Value and Business Strategies.

Market Position Part III: Focusing on Assets and Capabilities

Once clarity has been achieved on the value that the organization will strive to achieve for the healthcare system, a company's leadership will need to conduct a strategic alignment review of the assets of the organization, with a view to acquiring, divesting, or aligning with other organizations to drive the desired outcome. The restructuring of Novartis in 2014 offers an excellent example. With a clear vision and strategic focus, Novartis fundamentally restructured its portfolio, divesting its animal health business, setting up an independent joint venture for consumer health, and implementing an asset swap with GlaxoSmithKline plc, Brentford, United Kingdom (GSK), so that it could hone and redouble its focus on oncology. Within one year, Novartis repositioned itself in the marketplace with a new portfolio targeted at driving value for patients.

This new focus has driven and will continue to drive a reconsideration of foundational and differentiating capabilities. For this value-centric enterprise, these involve: accessing data on real-world outcomes; bringing these data into an advanced analytic environment to drive insights in the current standard of care, gaps and deficiencies in this standard, and opportunities to substantially improve patient outcomes and health system value; redefining the definitions of products to include services, technologies, and decision support tools; evolving far more integrated approaches to innovation management from late discovery through to full commercial management—bringing new forms of digital medicines that align therapeutics or devices with services and supporting technologies; a pricing and contracting capability that is synced to outcomes and value, where health economics is a tool for enterprise management as opposed to a niche capability; collaboration and partnership as a critical mode of execution; and a performance orientation that relentlessly looks for ways to improve patient outcomes and health system value as key drivers of company performance—outcomes and value, not volume.

Market Position Part IV: Divesting Existing Capabilities

As with any change, some existing capabilities, even some that are quite evolved and refined by today's standards, will not be the differentiators or source of distinctiveness in the future. Even worse, some highly evolved and large-scale legacy capabilities may promote a sort of lock-in where adopting the new ways of working and building the new capabilities are overwhelmed. Senior managers will need to be able to view these capabilities dispassionately and divest them progressively.

For example, traditional commercial analytics that focused on transaction data will provide no insights into the benefit delivered to patients or the value generated for risk-bearing providers or payers. The more specialized the pharmaceutical or biopharmaceutical company's product portfolio and pipeline, the more critical are real-world data sources.

Similarly, phase III clinical study data are having reduced influence on health reimbursement authorities and payers. Consequently, there is a growing need to reduce the size of these trials to just focus on those aspects required for regulatory approval, reserving more funding and new capabilities for post-approval clinical and observational studies.

The role of the sales force, too, is changing. In many therapeutic areas and regions, the access a traditional sales representative may have to physicians is now minimal. Even if they are afforded that access, the physicians themselves increasingly do not determine their own prescribing options—this is increasingly coming from an institutional committee and then rendered into the electronic medical record order sets. So, as Figures 2.1 and 2.2 demonstrate, where and how the sales force is allocated and integrated into new multichannel models becomes critical.

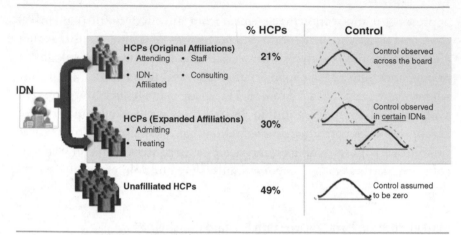

	% HCPs	Control
HCPs (Original Affiliations) • Attending • Staff • IDN- • Consulting Affiliated	21%	Control observed across the board
HCPs (Expanded Affiliations) • Admitting • Treating	30%	Control observed in certain IDNs
Unafilliated HCPs	49%	Control assumed to be zero

FIGURE 2.1   The Increasing Influence of Integrated Delivery Networks Through Employed and Affiliated Health Care Professionals

Source: Accenture research https://www.accenture.com/t20150608T044420__ w__/ us-en/_acnmedia/Accenture/Conversion-Assets/DotCom/Documents/Global/PDF/ Dualpub_15/Accenture-The-Doctor-Will-Not-See-You.pdf.

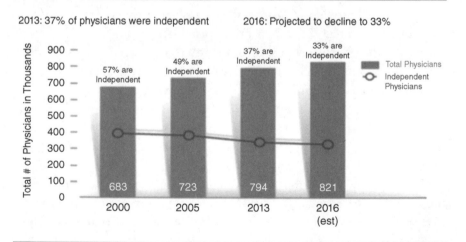

FIGURE 2.2   A Shrinking Minority of Physicians Are Independent

Source: Accenture research, http://www.accenture.com/SiteCollectionDocuments/PDF/ Accenture-The-Doctor-Will-Not-See-You.pdf.

Legacy pricing groups also warrant fresh consideration. Areas such as pricing traditionally focused on existing products in the same therapeutic category. The "case for superiority" thus supported increased pricing for newly launching therapeutics. Increasingly, multiple generics are upending this approach. There are more available that are highly efficacious in a wide number of diseases, with highly advantageous economics. Payers' expectations of real-world results consistent with the trial results also factor in, in a major way. Payers want to see assurance of actual benefit in support of their decision to allow access and reimburse at specific pricing levels. So historical pricing groups may be rendered obsolete by the new demand and the growing negotiations with business teams at risk-bearing provider systems, and increasingly sophisticated payers.

DIFFERENTIATING CAPABILITIES: "WHAT INTERNAL AND EXTERNAL CAPABILITIES DOES MY ORGANIZATION NEED IN ORDER TO GAIN AND MAINTAIN A LEADING MARKET POSITION?"

Once an organization's leaders have achieved clarity around market position and the asset structure necessary to drive that market position, they need to turn their attention to assessing the organization's core capabilities in even more depth. As we've noted, some may need to be divested. Others still may need major overhauls. The traditional R&D, supply chain, and commercial silos of healthcare products companies, for example, need to be objectively assessed in their "fit for purpose" for the next iteration of the competitive organization. And so senior managers across health services, digital technology, and life science companies need to answer several essential questions:

- What new capabilities are required?
- Do our existing capabilities need to be retired, reshaped, or restructured?
- Should the organization focus on one set of capabilities rather than focusing on all those that are required to deliver its strategic objectives?
- Are others better at filling strategic capability gaps?

Differentiating Capabilities: Pivoting to the Patient

Therapeutics companies are moving toward a value-basis for reimbursement, wrapping their therapeutics in a set of supporting services that fill in missing links in the healthcare ecosystem, integrate critical data on patients' responses to their therapeutics, and provide a range of patient engagement tools that strengthen the effectiveness of therapeutic approaches. This, along with other patient-centric developments, constitute a new core competency for leading healthcare organizations—the ability to pivot the organization to focus on the patient rather than the product and on the outcome rather than the sale. This pivot requires a restructuring of some of the traditional functions of R&D, supply chain, and commercial operations as well as the creation of new capabilities. Fundamentally the entity needs to move from being a product-focused organization to becoming a consumer- or patient-focused organization. This shift has happened in many other industries over the past decade but therapeutic companies in healthcare have been slow to adapt. With the pressure now on, future success rests on a significant rethink of organizational capability and alignment in areas such as:

Medical affairs: Consistent with the transition of healthcare to value, there is a need for a fundamental change in the role and relative importance of pharma and biotech medical affairs departments. Medical affairs historically provided brand neutral and study-supported information to clinicians and clinical communities and oversaw safety and pharmacovigilance processes. It was a critical function, but one that managed risks more than was considered critical for growth and revenue models. Increasingly, however, value-based medicine groups are creating new foundations for market access through chartered large-scale, real-world studies that can provide incremental outcome and value benefits of a therapeutic approach relative to a standard of care. These studies may even include services around the therapeutic (the drug or device) that significantly contribute to the outcomes realized.

A reconsidered medical affairs or value-based medicine organization would be the natural place to integrate new sources of data and insight, to consider sets of services that would contribute to the effectiveness of practice, or to be a digital attribute of a product. For example, in an emerging field such as neurodegenerative diseases, the collaborative collection of patient medical, neurofunctional, and patient-reported outcomes data could tune diagnostic and treatment approaches. This would work within currently marketed therapeutics, diagnostics, and functionality tests, using the broader data sets and power of a multicenter collaborative approach. Such approaches have been used through the years to achieve significant advances in patients' outcomes: childhood leukemia being a prime example of one disease that—through a persistent program of clinical and observational studies—evolved from having very poor outcomes for children to having treatments that are highly effective for the vast majority. Medical affairs would be the most likely group to be at the table for broad, population-centric collaborations with single payer or large regional health systems.

The sales organization: The sales organization stands in contrast to medical affairs. Historically the sales force was one of the key features and differentiators of the performance of one company from another, especially when comparing companies within disease or therapeutic categories. It justified mergers and acquisitions for the synergies that products might realize when being detailed by the same set of sales representatives. With the move to value, consolidation of decision-making authority within large health systems, and the shifting of risk and objectives to population goals, representatives in traditional models are declining in effectiveness and in the scope of their role. But what capabilities need to emerge in their stead?

For some companies, these legacy sales forces will become integral to articulating the value of a combined product and service delivering an improved value outcome to healthcare providers and making them aware of the services to inform their patients. The decision now confronting pharmaceutical, biopharmaceutical, and medical device companies is one of identifying and pursuing the distinctive operating characteristics and capabilities that will most align to value in the future, while assuring sustained performance today: a challenging remit for sure.

The ability to leverage real-world data and advanced analytics to predict opportunity and prove value: Real-world data are not new, but with the scope and scale of their availability over the past three to four years and their increased use by health providers and health insurers, they must also factor largely into strategic development. Think of real-world data as the foundation for an increasingly value-centric economy in healthcare. It would be impossible to understand the current standard of care in any meaningful way without real-world data. Optimization of outcomes for a population would not be possible without the insights into what is working, not working, or just missing—information that is provided by real-world data. No life science company or healthcare entity will be able to manage to outcomes or value without access to real-world data and deep expertise in advanced clinical analytics.

For the pharmaceutical, biopharmaceutical, or medical device company, real-world data are today available in a number of different forms. They can be purchased as data sets where the patients' privacy is protected (the sets do not identify patients). These data are generally made available through for-profit companies that have made provisions for accessing electronic medical records or health insurer claims data. These data are highly useful for understanding trends in a population, doing comparative analyses of the outcomes of one therapeutic approach (novel, innovator therapeutic–based) versus a standard of care (multiple-generic therapeutic regimen), understanding the patient pathway and treatment journey, or interpreting the prescribing and treatment decisions of clinicians in different settings.

Real-world data are also available through various patient organizations and through health-centric social sites and tools. These data tend to be more consumer-focused, sitting at the edge of the traditional clinical view and combining social, lifestyle, and behavioral aspects of a patient's life. This is an emerging and potentially high-value area of insight. Patients spend far more time away from formal health facilities and formal healthcare providers than they do with them. These data can provide information concerning the effectiveness or challenges of disease management for the patient and the patient's family, as well as insights into the aspects of care management that add the most value. For example, certain diseases such as multiple sclerosis, heart failure, and Alzheimer's may be accompanied by significant amounts of depression. The depression may lower a patient's ability to manage the more physically taxing aspects of disease self-management, leading to lower medical adherence and possibly detrimental lifestyle choices that accelerate degeneration or the return to acute disease state.

Increasingly, real-world data, clinical and social, are being made available through care provider and healthcare insurer collaborations. These collaborations are usually specific to a population or a set of clinical questions of benefit to patients. The value of this approach is that the full cooperation and collaboration of the healthcare provider generally allows for more complete access and a more complete view of a specific patient population, thereby accelerating insights as well as supporting more specific concepts or approaches to patient care management.

Organizations—be they biopharmaceutical, device, care provider, health services, or health insurers—will all need to have their strategies for accessing and collaborating around real-world data. This will be an area of deep competence and expertise in the future leaders of healthcare. It will be the source of insights around meaningful innovations that will be prioritized for commercialization. These data and supporting standardized analytics will be the currency for value contracting as well as the lever for insights into new treatment approaches and services that will transform the outcomes and value of healthcare.

The product offering: Pharmaceutical, biopharmaceutical, and medical device companies have defined terms—insider terms—to characterize and categorize their products. These therapies can be interventional in that they interrupt a disease state, restore functionality, or otherwise actively act on the biology of the patient and their disease. They can be supportive or complementary forms of therapy. They can be palliative, providing relief and comfort at end of life. All of this language, however, is disease and biology focused: It reflects the search for a chemical, biological, or electrophysiological way of treating an aspect of patient health. It is distinctly not holistic or focused on the total care management or total value requirements of the patient or provider system.

The move to value and the availability of broader, longitudinal health data are now enabling a new definition of "product" in healthcare, and that definition needs to become part of the vernacular in order to develop a viable strategy. The right definition of "product" can lead to a strong ability to deliver value, guide investments, and develop new capabilities. It can also provide a context for health provider and health insurer contracts or collaborations. These products—biopharmaceuticals or medical devices— should have active therapeutic, restorative, or preventative qualities in addition to supporting digital attributes. The attributes could involve specific tools for clinicians (e.g., real-time assessment of the highest responders to a specific therapeutic approach), patient engagement (e.g., medical adherence, lifestyle modification and management, response monitoring, etc.), and patient care management (e.g., remote-based and partnered approaches such as remote health monitoring of blood pressure, weight, pulse, activity levels, and diet, combined with an active platform of digital and personal interactions). In this way, the therapeutic product is a total product, increasing the value to patients and the healthcare system.

We see this redefined total product as the basis for competitive differentiation as well as the basis for a health system or insurer's preferred management approach. It may also become what underlies a patient's preference for a care or health management partner, in the same way a consumer might indicate a strong preference for the total proposition provided by Charles Schwab & Co., Inc. or Fidelity Investments (FMR LLC) in financial services or Apple Inc. for their personal electronics and lifestyle ecosystem.

Already we are seeing patients as consumers evolve in their preferences from whom and where they seek healthcare information. While their personal care providers clearly remain a primary source, online and digital channels are growing in credibility, increasingly viewed by patients as a needed and valued resource. The same is true of physicians, more than half of whom are consulting digital resource tools such as UptoDate® and ePocrates®, which support their diagnostic and treatment capabilities.

All healthcare-related organizations need a clear definition for their products and services as part of their overarching value strategy. This will lead to a redefinition of traditional innovation processes, how research and development is defined, the allocation of resources to innovation, and the role of key functions and partners. While many companies have evolved digital engagement and digital multichannel strategies as a more efficient mode of executing their classic commercial programs, the development of total products is something quite distinct. It is a therapeutic product intimately intertwined with digital medicine, where the digital and/or digitally enabled services are part of the product and not a commercial appendage thereof. Therapeutics, with the support of their digital medicine complements, are the basis for value, whether as a justification for price or as the basis for outcomes-based payment.

R&D: The traditional research and development business capability has been challenged for the past 20 years with declining productivity and rising costs. The new era of the patient-as-consumer and the availability of data provide both opportunities and challenges to the traditional capabilities. As we see, companies like Gilead self-disrupt the holy grail of patent protection and reach new heights on bringing out new products that "retire" existing products well before patent expiry and companies like 23andMe establish accelerated R&D capabilities that facilitate "*in silica*" research, the traditional bench research: Thus the clinical execution model is coming under pressure. The new R&D capability needs to be significantly more open, collaborative, external facing, data driven, technology enabled, and patient focused.

The supply chain: The traditional supply chains are coming under challenge. No longer is it good enough to have a compliant, global capability focused on product production and distribution. The traditional models were built for high-margin, patent-protected therapies and devices. In the new world, the patient will increasingly expect a service wrapper on a product, an interactive digital experience, and a two-way communications pathway that enables and facilitates innovation and continuous improvement.[7] The definition of the supply chain will embrace more than materials suppliers through to distributors; rather it will reflect the end experience of the health providers, patient, and potentially the patient's caregivers. The definition will integrate the therapeutic, devices, and information flows that enable the individualized experience and ensure outcomes and broader health system value. In the new world, the supply chain will act as the last mile of patient experience fulfillment. It will need service capability, patient and customer intimacy, data-driven processes, external partners, and an unprecedented level of direct connection with the hospitals, providers, caregivers, and other players in the broader ecosystem.

Senior managers need to consider overall capabilities not just function by function but also in the broad context of the raison d'être of the organization. They need to challenge traditional internal and external boundaries; they also need to establish new key performance indicators (KPIs), new measures of success, and a new level of integration across the enterprise that anticipates much more iterative evolution of products and service.

PERFORMANCE ANATOMY: PIVOTING THE OPERATING STRUCTURES TO PATIENTS AND ENSURING DIFFERENTIATING CAPABILITIES

The performance anatomy of a patient-focused, value-driven company servicing global healthcare markets is a fundamental departure from the product-oriented enterprises of the past:

- New performance structures are required that break down traditional barriers/silos and guide behaviors to the new norms of patient outcomes and value
- New metrics and key performance indicators (KPIs) are necessary to drive desired outcomes
- New talent and skills that guide decisions though analytics and drive value through technology and services
- Local/regional and global considerations need to be addressed to enable servicing of the different global markets that are themselves evolving at a different pace

Balancing the Global, the Regional, and the Local

Historically, large pharmaceutical and medical device companies were organized by brand and region. Brand was an overlay for separate legal entities, which were largely geographic and optimized for tax strategies, with different entities for intellectual property ownership in Ireland, Bermuda, or other locations. For reasons of legal separateness and because healthcare markets were often strongly local in their composition, purchasing, and decision making, the local organizations carried significant operational authority and control. The net effect was a "stickiness" to the local model that often reduced any meta-regional or global strategy to an advisory role.

Now, however, we see clinical and value analysis across geographies converging with value-based compensation. Consequently, the therapeutic and digital medical strategies of one geography have great relevance to another. Stated differently, as the basis of product pricing and reimbursement becomes more value-based, decisions become increasingly informed by real-world data and advanced longitudinal analytics, and products both intervene in the biology of a disease and provide digital medical benefits to patients and providers, we will see global platforms and capabilities take on greater importance. This will challenge the legacy role of localized, and often highly embedded, country and regional organizations as a primary performance unit.

All therapeutics companies, health services companies, and, increasingly, private healthcare insurers, need a differentiated approach to their regional strategies with clear implications for their operating models. The current evidence indicates that new roles in setting value strategies, creating real-world analytic capabilities, and redefining products will accrue to global entities. Clearly these changes will need to be approached with consideration of formal legal structures, work council requirements, and patient and provider data privacy requirements, among many related considerations. However, the consistency of the approach and the leveraging of difficult to replicate central capabilities will be key characteristics of the new leaders and highest performers.

Markets can now be defined as "value-based," fee-for-service, or transitioning. The focus may be a health system or a sub-region where the payer-provider combination creates a context for a specific reimbursement model. The big-picture view, then, will be a combination of the regional characteristic with an overlay for the population of patients benefiting from a specific therapeutic approach.

The implications for the pharmaceutical or medical device company commercializing their products into this situation are great. These organizations will be addressing a broader system that is changing and moving toward value and risk, even as they strive to be the better, cost-efficient operator in the traditional world of care reimbursement. They must balance the need to prepare for the coming future, while managing under the "old rules" that reflect the current operating model. Navigating through these two environments is tricky, as a few examples will illustrate. Consider:

Hospitals selecting an anti-infective to treat an acute infection usually begin with a set of generic alternatives to branded drugs. For acute infections, the costs of the therapeutics used are often borne by the hospital[8] as part of the procedure costs. Determining when to use generic acute anti-infective therapeutics versus branded is both an economic decision and a clinical decision.

Getting the diagnosis of the patient infection and selecting the right anti-infective matters a great deal. The wrong decision may result in a longer length of stay for the patient, a higher likelihood of readmission, or worse. Yet different hospitals will take different approaches to manage the decision process. For some that are already reimbursed on a value basis,[9] the risk is that they will not be reimbursed for the extra in-patient days and that they will bear the cost of the avoidable readmission. Here the hospitals have highly active programs looking to reduce readmissions across therapeutic areas, looking at infection control and other programs that may contribute to that goal. Other hospitals, however, may receive payment for extended length of stay days and even for what could be classified as an avoidable readmitted patient. Same problem, same options, but different responses in terms of internal capabilities, processes, and priorities in decision making.[10]

The classic adage "all healthcare is local" historically meant that the structure of all healthcare provider systems and the relationships across those providers were different in different geographies. Now we can say, "All value is local." The health reimbursement or financing authorities may be different across regions within a country. The policies and approaches of these authorities may also be different—some focused on population outcomes and others more focused on value measures.

Correspondingly, health providers in these regions will have very different structures, incentives, and measures of performance. For example, the hospitals that bear risk directly may be increasingly interested in an analytic solution that leverages data from their EMR, allows them to predict which microorganism is likely driving the infection,[11] and select the anti-infective with the highest likelihood of addressing the infection.[12] An institution that doesn't bear risk would certainly be keenly interested in that capability as well, but may place it at a lower priority relative to other initiatives, such as increasing rates of referrals to their acute hospitals from community providers outside of their own network.

Similarly, consider another example—a heart-failure patient who receives an initial diagnosis within the emergency department of a hospital, is then hospitalized and stabilized (e.g., fluid removed from the lung or a process called apheresis), and is then assigned a specific set of therapeutics and other lifestyle modifications (e.g., lower salt intake, diuretics, etc.). While risk-bearing hospitals may have significant incentives to maintain the patient safely at home (controlling actively for the risk of readmission and the overall health status of the patient), other health systems and other regions may place a different emphasis on the heart-failure patient population and choose to optimize the allocation of scarce program funds.

Commercial, medical, manufacturing, and supply chain capabilities all need to acknowledge these differentiated structures across therapeutic areas, broad regions, micro-regions, and the patient's own context to manage to value.

A RESPONSIBILITY FOR YOUR COMPANY'S FUTURE

The opportunity to drive higher performance through a value strategy and new operating models can be addressed on multiple levels—companies can look at the individual functional areas, alignment to new market definitions, and the new capabilities as outlined above to redefine value and drive results.

One of the emerging truisms of the digital business model era is that companies will not be able to be successful based on deploying the best practices of others or the past. Digitally enabled or entirely digital operating models are predicated on ever-improving responsiveness to customers and consumers, an increasing ability to anticipate and predict needs and requirements, and ever-improving economics of service value (top line) and service provision (bottom line). Think of this as the smartphone without "app stores," and then iOS and Android devices with broad application stores, content services, ecosystems of interactive remote blue-tooth enabled devices, and WiFi-enabled hubs accessing additional local networks of devices and services in the home and workplace. A 2015 analysis by Accenture Strategy estimated that digital restructuring of key functional areas can increase EBITDA by more than 27 percent for an $11B company.[13]

Pharmaceutical companies can grow their EBITDA by more than 27 percent ($1.04B EBITDA per $11B revenue) through partial digitization of the existing value chain:

- Manufacturing and supply   +11 percent (+$410M) EBITDA
- Marketing and sales   +10 percent (+$383M) EBITDA
- Research and development   +3 percent (+$124M) EBITDA
- Support functions   +3 percent (+118M) EBITDA

The analysis further projected that entirely new digital operating models could hold the potential to improve EBITDA by another 42 percent (+$1.62B EBITDA) through new digitally enabled, value-focused business models. This effect is independent of the individual company size.

- Digitization will contribute to changing demands patterns, blurring industry boundaries and enabling new business models (e.g. personalized healthcare, predictive healthcare, live healthy, and others).
- New business models will generate revenues from the traditional pharmaceutical market (41 percent; $1.6B), converging markets (0.9 percent; $34M), and enabling markets (0.1 percent; $5.6M).
- Only those companies investing ahead of existing and emerging competitors will capture this potential and establish the nucleus for the next generation of industry-dominant business models.

There is also a cost to "doing nothing." This study estimates that operating "business as usual" for an $11B pharmaceutical company carries the risk of losing up to 11 percent ($422M EBITDA per $11B revenue):

- Market share will be lost to competitors increasing their market share through partial digitization and emerging within and cross-industry innovators cannibalizing existing revenues with their new business models.

- In addition, average shareholder value for listed companies will deteriorate and cost structures will become noncompetitive compared to competitors with digitized operations by almost 24 percent of EBITDA.

Pharmaceutical companies serving this disrupted healthcare market in the new patient-as-consumer, data-rich, and digitally enabled world will benefit from keeping three main guidelines in mind.

First, real structural change is an imperative. "Business as usual" means losing revenue, market share, EBITDA, competitive strength, and shareholder value (for listed companies). In contrast, structural change holds the potential to grow EBITDA by $1.04B (27 percent) per $11B revenue through the digitization of various functions, and an additional $1.6B (42 percent) through new business models.

Second, broad-scale "functional digitization" *and* "new business models" are both needed. Combining both maximizes future EBITDA and revenue growth potential. Functional digitization provides a new cost and performance capability and new business models function as launching pads to catalyze the next generation of industry-leading business models.

Third, we recommend seizing the new opportunities with a highly differentiated strategy that provides competitive insulation. The most effective digitally enabled strategies for biopharmaceutical companies are tailored to the distinct characteristics of patients and their healthcare system. These are opportunities to reframe value, to stratify microgeographies and customers differently, and to differentiate the product, technologies, and services through partnerships and new digital capabilities. That differentiation is a growth driver and provides a measure of critical strategic protection during a period of great disruption and rapid shifts.

* * *

The presence of a few front-runners, their strategic decisions, and the moves that we have seen other organizations take as the new healthcare ecosystem starts to come into focus suggest that several business models have planted flags. Part II describes these models, first in summary, then in depth.

FROM STRATEGY TO VALUE WITH NEW BUSINESS MODELS

Chapter 3

Old Models and New

It's the end of one era and the beginning of another. Four new business models are emerging in the pharmaceutical field; companies with roots in other industries are crossing into the healthcare market; and entrepreneurs are coming on scene, powered by digital technologies and motivated by the promise of growth, profit, and bragging rights for expanding the definition of "care."

Some companies have already made significant strategic choices; as a result, several highly differentiated business models are solidifying. Some of these are opportunistic, leveraging managerial talent and capabilities with a focus on value for shareholders. Many represent substantial transformations—wholesale changes focused on improving patient outcomes and on creating value for the health system overall through high levels of engagement with patients and consumers, a redefinition of what a product offering includes (as the therapeutic, technologies, and digital enablement), and revenues tied tacitly or explicitly to outcomes.

Given the scope of these changes, most if not all of these new models will rely on new kinds of business-to-business relationships and collaborations, *some with long-trusted customers that will evolve into partners and risk-sharers, and some with entirely new companies and agreements.*

This chapter describes the four models we have observed at a high level; in Chapters 4 through 7, we will discuss each one in turn in more depth, assessing in greater detail how they work, providing examples, and examining their potential for sustainability.

*   *   *

Over the past five years we have seen tremendous challenges to business models long tested throughout the business world. Tesla Motors, Inc., for example, has transformed the economics of the auto industry and introduced an entirely new business model and customer experience grounded on product, infrastructure, and services innovation. Many of the traditional auto companies are now trying to follow suit by digitizing components of their business and rapidly innovating to electric vehicles, believing that they can leverage their existing infrastructure and brand to compete in the new world. Yet Tesla continues to outperform these companies even as they attempt to introduce all electronic vehicles.[1]

The Tesla difference lies in the fact that it is operating a fundamentally different business model. The retail locations are not traditional dealerships, being company owned, and are often located in shopping malls where people already go. Functionality is constantly improving as new features are "pushed" via wireless Internet connections that are constantly maintained. In the same way that Apple created an experience within its ecosystem of technology and applications, Tesla has created an ongoing relationship that listens, learns, and improves. There is little to no requirement for maintenance (aside from wiper and tire replacements as there are few moving parts). The durable, all-electric motors and long-duration synthetic lubricants allow most customer interactions to be positive about new sources of value from an existing investment. Just talk to a Tesla owner. Many of these individuals love to wax on about how different their experience has been from their experiences with any other car they've owned. From its inception, the business model was designed to deliver not only an innovative product, but also a fundamentally different, superior customer experience enabled by a virtual, global infrastructure that leverages modern digital technologies.

With the healthcare industry going through a similar revolution, life science companies are also reexamining their value proposition in the market and monitoring the shifting sands of their customer bases. These companies, too, face the stark reality that the business models of the past are not necessarily the right "chassis" for the businesses of the future. We haven't yet seen a "Tesla" of the healthcare industry. But some companies are moving far more quickly than others to assess the old approaches, and either adapt them to the new requirements, or create new models from whole cloth.

A PROFILE OF THE OLD WAY (THE STARTING POINT FOR MANY ORGANIZATIONS)

Historically, the operating approaches of pharmaceutical, biopharmaceutical, medical device, and medical diagnostic companies, and to a large degree even health providers, were relatively simple. They were based on a price for a product or a service, with greater payment when more product was used and more services performed. There were really three categories of businesses in this environment: generics, innovators, and service organizations. Therapeutics were priced like commodities (after patent expiry and six-month exclusivity), and, in large part, so were undifferentiated medical devices and supplies. Patent-protected innovator products were priced at a premium relative to prior products in the same category or some other comparable basis. And services were largely organized by acute (hospitals), non-acute (outpatient facilities or physicians' offices), long-term (rehabilitation facilities), and home care. Generally, institutions were organized around one segment of the continuum, though perhaps part of an integrated delivery system. They were volume oriented, not value oriented.

FUNDAMENTAL SHIFTS IN THE OPERATING ENVIRONMENT

But we know that the fundamentals of the operating environment are changing, with the basis of economics shifting from volume to value.[2] The basis for competitive differentiation is thus shifting from large-scale production (in pharmaceuticals, the production of chemical compounds) that dominated the past 30 years to a more stratified environment where a business model can "lead" with any of the following differentiators:

- Pure price in the case of over-the-counter[3] (OTC) and generic therapeutics

- An outcome driven primarily by product innovation (e.g., highly specialized medicines delivered to a patient identifiable via genetic mutation or specific pathophysiology of the patient's disease)
- An outcome driven by a combination of product and service (e.g., integrated therapies involving devices, products, and services focused on the patient, accommodating gaps in current provider care, or complementing the health provider's treatment approach in a remote setting such as their home)
- An outcome driven entirely by service (e.g., technology-driven products that work to change behavior or broader health/lifestyle outcomes integral with therapeutics, such as WellDoc, Inc.,[4] or purely digital companies that innovate leveraging data and capabilities rather than traditional science, such as 23andMe)

Accordingly, health providers that once influenced the prescription but did not pay for therapeutics are now becoming increasingly at risk for their prescribing decisions or are even becoming the purchasers of the therapeutics they prescribe.[5] Patients who once had highly standardized co-pays or were not directly responsible for payment with regard to their care, may now incur significant costs. Health insurers or payers that looked only for prescribing rules consistent with a U.S. Food and Drug Administration (FDA) or a European Medicines Evaluation Agency (EMEA) approval are now requiring demonstration of value based on real-world data. These buyers' expectations and constraints are shifting rapidly.

The pressures of healthcare costs around the globe, the increasing role of the patient as "consumer," omni-accessible and persistent digital channels for communication, and the availability of real-world patient data for both research and commercialization have all influenced expectations around value. And so there is an increasing requirement that price and payment forms reflect that shift.[6] Today:

- The patient as "consumer" has significantly more choice of over-the-counter (OTC) products.
- Health providers, authorities, and health insurers can increasingly direct use of the broad repertoire of generic therapeutics instead of one of the increasingly smaller number of branded or patent-protected innovator therapeutics through their coverage and reimbursement policies.
- Specialty therapeutics and devices are increasingly receiving value scrutiny from entities such as National Institute for Health and Care

Excellence (NICE) in the United Kingdom[7] and other advanced health payer analytic initiatives, or are being reimbursed in novel structures defined by entities such as the Center for Medicare and Medicaid Innovation (CMMI).[8]

- Patients as consumers expect to get more services around their products and are increasingly willing to contribute data to get better outcomes.[9]

As a result of these changes, we are seeing a new schema emerge for how pharmaceutical, biopharmaceutical, medical device companies, and health services will be paid. There are changes in how payment may be made—the fundamental basis of payments—and in who is responsible for the decision to purchase or pay.

There will continue to be a volume market where a large portfolio of generic therapeutics is purchased through tender or period supply contracts. We will also continue to see smaller-market and niche therapeutics opportunistically priced and purchased in smaller volumes. However, newer products being approved and launched will increasingly have payments made on the basis of value realized, verifiable through advanced population analytics.[10] Value-linked payments may be both, where pricing is supported by real-world evidence or where there are explicit linkages to health outcomes for patients and economic value for the health system. Figures 3.1 and 3.2 provide a conceptual

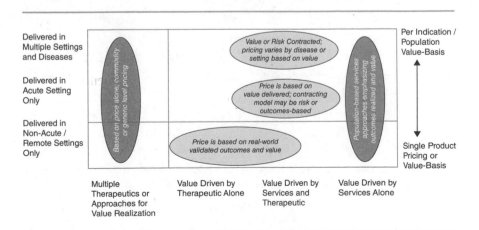

FIGURE 3.1   Emerging Schema of Pricing versus Value/Usage Matrix
Source: Accenture analysis.

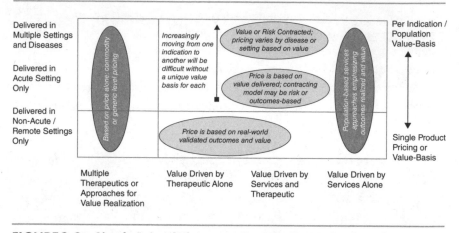

FIGURE 3.2 Single Priced Therapeutics Used in Multiple Settings and Indications Are Increasingly Challenged with Historical Uniform Pricing
Source: Accenture analysis.

view of this, where the focus will be on different groups of patients, populations, outcomes realized, the value of those outcomes, and allocated responsibility for that realization.

In the future, as we know, it will be difficult to secure reimbursement without a formal view of the value being delivered to specific populations of patients or even individual patients. We are now seeing formal health authority and private payer challenges to the universal pricing of therapeutics, as the same drug may be used to treat different diseases and have a different value for each distinct patient population.[11] The data for these sorts of assessments are accessible and are beginning to be used to make pricing "value-rational."

These new value-linked payment approaches require a tighter connection between the population or the individual receiving a new therapy, device, or procedure and the payment made. Stated differently, the local outcomes of a sub-region or tightly defined population will be the unit of analysis, payment, and decision. Increasingly this is meaning that financial risk is shifting from traditional health authorities and private payers to regional health systems, other providers, and new health services companies accepting whole or partial responsibility for outcomes.

THE NEW MODELS ARRAY THEMSELVES ON VALUE AND PAYMENT DIMENSIONS

In this context, key new emerging models are coming into focus. Reduced to their essentials, and with the strategic choices outlined in Chapter 2 as a backdrop, these models can be arrayed on two dimensions:

1. The value they deliver—that is:
   - The need for the product or service being sold and delivered (what it does).
   - The recipients (e.g., direct to patient, direct to consumer, to the health provider, to the financial risk bearer) and the method and form of delivery (e.g., by itself or in concert with, or embedded in, a partner's product or service, etc.).
   - The patient's necessary level of engagement (e.g., the patient's use of scts of engagement services, adherence to a regimen for a period of time, and/or use of remote sensors and monitoring to achieve the value outcome).
   - The basis of competitive differentiation (the incremental increase in the value that patients realize, compared with other offerings, in terms of outcome, ease of use, brand confidence, or another factor).
2. Who pays for that value, that is:
   - The customer (which may be the consumer but may also be a government, or risk-bearing healthcare provider system) that pays for the product or service, and the basis for that willingness to pay.
   - The pricing structure (e.g., pricing based on demonstrable benefit to patient and health system, outcomes-based contract, etc.).
   - The extent to which (or on what fronts) the company is equipped and differentiates itself as a better operator in this value-centric environment (e.g., value and outcomes, the total composite of therapeutic benefits and services arrayed to realize and ensure benefits, the basis for differentiation and competitive insulation).
   - The extent to which the company has adapted its revenue model from relying on the old business-to-prescribing influencer approach to the business-to-risk bearer approach. (For example, is this increasingly a business-to-business versus a business-to-prescribing influencer approach, where the business may be public or private risk-bearing entities such as payers or health providers that have

assumed clinical and financial risk for outcomes as a consequence of local payment reforms?)

- How the patient as a consumer is implicated in value realized and the willingness of the customer to pay. (For example, does there need to be a consumer or patient incentive for the total value to be realized?)

THE EMERGING BUSINESS MODELS

These models also range on a continuum from those that build on existing capabilities applied in a differentiated model to those that are disrupting themselves—and others—with new sources of value, delivered through a new operating model, and different bases of revenue derived largely from large risk-bearing provider systems or leading health insurers. In Chapters 4 through 7, we discuss each model in greater detail. Here we offer a brief outline of each, aligned to the framework developed in Chapter 2.

Emerging Business Model #1: Lean Innovators

With roots in the generics companies of old, this business model combines the best practices of efficient manufacturing, relentless cost management, return on investment rigor, advanced M&A expertise, and an eye for niche treatments where there may be significant latitude in pricing and market access approaches. While they maintain a broad generics portfolio, their financial performance is increasingly the result of their management of innovator products.

Market Position

In the post-patent cliff era,[12] generics/lean innovator companies have taken an increasingly dominant and important role in the new healthcare environment. They now offer the well-proven quality products of the past 20 years in off-patent format with an operating model that sustains competitive pricing for most governments and health systems around the world. They are no longer the "good enough" class but have now taken the position as the mainstay of the healthcare system. They offer affordable access to well-proven therapeutics. Their medicines are marketed toward large providers, governments, distributors, pharmacy benefit management companies (PBMs), and in some cases directly to consumers. Led by a new generation of "Lean Innovators," these businesses are excellent operators and cost managers, seeing sales, general, and administrative expenses (SG&A) and R&D as cost categories to be minimized and tightly controlled.

Differentiating Capabilities

The prototypical Lean Innovators are companies like Valeant Pharmaceuticals International, Inc. and Allergan PLC. (formerly Actavis). These companies are minimizing R&D while focusing heavily on optimizing product portfolios and leveraging mergers, acquisitions, and divestitures to drive shareholder returns. At the extreme, these companies behave like private equity organizations—investing and divesting with performance. From their heritage as inherently lean generics companies, they have highly efficient global manufacturing networks and highly integrated supply chains—something that most traditional large, innovator pharma are still struggling to assemble.

Given their heritage and their new commercial management paradigm, these companies can produce earnings before interest, taxes, and amortization (EBITA) as a percentage of revenue in excess of 20 percent and can compete well on the bottom line with the more diversified, patented portfolios of traditional innovator pharma.

Performance Anatomy

Lean Innovators are very global and very efficient. They have traditionally grown rapidly by acquisition and are less globally integrated than many of the innovator companies. While doing so, they have challenged the need for many of the traditionally high-cost functions fundamental to innovators (i.e., R&D and large sales force cost). As acquirers and highly optimized supply chain engines they have the potential to upend many models for how innovator therapeutic products can be managed for optimal profitability. They also hold the potential to use their enormous scope and scale in therapeutics to forward integrate with services. While many of their current strategies are financial and opportunistic, some will likely mature and differentiate as the value-centric environment of healthcare payment and consumer engagement advances and predominates. Those failing to make that transition in the coming years will find their acquisitions under increasing scrutiny and operations subject to broader oversight and controls by governments, health authorities, pharmaceutical benefit managers, and risk-bearing provider systems.

Emerging Business Model #2: Around-the-Patient Innovators

These businesses, still focused largely on producing drugs, seek to differentiate their offerings by developing ancillary services, algorithms, analytic capabilities, and more to create a new basis for product economics and add value for customers. In marketing terms, one could think of these ancillary elements as "line extensions"—they do not yet represent fundamental strategic shifts, although each has the potential to drive such a shift.

Market Position

In many respects these are among the most innovative companies. These companies are high science, high service, and high value. The Around-the-Patient Innovators are focused on the most devastating of diseases—those with the highest health burden on patients and high resource burden on health systems. They strive for insights into what is working and not working about the current standard of care. They have a willingness to "shape a market" by redefining modes of competition, bringing sets of technologies and services together to accommodate gaps and deficiencies in current care models and resources, and moving a market to value-based pricing and reimbursement approaches. They compete in multiple markets—for science and key R&D partnerships, for partners in technologies and digital infrastructure, and for share of value created for broad populations of patients with the highest unmet needs.

Differentiating Capabilities

Critical organization capabilities can be characterized as a form of relentlessness—an imperative to succeed now and in the future. The Around-the-Patient Innovators bring deep insights into current disease biology and the journey of patients in managing and treating their disease. While these are highly established companies, they have an unusual ability to be entrepreneurial in how they bring their scale, resources, and network to bear for the benefit of patients. They are increasingly global in the scope of their operations and vantage on the patients they seek to benefit. They recognize that the innovator therapeutics companies of the past were product-centric entities, while the imperative to benefit patient and health systems requires them to be solution focused and deeply competent in advancing the highest value new medicines, device technologies, advanced analytics, and digital infrastructure.

These companies are built on the traditional "diversified pharma" chassis but are leveraging and integrating their capabilities across the enterprise as well as harnessing new partners externally to fundamentally shift from an anatomy set up for optimization of individual product sales to one focused on selling a value proposition to a health system. Johnson & Johnson (J&J) and Novartis are blazing a trail in this area, focused on creating strong integrated backbones for innovation, operations, and sales. Where they do not have capabilities in-house they are reaching out to Apple, Google, Qualcomm, and others to drive partnerships that enable new offerings to the healthcare world. Their anatomics are in a state of change, but one that is being managed and funded by continual market success.

Performance Anatomy

The Around-the-Patient Innovators would rarely be characterized as lean. Yet they are incredibly strong stewards of their companies' resources. The most successful of the Around-the-Patient Innovators are the peak performers of life science companies. They focus on near-term performance, but not at the cost of long-run superior performance.

They view it as their responsibility to redefine the industry's operating models, even if others are the beneficiaries of their investments and experience. They are highly talent focused—creating an internal environment that recruits, develops, and continuously motivates the highest performers.[13] These are the companies pushing the industry to be increasingly analytic-driven, value-centric, and open to all forms of innovation that might bring benefit to patients. We expect to see significant changes in operating model metrics for these organizations as they blaze a trail over the coming years.

Emerging Business Model #3: The Value Innovators

By focusing completely on improving patient and clinical outcomes, this business model has great potential to make the healthcare system more efficient and effective overall. Companies using this model have formally accepted that the healthcare system is shifting to value and, rather than waiting for the entire market to complete this transition, they are going to be the "better operator" for this future state today, actively shaping its course and pace.

Market Position

Integrated therapeutics companies focus on integrated solutions that deliver individual, population, and health system economic outcomes. These companies integrate across care settings with technologies that bridge the divides between physicians and patients. They are integrating interventional technologies (e.g., medicines and devices) with monitoring and engagement tools. They are providing solutions that were not possible before and filling critical gaps that thwarted efforts to advance value even where this was attempted with the most sophisticated therapeutics. These companies recognize that they are no longer solely therapeutics or device companies. Instead, they deliver value through their ability to close gaps and remediate deficiencies in legacy healthcare models.

They are true value innovators. Their customers are risk-bearing health providers and health insurers. Their programs focus on specific patient populations with a set of quality outcomes targeted for realization. These value innovators are evolving the basic definition of a product-centric company into a new, outcomes-centric mode. And they are seeking to be paid for these outcomes, not the products they deployed.

Differentiating Capabilities

These companies require R&D capabilities comparable to the innovative medicines companies, but equally advanced medical affairs or evidence-based medicine groups that can substantiate value. They are analytics-centric and driven—requiring real-world insights to define their services, inform their contracting and risk models, and act as a new "language" for their health authority and provider system interactions. They also need new services units that will function as next generation commercial organizations. In the current climate, we find many of these companies collaborating with other parties in the ecosystem—with device manufacturers, therapeutics companies, digital disruptors, service providers, and data analytics players—all with the aim of creating and supplying superior services to patients and risk-bearing health systems. In short, these organizations are accelerating their evolution into integrated services organizations, focused on an array of levers that deliver outcomes.

Performance Anatomy

Most of the emerging Value Innovators we've observed were highly successful product companies, with leading sales forces and highly productive sales representatives with close working relationships with specialist clinicians and senior administrators. They are now focused on their relevance to health authorities and the top teams at risk-bearing entities. This relevance comes from their ability to generate unique insights into patients and populations, and their ability to offer solutions that predictably bring value to patients and the health system. They are learning how to measure value, direct their overall strategy and corporate resources to new value-delivering services, and incentivize their organization to value realization from the most senior corporate leaders to the frontline associates. While this is beginning within their new services units, it will rapidly move across product groups, regions, and functions.

Emerging Business Model #4: The New Health Digitals

The companies using this model are leading digital companies that are "going healthcare" by deploying their technologies, infrastructure, and developer networks to health, wellness, and care management. They are also technology-savvy healthcare companies that have "gone digital" by putting digitally powered initiatives at the center of their strategies, and start-up entities that are entering the healthcare market as they see opportunities to bring digital solutions to bear on any gaps in the system they spot—whether for patients, providers, payers, life science companies, other health-related businesses, or all of the above. And, they are start-up organizations, seeing gaps in the market and racing to fill them before one of the other two types steps in.

Market Position

New Health Digitals use their technological expertise and scale to enable services, often operating independently or in conjunction with the Around-the-Patient and Value Innovators companies above. We're seeing two primary variations on this business model. The first, which we call "Digital Gone Healthcare," are consumer and infrastructure-focused technology firms (including Google, Apple, and Qualcomm) that are now placing a major focus on healthcare services. These companies are providing services in the digital world in a manner that leverages technology to become more intimate with patients and their conditions. Combining this intimacy with digital technology can disrupt many of the traditional healthcare companies' functions of discovery, development, product launch, fulfillment, and service.

We call the second variation on this business model "Healthcare Gone Digital." These are healthcare-centric firms that are now digitally enabled and savvy, seeking to disrupt themselves and others with new strategies and new mandates (including Philips Medical and GE Medical[14]). For both of these types of digital disruptors, the customer is the consumer-as-patient and consumer-as-health-self-manager who sees value in consistently and conveniently acquiring contextual information about their health condition.

These firms have the potential to transform what is meant by healthcare. They are bringing together traditional elements (e.g., data from electronic medical records) with new sources of insight (e.g., personal monitoring devices and social tools) and providing them within devices and applications the consumer already owns and is trained to use. While these may appear to be inferior solutions today (e.g., the cardiac monitoring on a wearable may be less accurate today than the unit in your physician's office), they are early and improving rapidly. They also collect data in a way clinicians never could—continuously or at least with much greater frequency. All in all, these companies may play the role of classic disruptors for some and emerge as the critical partners for others.

Differentiating Capabilities

Healthcare Gone Digital businesses are using digital to reinvent and redefine their prior business models such that new value is offered but paid for by legacy customers. In contrast, the Digital Gone Healthcare organizations bring a scale of consumer device and application penetration that no healthcare company has ever achieved. They have strong, high-affinity relationships with consumers who have demonstrated a sustained willingness to engage and pay.[15]

Performance Anatomy

We are already seeing the New Health Digitals' strategies branching in different directions. The Digital Gone Healthcare businesses have a set of operating economics that assume enormous scale—50 percent of a country, hundreds of millions of customers, and petabytes of data. Their economics are equally digital in that they can assume an asset-free business model that can influence bricks and mortar or other physician assets (e.g., Uber providing transportation but owning no cars). Their marginal costs are low, implying that the investment requirements to gain another consumer or patient within their health ecosystem are exceptionally low. They come from a focus on the patient as a consumer, and they believe in the empowerment and protection of that consumer—giving the patient the power, authority, and confidence of an expert.

In contrast, the Healthcare Gone Digital businesses have brought with them infrastructure and costs from their legacy operations within hospitals and ambulatory clinical care facilities. They are extending out to remote settings and integrating across the continuum. Still, their costs are "healthcare" in their origins and centered on expertise and precision. They focus on the care providers and clinicians—they bring the experts to the patients.

Each model focuses on providing a system and service solution for patients and the healthcare system that provides value—none of these volume-based models. Yet one is focused on the consumer as personal health manager and the consumer as empowered patient. And the other provides digital infrastructure and tools that enable clinicians, health providers, and risk managers to extend beyond their historical walls and spheres of influence to remote settings where costs are lower and patients regularly spend their time. The Digital Gone Healthcare set is deeply disruptive and the Healthcare Gone Digital set is strongly transformative. It is still early; the ultimate digital winners are unclear.

HYBRIDS AND OTHER NOVEL SOLUTIONS

In addition to these four distinct models, we're also seeing some of the distinctions between healthcare providers and health payers begin to blur. In the United States, some providers now offer healthcare insurance products and coverage—and the trend is accelerating.[16] Regional ACOs are a further hybrid, using technology integration to oversee the care of specific populations of patients across multiple provider entities. Some of the largest health insurers, such as UnitedHealth Group Inc., have also forward integrated into primary care medical practices and health management. Finally, there are more consumer-centric changes underway, such as an expansion of personal lifetime health savings accounts (which already exist in the United States, though they are only attached to specific health insurance plans) that are a micro self-insurance mechanism that will ultimately represent a sizable pool of funds within the United States and potentially other markets. Some believe that this could catalyze for health insurance and health services the same revolution in products and services that transformed personal financial services.

This additional contextual wrinkle will ultimately expand the strategic options available to pharmaceutical, biopharmaceutical, medical device, health services, and health digitals. The character and form of contract structure and collaborative models are only just beginning to be explored. Similarly, the range of new company and service options available to the newest risk bearers (e.g., health providers taking risk or working in value contracts) and the newest health service providers (health insurers directly providing clinical and health management services) indicate that they have wide latitude to reconsider their models; they will not view history as the best guide to their futures. They will find that the increasingly value-focused, services-centric, and digital companies of the future are some of their best partners for meeting population and patient engagement goals.

In the value era, there is significant latitude for differentiated strategies. The definition of the product is broadening to include more dimensions than just the therapeutic entity itself. The assumption that healthcare occurs within healthcare facilities is also giving way to a view that much care needs to take place away from those settings in order to reduce costs, fill notable gaps, improve overall quality, better engage the patient and their caregivers, and more broadly drive value. We are already seeing product-centric organizations become focused on services as a source of future growth and revenues. The early results reflect that these service models are more profitable than the legacy product business and can access far larger markets. This parallels the trend in other industries—including insurance, media and entertainment, jet propulsion, transportation, and IT cloud services. Just as we have seen in these other industries, the opportunity to price to value delivered, to integrate new services continuously, and to move rapidly into new markets all enhance prospects for revenue and income growth. Since this is a new era, with new and broadly accessible technologies, the scope of strategic options available has accordingly expanded.

Chapter 4

Lean Innovators

With roots in the generics companies of old, this business model combines the best practices of efficient generics manufacturing with merger and acquisition (M&A) expertise and an eye for niche treatments.

Lean Innovators are product-centric businesses. Companies evolving toward this model as their primary modus operandi started out as generics companies, but they are no longer focused only on generic products; market pressures and new opportunities have encouraged them to reinvent themselves and enter new worlds of unmet medical need with patented and off-patent products. As of this writing, they have been profoundly successful financially—although increasingly under scrutiny.

Their distinctiveness lies in the fact that they often bring best practices from the world of generics to their work—large-scale efficiencies, a global scope, and a lean organization. Many members of the leadership teams at these companies have deep M&A and post-merger integration skills.

The Lean Innovator model is centered on acquiring companies that specialize in developing treatments for niche illnesses; that's what has made them the focus of many governmental and private payer reviews. Lean innovators capitalize on acquired organizations' growth and margin potential through broad cost-efficiency initiatives and strategic pricing increases.

Increasingly, they are focusing on innovation, with conservative approaches to research and development (R&D) that emphasize indication expansions and lower-risk, late-stage development programs.

*   *   *

The Lean Innovator is the successor model to the classic large-scale and global-scope generics company model. It is built on the foundation of a generics business, but adds the growth and margin improvements of the innovator companies it acquires. Yet it is more than a mixed breed. By applying a combination of low selling, general, and administrative (SG&A) expenses typical of generics with the performance mindset of a private equity player, it creates something new and very competitive, something that creates great value and is also disruptive to traditional business models.

Nonetheless, in order to understand the Lean Innovator model, it's important to know about the way in which pure generics companies evolved, grew, and prospered, and about the pressures they now face.

THE GENERIC CHASSIS AND HOW IT EVOLVED

Generic pharmaceutical manufacturers make medicines available at low prices to the broadest possible population of patients. As such, they have played an important role in the evolution of the entire healthcare system. Some have gone as far as crediting them with improving the health status of the population overall.[1]

First introduced in the United States in the 1920s (after Bayer AG lost a court battle to prevent the sales of generic aspirin), the generics market grew steadily until 1962, when the Food and Drug Administration (FDA) began requiring that pharmaceutical companies prove that their drugs were safe and effective before putting them on the market. The high expense of testing kept many would-be generics producers at bay—until 1984, that is, when the Drug Price Competition and Patent Term Restoration Act (known to most people as the Hatch-Waxman Act) went into effect. Hatch-Waxman extended the amount of time that companies could hold patents on new drugs; it also granted pharmaceutical manufacturers 180-day exclusivity over a generic drug after proving that the offering had the same active ingredients as the patented drug it was mimicking and worked in the same way. (Generics didn't have to go through the same lengthy trials as patented drugs before entering the market.)

Predictably, demand for generic drugs began to grow exponentially, and the market experienced years of continuous growth. Generics companies found it advantageous to broaden the number of therapeutics that they could offer and the number of geographies they could serve, leveraging the global scale of their manufacturing base and supply chains.

So while names like Pfizer Inc., Merck & Co., Inc., and F. Hoffmann-La Roche AG (Roche) may be more familiar to most people, the operations of some generics companies, such as the Israeli generics manufacturing company Teva Pharmaceutical Industries Ltd., are equally large and diverse.

For perspective, consider that each year 2.6 billion generic prescriptions are filled in the United States, and one of every eight of those prescriptions is a Teva product.[2]

Teva, interestingly, is a product of a series of mergers dating back to the early 1900s; to become Israel's largest pharmaceutical company, it joined forces in 1976 with two other businesses, Assia and Zori.[3] Soon after that, the merged entity began an ongoing series of acquisitions—more than five in the 1990s alone—which made it the global giant it is today. Teva expanded into the U.S. generics market shortly after the Hatch-Waxman Act went into effect.

Other top generics companies such as Valeant and Actavis also achieved a consistent pattern of growth through acquisitions within the United States, Europe, and (more recently) Asian markets. And not surprisingly, as they grew, they developed highly efficient management skills in the areas of due diligence and contracting—key levers in strategies that depended on efficiently assessing and assimilating other organizations.

They also became fluent in the art of balancing change management and the continuous operational improvement needed to maintain high-quality performance. Leading generics companies today are focused and forceful in meeting post-merger integration cost and growth targets, and especially adept at managing the high volumes and relatively narrow margins of the traditional generics industry. In part, that may be because they embraced the idea of efficiently managing highly diverse product portfolios within relatively lean and highly experienced management structures when compared with their pharmaceutical and bio-pharmaceutical company peers. An added advantage: Many executives at generics companies have worked together across successive acquisitions or even at other companies; as a result, they often come to the table with a high level of intra-team experience and trust, and a predisposition to work with one another as equals.

SHIFTING OPPORTUNITIES AND RISING PRESSURES

The great problem for generics companies is that the opportunities available within the traditional generics field are changing rapidly. The sector's growth was originally driven by the patent expiry—or by successful strategies to invalidate the core patents—of drugs that are used for the most part to treat conditions such as high blood pressure or high cholesterol that affect large numbers of people (also known as large-population therapeutics).[4] When patent-protected, these therapeutics were usually multibillion dollar revenue products. So the value of being the first to claim the right to produce the generic—and thus capturing six months of profits from exclusive generic marketing—was enormous.[5]

However most of these patent expiries have now taken place—many within the past 15 years in a circumstance known in the industry as the "patent cliff." Most of the broad-population chronic diseases and conditions that the medical field is aware of are now "covered" by generics. Also, an increasing proportion of the highest value, near-expiry pharmaceutical products are significantly different from the drugs that have been copied by generics in the past. These newer drugs, known as biologics, are derived from living organisms such as human, animal, or microorganism sources and are therefore much more difficult to replicate.[6] (Figures 4.1 and 4.2 provide additional detail on the patent cliff.)

And that isn't all. Generics companies additionally face another conundrum in their core business—the relative lack of leverage they have on their markets overall considering their enormous portfolios. They may supply the majority of therapeutics taken by patients in the United States, but pharmaceutical distributors such as McKesson Corporation, Cardinal Health, Inc., and AmerisourceBergen Corporation, and pharmaceutical benefit managers (PBMs) such as ExpressScripts Holding Company, Optum—an affiliate of United Health Group Inc., or CVS Health have had increasingly more power to determine which generic manufacturers' products are made available to patients. They do this by controlling which generic product is made available at the point of dispensing. In China (the second largest pharma market in the world), the government-controlled Essential Drug Lists (EDLs) control the prescription of specific drugs for reimbursement in each of the regions.

Pharmacy retailers and PBMs also manage the mail-order fulfillment of many chronic-use therapeutics renewals on behalf of patients who are

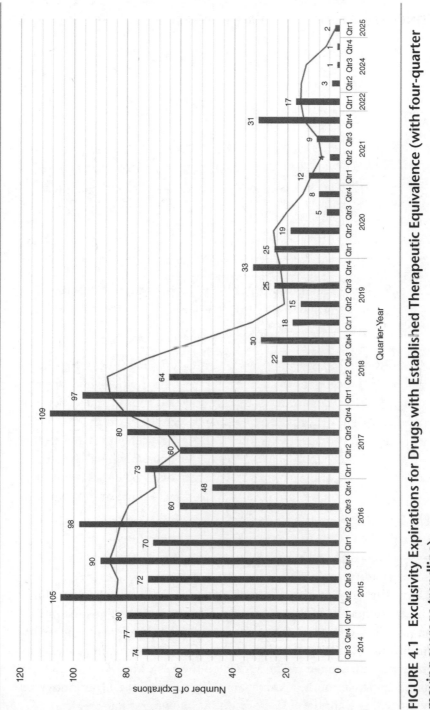

FIGURE 4.1 Exclusivity Expirations for Drugs with Established Therapeutic Equivalence (with four-quarter moving average trendline)

Source: FDA Orange Book, www.fda.gov/Drugs/InformationOnDrugs/ucm129662.htm.

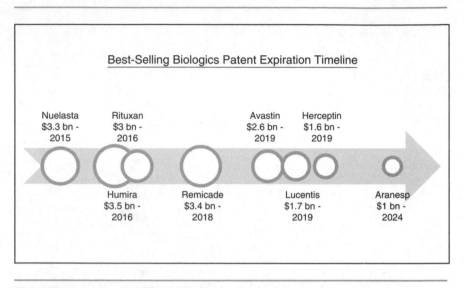

FIGURE 4.2   Best-Selling Biologics Patent Expiration Timeline
Source: Forbes http://www.forbes.com/sites/peterubel/2014/10/16/the-best-selling-biologic-drugs/.

reimbursed through their employers' health plan programs. Often these distributors will negotiate exclusive or preferential pricing on specific products or portfolios of products, forcing constant control and sometimes declines on margins in the highest volume categories of drugs.

Cardiovascular therapeutics is one of the largest categories and examples of where this occurs.[7] Generics companies possibly have the largest scale and scope of operations within a category of therapeutics here but at the same time, they have limited ability to direct where and how those therapies make their way to patients.

ENTER THE LEAN INNOVATOR MODEL

Faced with these realities, the classic choices for generic manufacturers have been: exit the market, differentiate in the current market, or innovate to create a new market. The companies that have chosen to pursue differentiation and innovation strategies, while leveraging their core competencies as generics, are the ones we say have created the Lean Innovator model.

Using what we term the "Value Curve" construct, the Lean Innovator model fits neatly into the "A" position, as shown in Figure 4.3.

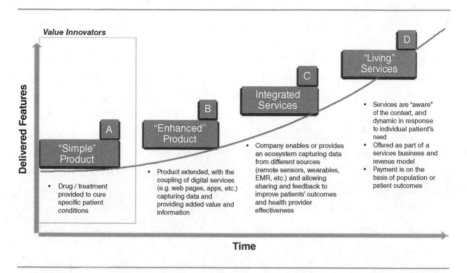

FIGURE 4.3   Lean Innovators Are the First Step on the Value Curve
Source: Accenture analysis.

Importantly, though, Lean Innovator businesses are new in two respects. First, they target smaller innovative products for acquisition that are undervalued by the market. Their focus is not on the therapeutic value of the product and securing reimbursement commensurate with that value, but rather on understanding the full financial potential that can be realized based on relative exclusivity, limited therapeutic choices, and the limited visibility the product may have to healthcare financial payers. It is akin to the small part in an electronic manufacturer's "bill of material" that is critical, can't be replaced with a substitute, but may represent only a very small percentage of total product's cost. These factors allow Lean Innovators significant latitude to set prices as they'd like. This is a form of pricing arbitrage, in that there are few controls or resources allocated to scrutinizing the prices of these smaller and more niche "miscellany" therapeutics. And, as with any arbitrage opportunity, it will be closed by Lean Innovators or through interventions by insurers/payers.[8]

Second, Lean Innovators are increasingly diverse companies operating across therapeutic areas, geographies, and contracting models. Relative to classic pharmaceutical innovators, their revenues are far less vulnerable to the performance of any one product but realize margin performance significantly greater than the historical generics companies. It is a potent combination.

Teva

Teva, for example, has increasingly taken advantage of its position within the Israeli life sciences sector to access opportunities outside of generics. As early as 1989, the company began working with the Technion-Israel Institute of Technology to develop Azilect®, a drug for the treatment of Parkinson's disease. Its first major new drug, Copaxone®, was approved by the U.S. Federal Drug Administration (FDA) in 1996, for the treatment of multiple sclerosis (MS). Teva launched this product with patient-centric programs that were leading edge in the 1990s. The company developed and built up an active online community, provided support to patients, and surrounded the product with services for the caregivers. All of these offerings established loyalty and trust.

The strategy served Teva well for 20 years and allowed it to enjoy the top and bottom line growth associated with a patent-protected niche product through 2014. And while the product has now lost patent exclusivity, the company's approach provided a solid foundation on which Teva can move forward with a new and balanced business model that can accommodate a diverse product base.

After Copaxone's patent expiry, Teva experienced an immediate decrement in financial performance, which was to be expected and serves to reinforce the compelling economics of the Lean Innovator versus generics pure-play model. Teva's ability to combine lean global operations with patient-centric programs is part of its secret to success—a success that allows it to enjoy an EBITDA equivalent to other large pharma with much larger patent-protected portfolios. (Figure 4.4 shows Teva's performance by specialty versus traditional generics 2009 through 2014.)

Valeant

Valeant, based in Montreal, Canada, provides another example. Valeant has long focused on adding small niche therapeutics products to its considerable portfolio, in addition to pursuing a few larger scale acquisitions. In recent years, Valeant (like Teva) sought opportunities where it would have broad latitude to increase prices, or where a product's former economics could be optimized for higher profits and improved cash flows from R&D, commercial, and G&A expense reductions.

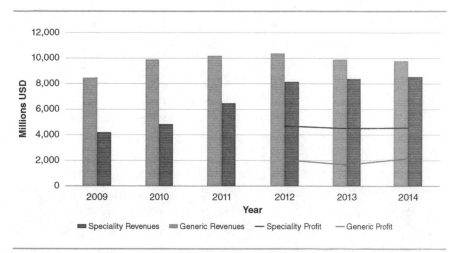

FIGURE 4.4   Teva Product Segment Performance
Source: Accenture analysis.

These moves paid off. By the spring of 2015, Valeant had achieved a distinctive reputation among financial managers and hedge funds, and was included on Goldman Sachs's list of the favorite stocks of hedge fund managers.[9] But in October 2015, Valeant management approaches became the subject of new headlines noting investigations into its pricing and distribution practices.[10] These led to the CEO, J. Michael Pearson, declaring on October 20, 2015, "Given the evolution of our product mix, coupled with the recent events, it is likely that we will pursue fewer, if any, transactions that are focused on mispriced products."[11] He further noted that R&D spending would rise from less than $100M to between $400 million and $500 million by the close of 2016. That, to us, signaled that the company was completing the cycle of innovation into a Lean Innovator.

There is a growing recognition that some Lean Innovators have significantly increased generic drug prices across broad categories (and in specific circumstances, as a result of market consolidations, supply constraints, and explicit company strategies).[12] But the mechanism for those actions warrants some explanation:

In the United States, consumers generally initially acquire therapeutics through their local pharmacy retailer and ultimately through a pharmaceutical benefit manager (PBM). The pharmacy retailer (a company such as Walgreens or CVS Health) enters into a contract with the PBM or uses its own. There is a specific formula for reimbursing branded or innovator (patent-protected) products, generics, and specialty pharmaceuticals. For innovator and specialty products, that is the average wholesale price (AWP), less a percentage representing distribution margin, plus a dispensing fee. For generics, though, the PBM is likely to introduce a maximum allowable cost (MAC), which is the maximum amount that a plan will pay for generic drugs. In general, the PBM will reduce the MAC for a generic class after six months of generic exclusivity, when competition among generic manufacturers increases.

PBMs thus operate within a spread: the consumer's health and drug reimbursement plan sponsor (e.g., an employer) is charged for a drug; the pharmacy is reimbursed a lower rate; and the PBM maintains the "spread" as its margin. The higher the generic cost, the higher the overall pricing to the sponsor and consumer, the greater the spread. For example, for a month's worth of a daily 20-milligram dose of a generic statin, prescribed to treat high cholesterol, consumers or their employers would pay $21.60; retail pharmacies would be reimbursed $10.83, and the PBM spread would be $10.77.[13] In recent years, generic manufacturers have noted that payers are quick to act on price decreases, but slow to readjust or respond to reimbursement levels when prices go up.

The conundrum for the large pharmacy retailers is that they have to choose the extent to which they maintain large inventories to manage their supply chains, forge broad relationships with pharmaceutical distributors (the leading companies being AmerisourceBergen, McKesson, and Cardinal Health), or forward-integrate into PBMs. Where they manage their own supply, they see losses at the system level when generics cost more and reimbursement levels are lower. (For smaller and independent pharmacy retailers, this is less of an issue, as these prices are more transparent and costs not reimbursed can be more directed flowed to the consumer or others.)

The recourse is a MAC appeal process, which in itself represents a lag. It is also why each of the large national pharmacy retailers is considering, or has executed, forward integration into PBM services or broader relationships and equity investments into therapeutics distributors.

This is the root cause of the problem. The generic therapeutics that were intended to provide patients and health providers broad access to needed medicines at reduced costs, thereby opening up capacity in the system to fund the increasing number of new specialty therapeutics, are actually increasing in cost. The economic consequences are at odds with current cost containment and reform initiatives. As a result, we're seeing formal investigations of these practices.

As of this writing, in December 2015, the U.S. Justice Department is broadly investigating pricing practices.[14] The bipartisan U.S. Senate Special Committee on Aging has also launched its own pricing investigation, prompted by Turing Pharmaceuticals AG's acquisition of the anti-infection drug Daraprim and subsequent 5,000 percent price increase.[15] The drug, which Turing acquired in August 2015, is the only U.S.-approved treatment for a deadly parasitic infection that can affect pregnant women and patients with HIV.[16]

As the U.S. presidential and congressional cycle accelerates in advance of the November 2016 elections, these kinds of investigations and their visibility will likely increase. A recent Kaiser Family Foundation consumer poll confirms that the affordability of prescription drugs continues to be at the top of the U.S. public's priority list for the president and Congress, making it extremely unlikely the investigations and public debate on pricing will diminish in the near term.[17]

Actavis

Finally, consider Actavis PLC. From a pure-play generics business that grew largely through acquisitions and mergers, Actavis has become a global pharmaceutical company with a market capitalization greater than Bristol-Meyers Squibb Co., Eli Lilly & Co., and AbbVie, Inc. It develops, makes, and sells a range of branded pharmaceuticals, over-the-counter medicines, and biologic products. (Botox may be the most widely recognizable of its offerings.)[18] Over the past 15 years, it has acquired 10 major companies, five of which were innovative therapeutics companies or products—assets that fall outside the category of its generics business—that broadened its product portfolio dramatically. In February of 2015, after acquiring the Forest and Allergan businesses, the company announced its intention to change its name to Allergan PLC, signaling a shift from thinking of itself as a generics company with other lines of business, to a specialty pharmaceutical company. Then, in July of 2015, the company completed its transformation into a Lean Innovator with the $40 billion sale of its generics business to Teva.[19,20]

The relative success of Teva, Valeant, and Actavis in acquiring and leveraging innovator products, as well as fundamental changes and trends in the generics industry, is hastening a broader evolution in the business model and strategy of other leading generics—one that could represent

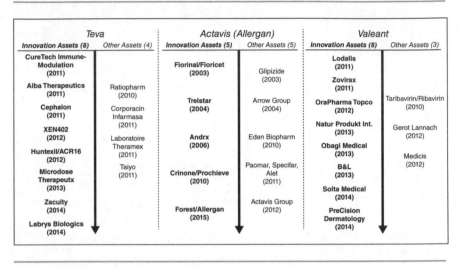

Teva		Actavis (Allergan)		Valeant	
Innovation Assets (8)	Other Assets (4)	Innovation Assets (5)	Other Assets (5)	Innovation Assets (8)	Other Assets (3)
CureTech Immune-Modulation (2011)		Fiorinal/Fioricet (2003)	Glipizide (2003)	Lodalis (2011)	
Alba Therapeutics (2011)	Ratiopharm (2010)			Zovirax (2011)	
Cephalon (2011)	Corporacin Infarmasa (2011)	Trelstar (2004)	Arrow Group (2004)	OraPharma Topco (2012)	Taribavirin/Ribavirin (2010)
XEN402 (2012)	Laboratoire Theramex (2011)	Andrx (2006)	Eden Biopharm (2010)	Natur Produkt Int. (2013)	Gerot Lannach (2012)
Huntexil/ACR16 (2012)	Taiyo (2011)	Crinone/Prochieve (2010)	Paomar, Specifar, Alet (2011)	Obagi Medical (2013)	Medicis (2012)
Microdose Therapeutx (2013)				B&L (2013)	
Zacuity (2014)		Forest/Allergan (2015)	Actavis Group (2012)	Solta Medical (2014)	
Labrys Biologics (2014)				PreCision Dermatology (2014)	

FIGURE 4.5   Lean Innovator Acquisition Strategy
Source: Accenture analysis.

profound change for innovators and health systems alike. (Figure 4.5 illustrates the companies' acquisition strategies.) While many of the leading generics companies continue to broaden their geographic reach through their traditional generics business, they are more importantly taking their acquisition and post-merger integration skills into new areas.[21]

EARLY CHALLENGES TO THE LEAN INNOVATOR MODEL

The Lean Innovator model is not a foolproof path to success. As we have described, it is already facing some of its first challenges in the form of insurance companies and risk-bearing provider systems that are balking at rising prices. Given that these increases are not negotiated with payers, nor are they supported by new clinical evidence generated post-approval that would justify premium pricing due to improved outcomes, it is not a surprise they're eliciting strong reactions.

In addition, Lean Innovators are facing other challenges, including national governments' rising investments in advanced analytics and value-based pricing constructs; private payers with horizontally and vertically integrated operations that will analyze patient population risk, pricing, and manage their services accordingly; and regional and national health-care providers that are forward-integrating.

This is a marketplace where advanced analytics (guided by expert individuals and machine models and focusing on populations, individual patients, and products) will identify opportunities to reduce costs and improve value in the healthcare system. And so the ultimate vulnerability for Lean Innovators lies in the possibility that the data on outcomes won't be positive and consistent with rising prices.[22]

Nevertheless, there are too many inefficiencies in current innovator models and so much fragmentation among small specialty marketed therapeutics to diminish the returns to this strategy in the short term.

Figure 4.6 illustrates that point. The classic set of big pharmaceutical companies has an average EBITDA (Earnings Before Interest, Taxes, and Amortization) margin of 28 percent. Pure-play generics companies as a group come in two percentage points lower on this metric, at 26 percent. Lean Innovators, however, have exceeded both, with an average EBITDA margin of 35.6 percent. This is tremendous progress in

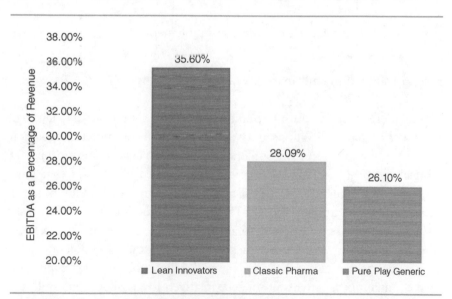

FIGURE 4.6   Average EBITDA Margin, 2014
Source: Accenture analysis, High Performance Business Study, 2015.
The Lean Innovators represented here are Actavis, Teva, and Valeant;
Classic Pharma are Novartis, Sanofi S.A, Merck, GlaxoSmithKline PLC (GSK),
AstraZeneca PLC, Bayer, AbbVie, Eli Lilly and Company, Bristol-Myers
Squibb Company (BMS), and Astellas Pharma Inc.; Pure Play are Dr. Reddy's
Laboratories Ltd., Mylan N.V., Sun Pharmaceutical Industries Ltd., and Aspen Medical
Group, Inc. Averages reported for year 2014.

driving substantial growth and operating performance in a very short period of time.

THE TECHNIQUES OF A LEAN INNOVATOR

Overall, the companies we observe engaging fully as Lean Innovators are just beginning to achieve the scope and scale they need in order to see their overall financial strength and value-management model resonate across markets. As they do, differentiated strategies among Lean Innovators are becoming apparent. We see three promising meta-strategies emerging that companies can emphasize to employ Lean Innovator techniques:

1. Utilizing strong transaction and financial management skills
2. Broadening the scope of therapeutic area coverage
3. Developing new partnering skills to broaden influence

These strategies can be discrete or complementary.

Strong Transaction and Financial Management Skills

Companies aspiring to use a Lean Innovator model should strive to leverage their current market positions and capabilities with a continued emphasis on mergers and acquisitions, post-merger integration, cost management, and strategic pricing. Lean Innovators are deal-focused companies that have highly evolved transaction and post-transaction management skills, but their principles can be applied widely. They look at other companies and ask, "What assets are stranded, undermanaged, or under the radar and thereby offer us significant value improvement potential?" If they spot that potential, they move ahead and marshal differentiated skills and capabilities supported by the contemporary environment, with relatively low cost of capital and tax-advantaged operating structures. Shareholders benefit as well, as acquisitions provide a payout that historical management teams, with more traditional, innovation-centric approaches, may never have realized.

A Broad Scope of Coverage

The second major strategic option for Lean Innovators is leveraging their scope across three key dimensions: disease coverage areas, geographies, and health system relationships. In addition to highly evolved transaction skills, large generics companies have enormous global scope, strong health system relationships, and wide therapeutic area coverage. Historically this has proven hard to use in any financially beneficial way beyond a low margin cost for an incremental therapeutic or to add volume to an account. However, in the model of the future, the focus will no longer be on units sold but rather on population disease management. Lean Innovators are well positioned to excel in this area. Their breadth of disease coverage allows for holistic patient care, rather than narrow, disease-specific care. In addition, their global coverage and relationships allow for rapid expansion of this model internationally.

Interestingly we see similar firms using this strategy; the recent Medtronic PLC/Covidien PLC merger offers just one example. Medtronic CEO Omar Ishrak said that the rationale behind the merger was to make the combined entity more relevant to the top teams at large health systems (e.g., Kaiser Health System, Partners Healthcare) and health authorities responsible for payment and health system financing.[23] Stated differently, in order to have an executive team of a large provider system, payer, or government discuss a deal or contract model, the life science company would have to matter. The larger the company is as a percentage of total purchases, the more they matter. The combination of Medtronic and Covidien increased its percentage of total sales in cardiovascular and allowed it to look at a number of differentiated contracting and population or disease management opportunities. Their product lines are diversifying to increase sales in related therapeutic services—remote patient monitoring services, diagnostics to better oversee a broader population—versus the traditional interventional devices and hospital supplies.

Similarly, the combination of Novartis and Sandoz has created one of the latest Lean Innovator companies, one able to provide a broad set of solutions across oral therapeutics, biologics, and highly focused innovator therapeutics. A view of its combined portfolio in oncology and cardiovascular diseases creates the picture of a single entity able to contract for a significant proportion of a health system's or patient population's requirements. To date this portfolio of therapeutics has functioned independently across innovator, traditional generics, and biosimilars,[24] but the company is advancing with a number of novel reimbursement initiatives emphasizing the outcomes achieved for specific patient populations and payment explicitly linked to that.[25] Solutions that combined therapeutics across their portfolio could be a natural next extension.

We expect that the larger generics companies will create sets of differentiating services that allow them to bridge their global and therapeutic area scope to a broader participation in the total value that can be delivered. The combination of generics and innovator therapeutics that are transforming the pipelines of these companies allows them to increase their relevance over single product companies or pure services entities. For example, a fully diversified Lean Innovator with sets of population services and clinical decision support tools could effectively "cap" or guarantee the cost for a patient population. Again, this form of contracting would support a longer-term perspective and sets of investments consistent with the capital intensity of their business. These Lean Innovators could ultimately become the main companies serving large global health systems, being the conduit for non-acquired, smaller innovators gaining market access.

New Partnering Skills

The third strategic option focuses on cultivating non-traditional partnerships that bring new capabilities to the scope and breadth of generics to deepen relationships with key, large risk-bearing health systems and potentially large private or public payers. This approach is about leveraging the customer and therapeutic area coverage that the largest players have accumulated over the past few years. These companies are looking at the entire value chain and sets of current and potential participants around a patient population or health system and asking, "What combination of capabilities and companies could remedy critical care continuity gaps and together provide a turnkey solution for some of the highest cost and highest medical need patient populations?"

As we've said, we are only beginning to see these strategies emerge. Our belief is that they will focus on large risk-bearing hospital systems and mid-tier payers where the costs and economics of specific therapeutic areas can make or break their profit and loss (P&L). These will focus on managing the risk of therapeutic areas by guaranteeing therapeutics spending rates or caps on spending for broad patient populations. These will combine therapeutic decision support tools with the ability to deliver those therapeutics. Because the vast majority of therapeutics used are generic, and there are wide treatment options for most diseases, this will contain incentives to use generics wherever possible. The normal conflicts of an innovator manufacturer are not there as these are not proprietary but widely available—and there is a risk-bearing component to these relationships.

These will ultimately involve new forms of formal joint ventures, joint risk contracts, or even consolidations—distributors with pharmaceutical benefit managers (PBMs); generics companies with PBMs (e.g., Express-Scripts); generics companies with hospital IT and supplies companies (e.g., Becton, Dickinson and Company); and generics companies with health IT companies (e.g., athenahealth, Inc., SureScripts, LLC, Cerner Corporation, Epic Systems Corporation).[26]

THE "LEAN" OPERATING MODEL POSITION: EXECUTION, EXECUTION, EXECUTION

Most Lean Innovators to date are, at their core, volume-based competitors. This is their primary lens for the attractiveness of specific geographic and health system tendering opportunities, niche innovator therapeutic markets, and justification for capital and capability investments.

The generics origins of the Lean Innovators provided their foundational capabilities and guide those being honed for the future. Lean Innovators manage current operations for ongoing productivity improvements and continuously improving cost efficiencies. They recognize where there is performance improvement potential and merger synergies to be realized. They have execution skills to predictably and confidently claim the value of performance improvements. They have an internal apparatus to identify acquisition targets, conduct diligence, and run post-merger integration with a minimum of external support.

Companies such as Valeant have done as many as 20 deals on average per year, for the better part of the last decade. This is central to their strategy and core to their performance model. The performance management system of the Lean Innovators focuses on year-over-year organic and inorganic growth, post-transaction growth and margin improvements, M&A transactions initiated and closed, aggregate revenue, and overall cash EPS improvements. They understand that larger deals offer more potential for post-merger synergies and allocate resources accordingly. They understand that knowledge of the businesses yields synergies, and they work to identify and formally target those synergies. The Value Innovators are the apex of the volume model that evolved over the last few decades. They only value "best-in-class" goals realized.

The accompanying "Harvey Balls" graphics, Figures 4.7, 4.8, and 4.9, illustrate Lean Innovators' market positioning, differentiating capabilities,

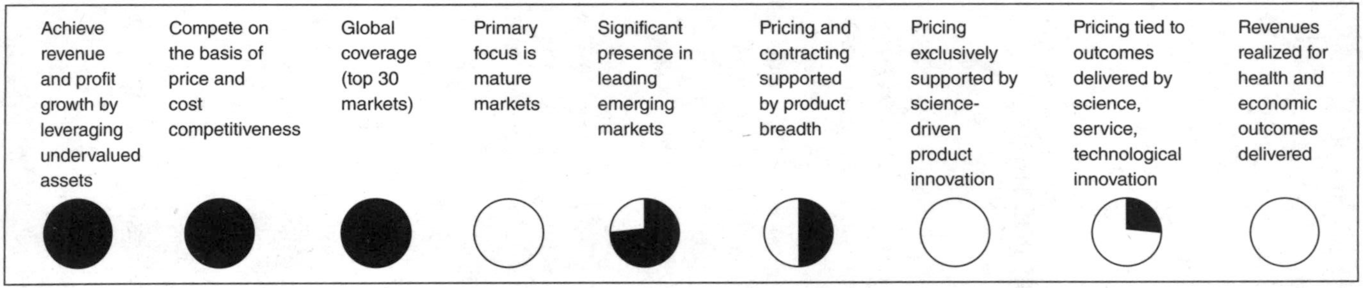

Achieve revenue and profit growth by leveraging undervalued assets	Compete on the basis of price and cost competitiveness	Global coverage (top 30 markets)	Primary focus is mature markets	Significant presence in leading emerging markets	Pricing and contracting supported by product breadth	Pricing exclusively supported by science-driven product innovation	Pricing tied to outcomes delivered by science, service, technological innovation	Revenues realized for health and economic outcomes delivered
● (full)	● (full)	● (full)	○ (empty)	◕ (three-quarter)	◑ (half)	○ (empty)	◔ (quarter)	○ (empty)

FIGURE 4.7 Market Positioning (What Unique Position in the Market Does the Company Want To Occupy?)

Source: Accenture analysis.

Figure Key: The circles in the graphic, known as "Harvey Balls," provide qualitative comparisons across categories and items. They indicate the extent to which any given component (or category) is complete, meaningful, representative, or fulfilled. A blank circle indicates that the criteria are not met; a circle that is completely filled in indicates that the criteria are fully met.

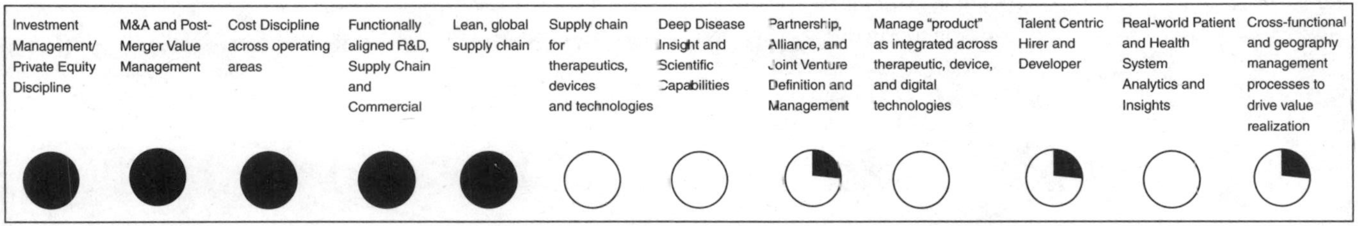

FIGURE 4.8 Differentiating Capabilities (Critical Capabilities Needed to Drive the Market Position)

Source: Accenture analysis.

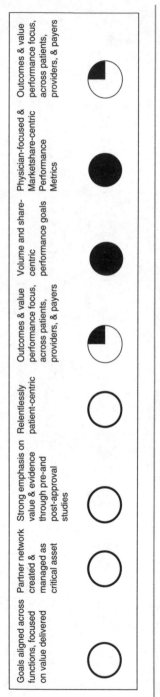

FIGURE 4.9 Performance Anatomy (How to Organize for Success)

Source: Accenture analysis.

and performance anatomy, in accordance with Accenture's High Performance Framework, described in Chapter 2.

LEAN INNOVATORS: SPOILERS OR VALUE VANGUARD?

Lean Innovators hold the potential to be one of the better operators in the emerging healthcare landscape. Their economic impact is already demanding the attention of leading health insurers and risk-bearing provider systems. Health insurers—whether they are health insurance companies or PBMs—are focused on the increasing costs in their base business, in particular those associated with current therapeutics for patients in their programs. When there are substantial increases in prices, other market intermediaries, such as large chain pharmacy retailers, may be absorbing some of the costs, with PBMs and payers passing them on in the next fiscal period, often shifting risk back to private employers that are self-insured and providing healthcare and pharmaceutical products coverage as a benefit to their employees or to the consumers themselves. These costs will cascade through other reimbursement programs and impact other patient groups as well. Regardless, these incremental pricing changes, in aggregate, represent a significant increase after a period of relatively flat overall costs and counter to the goal of trending overall healthcare expenditure increases in line with overall CPI.[27]

But consumer concern over the trend toward higher prices for new and generic therapeutics continues to grow,[28] even as the number of therapeutics prescribed per consumer increases. With the increased political scrutiny of pricing practices by government and private payer review bodies, and a presidential election year in the United States, it is likely that current pricing arbitrage practices will be curtailed through legislative actions, payer policy changes, investor pressures, and broader pressures coming from adverse public response.

During the past decade, pure innovators were fortunate that patent expiries aligned to new product launches, supporting the ability of new innovations to reach targeted patients with no significant aggregate decreases in spending. We therefore expect significant responses to the accelerating cost trend, either in terms of reduced access, tighter criteria for prescribing, cost shifting to patients, or even delisting of coverage.

For health providers that increasingly bear risk, this is already driving an uncontrollable spending level and contributing to declining operating margins. Because it is hitting many smaller products and a few larger ones, it is difficult for them to identify the specific therapeutics and even more difficult to control spending given the limited management oversight and technical rules in EMR or electronic prescribing environments. Here too we expect to see formal responses as certain therapeutics are considered less clinically essential or as having insufficient value relative to the acuity of the disease or health state they address. We are already seeing circumstances where innovator therapeutics are being switched to oral generics wherever possible.[29]

Ultimately, the Lean Innovator model that's now emerging will evolve, possibly with some organizations focusing on aggressive cost management and opportunistic pricing, and others leveraging their combined portfolio of generics and innovator therapeutics, relying on partners' expertise to become better providers and managers of broad population and disease management services. Longer term, our view is that the more value- and population-centric Lean Innovators will predominate, but the more opportunistic approaches will likely be yielding highly positive returns for several more years.

Chapter 5

Around-the-Patient Innovators

This business model, still centered largely on producing drugs, also calls for developing ancillary services, algorithms, analytic capabilities, and more to create a new basis for product economics and to add value for customers.

Still product-centric at heart, the businesses embracing the "Around-the-Patient Innovator" model understand that developing and commercializing therapeutics is no longer enough to sustain them as innovators. They know that in order to make enough money to offset the risks of being an innovator, they need to pivot to a patient outcome–centric business model, which will not only enhance the value of the science but also equally satiate the needs of the emerging patient-consumer and the payer systems that are looking for value for their reimbursement dollars.

To do this, they are creating sets of services, algorithms, analytic capabilities, and more, and packaging them to create a unique benefit for clinicians, provider/national health systems, and patients. In other words, Around-the-Patient Innovators are making bold moves to broaden the definition of their product offering beyond the device, or the chemical or biological entity they produce. By adding digital and service dimensions to their offerings, they can provide a robust scope of value to customers—and create a new basis for their product economics.

*   *   *

Healthcare and business strategist Clay Christensen some years ago introduced a construct called the "jobs" framework whereby customers "hired" products to do jobs.[1] The idea was not that these customers wanted products per se, but rather that they wanted to get various jobs done, and the products did those jobs.

Christensen's construct applies increasingly in healthcare, the difference being that the customers—patients, healthcare providers, and payers—can't get the job done solely with products—therapeutics, devices, and diagnostics. With regard to health, the job—the best possible outcome—requires a holistic and integrated approach. That is, a therapeutic alone cannot usually complete a job without additional support from physicians, payers, possibly other caregivers, the patient, and possibly the patient's family. Around-the-Patient Innovators are some of the first organizations to engage with the notion of providing a set of tools and capabilities to supplement their products.

As the early chapters of this book discussed, health payers—private and public—are becoming ever more demanding of the value of the clinical services clinicians provide, the therapeutics they prescribe, and the devices they use. Patients are increasingly engaged in their own healthcare—sometimes because they are forced to bear more of the cost burden of care, sometimes because they have incentives, financial or otherwise, to sustain or improve their own health status, and sometimes because they are gaining increasing sophistication in their understanding and control of their own care, the result of access to a wealth of information on the Internet, health applications, and other consumer health devices. And physicians and health providers, increasingly bearing financial risk, are relying increasingly on a sort of economic calculus that involves considering both the potential health outcomes of an intervention alongside its costs in hopes of maximizing the former while minimizing the latter to inform their treatment decisions.

This convergence of factors is driving fundamental transformations in the business and operating models of therapeutics, diagnostics, and device companies in the United States, in Europe, and in other regions of the world. Some—mostly former pure-play generics companies—are morphing into Lean Innovators, as the previous chapter explained. In the construct we introduced in Chapter 3, businesses embracing the Lean Innovator model are located at A on the Value Curve, making the economics work by targeting niche areas of need, and by trading on their ability to produce products with extreme efficiency.

But other companies are beginning to operate between B and C on that curve (as shown in Figure 5.1). These organizations are packaging sets of services or ancillary products with their therapeutics—services and products that can help patients, providers, and payers achieve the highest value outcome (the best possible patient health at the lowest cost).

Consider, for example, a person who suffers from a particular type of heart ailment that requires an implanted pacemaker. The pacemaker monitors heart rhythm and delivers interventions automatically as required. But if the patient does not lower salt intake and take diuretics, he or she will surely be rehospitalized. The outcome we want—the job at hand—is to keep the patient healthy and out of the hospital, and the pacemaker can't do it alone.

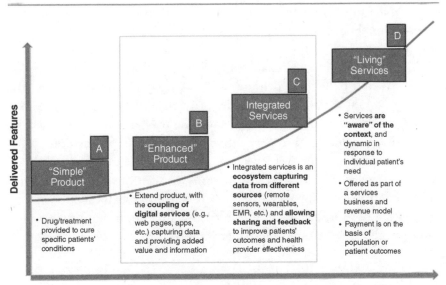

FIGURE 5.1   Around-the-Patient Value Curve
Source: Accenture analysis.

Similarly, if a doctor assesses a patient and finds that he has a high body mass index (BMI), A1C (blood glucose) levels above 5.7, and low levels of physical activity, the doctor may say with confidence that the patient has a significant risk of developing diabetes. The doctor may then suggest lifestyle modifications that could prevent a disease state. But if a patient who has diabetes does not follow the doctor's advice with regard to exercise, diet, appropriate prescribed therapeutics, and the like, the disease will progress.

Likewise, if a patient with advanced diabetes undergoing insulin therapy does not test his blood glucose levels, monitor for sores, and titrate (provide the right amount of medicine for the patient at the right time) appropriately, he risks prophylactic amputations and increased rates of hospitalization. In each of these cases, the patient's provider taps products and devices to assess a health status and inform suggestions and prescriptions that will get the job done. The payer assesses risk, and provides the support it determines is appropriate. And yet the solutions— the jobs themselves—involve more time away from providers and health-care facilities than within them. The patients—and the immediate support they have, allow, or enable—determine the outcomes (to the extent that such a determination is possible). The necessary *system* includes anyone and anything that contributes purposefully to the patient's overall health and positive outcome.

Current trends in healthcare shift risk increasingly from payers to physicians and patients (redefining value as well, as we have discussed). But these trends do not automatically provide added capabilities so that physicians and patients can manage and meet the demands of this risk, so we need new solutions and new capabilities. Providers alone don't have the scope of operations or even capabilities to take on all the roles required. Payers don't have the continuity of relationship with patients or the mandate to fill the gap. These needs and gaps create an opportunity (and in the not-too-distant future, probably an expectation) for organizations to become Around-the-Patient Innovators.

IDENTIFYING UNMET NEEDS

Accenture recently completed a survey of 10,000 patients in five global regions and seven major therapeutic areas to gain a better understanding of how some of those needs and gaps might be closed through focused sets of services that beneficially engage the patient throughout the entire journey—from symptoms and prediagnosis of an illness or condition to active treatment and recovery. (Figure 5.2 offers detail.)

Here's what the survey revealed:

A patient's information and support needs are quite high before being treated—and even before being diagnosed.

Patients for the most part believe that their personal experiences with an illness or a condition begin prior to a consultation with their physicians and any formal diagnosis. In fact, this is one of the stages where they report experiencing the greatest overall frustration. Nearly two-thirds (65 percent) of all patients surveyed indicated that the pretreatment interval is the most frustrating period for them, and that their single biggest frustration is the lack of notification of being at risk for a condition. As Figure 5.3 shows, the survey found 34 percent of respondents were frustrated that they had little warning that they could be diagnosed with a condition. This percentage rose to 44 percent for patients who had autoimmune diseases (diseases in which the body attacks its own tissues, such as rheumatoid arthritis, lupus, multiple sclerosis, and inflammatory bowel syndrome).

The roots of this frustration are in part the unknowns—patients feel that they have no real understanding of the potential health problem, root cause, possible remedies, and implications of those remedies. The health-care ecosystem appears to be asking patients to take more responsibility for their health; to be preventative by being proactive. Yet they see sources of data and counsel as inaccessible and/or incomprehensible.

Patients are generally not aware of the services that are available to help them.

Between news reports of the latest clinical studies, profiles of surgical breakthroughs, and coverage of health-related threats, it may seem as if every media channel and platform around the world provides a steady stream of information about health. But the opposite is apparently true when it comes to information about patient services. The survey found that, on average, fewer than one out of five patients (19 percent) are aware of the services available to them. What's more, awareness is low across all therapeutic areas, ranging from a low of 18 percent for bone, lung, and heart conditions to a slightly higher 21 percent for cancer and immunological diseases.

FIGURE 5.2 Accenture Global Patient Survey

Source: Accenture, 2015. https://www.accenture.com/us-en/~/media/Accenture/next-gen/patient-services-survey/mc814_Patient%20ServicesLS%20Research%20Note2015_v7.pdf.

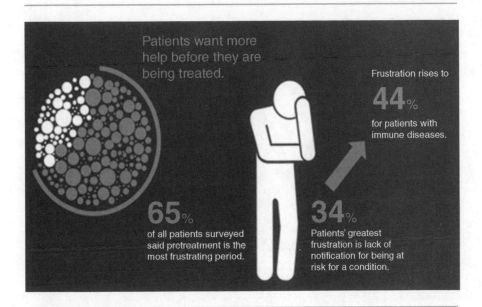

FIGURE 5.3   Pretreatment Frustrations

Source. Accenture, 2015. https://www.accenture.com/us-en/~/media/Accenture/ next-gen/patient-services-survey/mc814_Patient%20ServicesLS%20Research% 20Note2015_v7.pdf.

When patients are aware of services, they use them.

The simple fact that patients make use of services that are made available makes the opportunity revealed by such low rates of awareness particularly compelling. As Figure 5.4 shows, the survey found that nearly six out of 10 patients (58 percent) use services when they are aware of them. While usage of specific patient services varies, utilization is still generally high across all services provided. Within the survey population, the use of services ranged from a high of 69 percent for services that helped patients obtain information on a condition, to a low of 47 percent for information on support groups. As Clay Christensen would say, patients are trying to get a job done—they want information on their health condition, to know the options and implications thereof, and to regain their health or manage their condition more effectively. They are willing to, or at least trying to, be proactive and vigilant in managing their health.

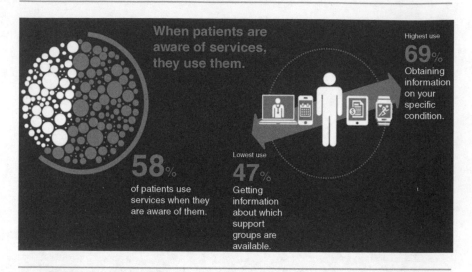

FIGURE 5.4   When There Is Awareness, Patient Services Are Used

Source: Accenture, 2015. https://www.accenture.com/us-en/~/media/Accenture/
next-gen/patient-services-survey/mc814_Patient%20ServicesLS%20Research%
20Note2015_v7.pdf.

Patients value services across all major diseases.

Patients not only use services once they are aware of them, but also value them— no matter what health condition they are facing. The vast majority (79 percent) of survey respondents said the services they used were "very" or "extremely" valuable. This high level of satisfaction was seen across all disease states, with patients contending with diagnoses that range from life threatening, as in cases of cancer, for example, to chronic, as in the case of autoimmune or hormonal disorders.

Patients want their healthcare professionals to be the primary source of information on services they need to manage their health, but they also see digital channels as increasingly credible and important.

As Figure 5.5 illustrates, an overwhelming majority of patients (87 percent) stated they wanted a single point of contact to provide services to help them manage their condition. The vast majority (85 percent) would like that point of contact to be their healthcare professional. Only six percent would seek information about services from their insurance company, while that number drops to 1 percent for pharmaceutical companies.

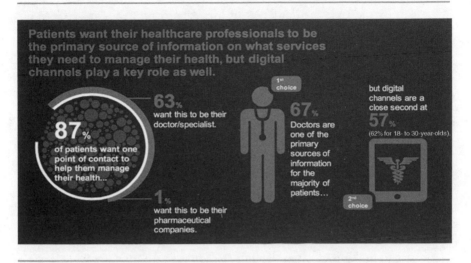

FIGURE 5.5   Patients Prefer Information from their Healthcare Providers, but Digital Sources Are Advancing Rapidly
Source: Accenture, 2015. https://www.accenture.com/us-en/~/media/Accenture/
next-gen/patient-services-survey/rnc814_Patient%20ServicesLS%20Research%
20Note2015_v7.pdf.

However, while in-person visits with doctors remain the top means from which patients gain information (67 percent), digital channels are gaining ground and are a close second, mentioned by 57 percent of respondents. Further, younger individuals (18 to 30 years old) are even more receptive to digital channels with 62 percent ranking them in the top three preferred sources of information.

As the results of Accenture's survey reveal, addressing the needs of patients with chronic and acute diseases effectively involves not only a deep understanding of the biology of the illness, but also a thorough understanding of how that disease impacts the life of a patient and his or her family, and equally how their life choices on nutrition and exercise are likely to affect the outcome. Around-the-Patient Innovators recognize this reality and focus on it, aiming to provide value to patients as individuals at a big-picture level. The Around-the-Patient business model explicitly recognizes the fact that if patients are armed with new tools and sources of support, and these resources are made integral to their lives, they may be more successful in addressing or managing their disease and more successful in meeting the demands of life. As a result, they may be more likely to enjoy their lives.

One of the Around-the-Patient Innovator's key competencies, then, must be developing the ability to analyze an individual patient's situation. An example of what such an analysis might entail and reveal is shown by the Accenture survey. Like the survey, the goal of these analyses would be to understand the activities most valued by patients and family or personal caregivers, healthcare providers, and potentially even health risk bearers or payers, and then to build a compelling business case for providing or coordinating a set of those capabilities.

Again, most of the patient's care occurs outside of health facilities and away from healthcare professionals. Most care is coordinated by the patient and his or her family. The key to adding value in these circumstances is to make that an easier job to manage and manage well. That's why for Around-the-Patient Innovators, the product is not simply a chemical or biological entity. Instead, the product is a proposition that delivers a therapeutic, economic, and life outcome. Innovations "around the patient," for these organizations, may have a great impact—on the patient, and on the bottom line.

INNOVATING TO MEET NEEDS, FILL GAPS

This isn't a traditional role for the pharmaceutical or device company. In our research for this book, in fact, as we engaged in extensive conversations with all types of participants in the healthcare system, we found that the idea of a potentially increased, more visible, and more personal role for pharmaceutical or device companies was among the more controversial topics.

Nevertheless, we believe that these organizations may have the greatest incentive and ability to take on this role and do it well. The success or failure of their therapeutics or devices ultimately determines their compensation and whether their products will be available broadly to patients. Their knowledge of a disease is contemporary and forward-looking.

They do not necessarily have to have all of the answers to managing a patient's life but they can provide solutions that will enable the entire ecosystem to operate more effectively to drive the outcome. An analogy can be drawn with Apple's introduction of iPhones, iPads, and the iTunes universe. All are great products in their own right but one of their key contributions to society is that they facilitate ecosystems coming together (music industry/movie industry/books/games industry with the global virtual consumer). They define new operating models, new businesses, and new ways of working. They increase/change expectations and generally make life more livable. Around-the-Patient Innovators have the opportunity to play an equally pivotal role in the life of the patient and the treatment/prevention of disease.

With real-time data, analysis, and insights at hand, there are a number of ways that the Around-the-Patient Innovators will enhance the engagement and value realized by patients and will partner more effectively with health providers and payers. Most of these Around-the-Patient offerings are focused first on patients—providing information, and ultimately offering sets of focused patient services that begin integrating into patients' lives much earlier in the patient journey than has historically been the case. But stepping back and taking a broad view, we see emerging Around-the-Patient Innovators developing the following characteristics:

1. **They will have a strong focus on the prediagnosis period, and offer pretreatment services.** By providing critical services and resources at the point when physicians and patients are seeking the most relevant data and have the greatest angst, these companies have an opportunity to influence value for the patient and health system—selecting the right treatment for that individual and gaining his or her active engagement in achieving optimum outcomes.

2. **Leveraging digital engagement as a complementary, but not exclusive, channel for communicating with patients, these businesses will strive first and foremost to build high-credibility and high-trust partnerships with healthcare professionals, offering these providers tools that they can deploy on their own or tap to help patients manage their care.** As of this writing, there are more than 1,000 digital apps broadly available to patients (offered directly to them by life science and health services companies) but minimally used. As a result, we don't believe that putting another app out there represents an innovative solution. With healthcare professionals remaining patients' most trusted advisors, these individuals are the natural conduit to making patients aware of the services available to them.

3. **They will invest in the quality and effectiveness of patient and physician services.** The costs and barriers to development and launch of digital service and apps are both low. Pharmaceutical, medical

device, and health services companies that aspire to the Around-the-Patient model will rethink how they conceive, launch, support, communicate, and coordinate their services with healthcare professionals and the other key stakeholders including payers, providers, governments, and pharmacies. These services need to be integral to the health ecosystems and not skirt the periphery. They need to be guided by advanced analytics and integrate across services and partners. In that spirit, strategic conversations will no longer focus on products, but on overall patient value and health system outcomes (outcomes based on how well various elements come together to treat the disease and improve patients' lives) and how the combination of products and services can help achieve those goals.

Though they are clearly on a path that seems to lead toward embracing a service-based business model, Around-the-Patient Innovators do not make that leap (or engage with the strategic considerations that such a move would catalyze). The Around-the-Patient Innovators remain product companies that have developed services that can attach to their products; they are still, at their essence, devoted to product sales. (By contrast, Value Innovators, coming up in the next chapter, do make the leap, selling integrated services and tying their compensation to the success of those services with regard to targeted population outcomes.)

We can illustrate the changing capabilities and approach to ensuring value of the Around-the-Patient Innovators with an example of a large population chronic disease, diabetes. Consider: We know that 20 to 40 percent of newly diagnosed diabetes patients never initiate therapy. Of those who do start therapy, 40 percent stop taking their medication within eight months.[2] As Figure 5.6 shows, this is a complicated disease that comes with a myriad of clinical, financial, and social issues to ensure treatment is initiated and sustained.

Under the old approach, the health provider (the doctor or hospital) would suffer a decrease in reimbursement revenues if the diabetes patient stopped coming to healthcare visits. In certain regions with high mobility and high switching across private health insurers, there were few to no consequences for the patient's health insurance payer (usually contracted through the patient's employer). In fact, there might have been an unintended "adverse benefit" for payers in that the health insurer was saved the expense of covering the nonadherent patient's visits and drugs. What's more, the health insurer likely wouldn't face any long-term

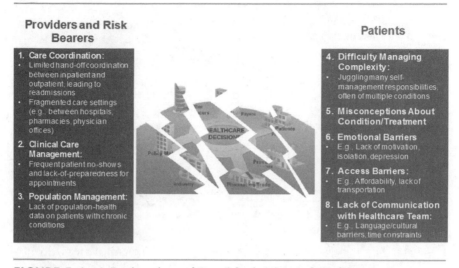

Providers and Risk Bearers

1. **Care Coordination:**
   - Limited hand-off coordination between inpatient and outpatient, leading to readmissions
   - Fragmented care settings (e.g., between hospitals, pharmacies, physician offices)

2. **Clinical Care Management:**
   - Frequent patient no-shows and lack-of-preparedness for appointments

3. **Population Management:**
   - Lack of population-health data on patients with chronic conditions

Patients

4. **Difficulty Managing Complexity:**
   - Juggling many self-management responsibilities, often of multiple conditions

5. **Misconceptions About Condition/Treatment**

6. **Emotional Barriers**
   - E.g., Lack of motivation, isolation, depression

7. **Access Barriers:**
   - E.g., Affordability, lack of transportation

8. **Lack of Communication with Healthcare Team:**
   - E.g., Language/cultural barriers, time constraints

FIGURE 5.6   A Patient's and Provider's View of Diabetes
Source: Accenture research.

consequences either, since the patient would probably switch insurers, switch employers (or the employers would switch insurers), and so on. The result is that the patient likely wouldn't be covered by any of its plans after two to three years.

Meanwhile, the patient probably didn't experience an immediate health impact, as type 2 diabetes tends to progress slowly. And we wonder why we didn't make any progress against slowly progressing, chronic diseases? Gaining real and actionable insights requires working directly with real-world data from a number of sources to understand the current standard of care, its effectiveness, and the gaps that may be gating against value for the patient and health system. As Figure 5.7 shows, the Around-the-Patient Innovators are increasingly defining formal methodologies and teams for gleaning these insights and translating them into services architectures.

The "value-focused" patient journey can yield key insights in "interests" where these are a combination of (1) the patients on whom we should be focused to develop actionable insight; (2) the gaps, deficiencies, and even moments of emotional difficulty where we could beneficially intervene or offer more explicit support; and (3) the "outcomes of interest" in the micro-region in which these patients are living and receiving treatment. Outcomes of interest will vary by country, sub-regions within these

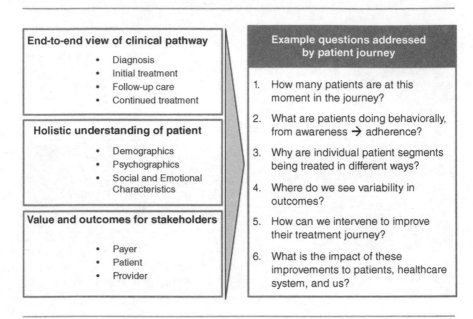

FIGURE 5.7 Defining the Patient Journey
Source: Accenture research.

countries, and even by health authority/risk-bearing healthcare provider combinations.

This framework allows the Around-the-Patient Innovator to bring that all together into a coherent view with clear targets of value and implications for actions. It also becomes the framework (and provides the vocabulary) for various health agency or risk-bearing health provider collaborations, as the key actionable insights align with the Triple Aim framework, shown in Figure 5.8.

These are rigorous analyses that can bring together critical clinical data and perspectives with the behavioral and practical (e.g., eligibility for specific reimbursement programs, accessibility of childcare to attend physician appointments). Together these can create the "pathway of interest," which becomes the population and individual care coordination construct for the services to be deployed by the Around-the-Patient Innovator (see Figure 5.9).

We now know that the treatment and care of diabetes and other chronic illnesses is complicated. It's not just about patients taking their medicines, but it is also about modifying lifestyle, diet, and so on. In order to do this

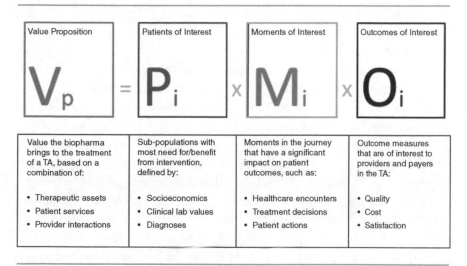

FIGURE 5.8   The Value Strategy Guided by Insights into "Interests"
Source: Accenture research.

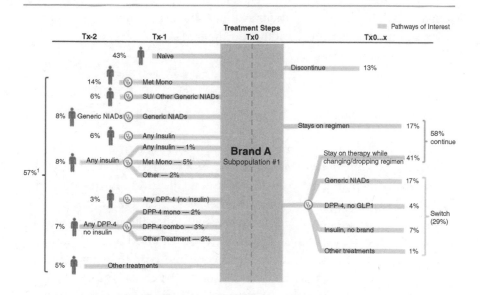

FIGURE 5.9   Accenture Patient "Pathways of Interest" Model
Source: Accenture research.

successfully, patients require customized services and support to meet them where they are in their healthcare journey and break down barriers to adherence.

Ultimately, as a result, Around-the-Patient Innovators hold the potential to be stronger operators in the new healthcare ecosystem. Their positions will be difficult to achieve and difficult to maintain, but the overall rewards and value of achieving a solid status as an Around-the-Patient Innovator are clear: deeper partnerships with key, high-influence, and luminary health providers and the ability to interact directly with patients, deploying services as a formal partner in the treatment of disease.

Product-focused companies that are struggling, take note: This model cannot work for an organization that tries to wrap services around an inferior product or treatment to make up for its shortcomings. Before even considering a move toward an Around-the-Patient model, a company's senior management must first assess the product and the company's organizational strengths and weaknesses on their own merits.

This model is also not a shortcut to a strong position in the emerging healthcare ecosystem. It is about having solutions that unambiguously address or resolve an unmet medical need. It is about tapping patient experience to inform new research. And it is about recognizing that the journey of the patient, the patient's family, and even other caregivers may be complicated, disjointed, and uncoordinated—and responding in a way that makes their lives easier.

EXAMPLES OF EMERGING AROUND-THE-PATIENT INNOVATORS

Emerging Around-the-Patient Innovators as of this writing include:

The Swiss pharmaceutical company, Novartis, Basel: In 2015, this company launched a new heart failure medication, Entresto™, also known as LCZ696. It is the first new therapeutic for patients with heart failure, a condition for which currently available therapeutics provide limited therapeutic protection.[3] However, the standard of care therapeutics are largely generics and therefore very low cost. Novartis' pricing would represent about $12.5 per day or $10 per day more than the generics. Even with an advanced therapeutic, there are other needs of these patients to ensure their disease is being tightly managed and they avoid a potentially acute event. They need to modify their diets and salt intake. They need to maintain a modest but specific activity level. They further need to monitor their blood pressure and weight to ensure there is no fluid build-up in their lungs, a sign of deterioration and potentially predictive of an acute event.[4] Novartis sought to emphasize and ensure the value through two means: The first was value-linked reimbursement and the second was an Around-the-Patient approach of including remote monitoring.

David Epstein, head of the Novartis business developing and commercializing Entresto™ noted in a June 30, 2015, interview with Reuters,[5] "We are beginning to share the risk. When you buy other goods that don't work you either take them back or get your money back. Our industry is a bit unique because historically if the drug doesn't work it still gets paid for. I think that model will have to shift."[6] So by providing risk-shared and value-priced approaches, the benefits of the innovation can be made more accessible to patients and the health systems assured that the value is realized. In a separate interview with the *Wall Street Journal*, July 10, 2015, Novartis corporate CEO Joe Jimenez said that healthcare payers have expressed an interest in "pay for performance" versus pay per pill.[7]

Jimenez further said, "We're going to have to get smarter about services around the pill . . . and move into some areas that are different from just discovery of the drug. You're going to see Novartis go to payers with multiple services." The idea would be to be able to monitor patients remotely for any signs of deterioration. As Jiminez explained: "If you had a remote patient-monitoring device that the patient could use in their home together with Entresto™, we could make an even more serious dent in hospitalization."[8] Novartis plans to develop and offer these services through a set of partners who can enable and deploy the technologies in the different regions where these health authority and provider system models are put into place.

Biopharma company UCB S.A., Belgium, is partnering with PatientsLikeMe, a company built around a healthcare data-sharing platform to create a free, online open community dedicated to capturing the experiences of people living with epilepsy in the United States. Patient members will be able to create profiles and record and share their symptoms (including seizure type, frequency, and severity) and their treatments. The patient members will also be able to report adverse effects associated with approved UCB epilepsy therapies to the U.S. Food and Drug Administration (FDA). UCB leaders hope that through the information that members share, the company will be able to better focus its research and improve its treatments, as well as spot (and take advantage of) other opportunities to improve the lives of people who suffer from epilepsy.

Johnson & Johnson Services, Inc., which is partnering with IBM's Watson Health, is creating a patient concierge service that provides highly individualized assistance to patients preparing for knee surgery with the goal of being their partner through all the post-treatment activities that directly contribute to the success of the procedure. This service brings the cognitive expertise of Watson Health to interpret and anticipate the needs of these patients where pre- and post-treatment preparations contribute significantly to outcomes and satisfaction.[9]

Biogen, Inc., has also worked with PatientsLikeMe to reap the benefit of integrating wearables into the care and lifestyle management approaches of multiple sclerosis (MS) patients. In an interview about the wearables study conducted with PatientsLikeMe, Dr. Richard Rudnick, Biogen's head of value-based medicine, said, "MS impairs the ability to walk for many people with MS, yet we only assess walking ability in the limited time a patient is in the doctor's office. Consumer devices can measure number of steps, distance walked, and sleep quality on a continuous basis in a person's home environment. These data could provide potentially important information to supplement office visit exams."[10] (See Figure 5.10.)

AstraZeneca, is partnering with Vida Health, Inc. to offer an app called "Day by Day" designed to help cardiac patients connect with coaches who will encourage them to follow through on their doctors' recommendations after they are discharged from the hospital, and in between visits to the doctor's office. For AstraZeneca, the app (which does not bear its name) will provide a way to track how well patients follow their medicine regimens when recovering from a heart attack or a cardiac operation. And it will work with other companies' drugs as well as AstraZeneca's offerings. So while AstraZeneca might not derive an exclusive benefit in terms of increased drug sales through "Day by Day," the app will provide valuable information that will facilitate AstraZeneca's push to create a care platform for patients with chronic illnesses.[11]

In certain highly specialized disease states, getting real-world data that can advance these insights can be challenging if not impossible from secondary use sources[12] given the dearth of standardized data sets. For example, certain degenerative neurologic diseases may see only a few

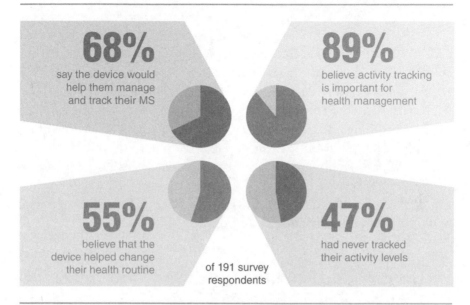

FIGURE 5.10   Results of Biogen/PatientsLikeMe Wearables Pilot
Source: PatientsLikeMe.

thousand patients even at the largest health systems and the data collection and mechanisms for capturing those data may vary tremendously across health systems. In response, one biopharmaceutical company developed a highly collaborative model across multiple regional healthcare delivery systems as a novel, standardized solution. While still in its development stages, the intent of this advanced analytic resource is to allow for improved insights and outcomes in the treatment of care on a statistically significant sample size. Furthermore, this database allows for sub-population analysis by key demographics (gender, race, age, etc.) and key clinical features (e.g., imaging studies, patient-collected functionality), which previously would not have been possible. The end goal will be to apply these insights to improve the overall standard of care and the insights any provider can have for the individual patient, thereby improving the value delivered for currently available therapeutics for the population overall.

Nor is it only chronic diseases that see the need for value-based innovation. The hepatitis C (HCV) space has received a lot of media attention this past year for its new drugs with cure rate in the high 90 percent range and equally high price tags running upward of $100,000. To differentiate in this space, HCV companies looked to provide patient services to bolster adherence required for drug efficacy. The value proposition to payers is clear: If a program provides adherence support, and therefore improved cure rates, the drug at the center become much more appealing, even if it has characteristics that make it less competitive off the shelf (duration, side effects, clinical trial efficacy, method of distribution, etc.).

From the Patient Pathways and "Moments of X" analyses, the Around-the-Patient Innovator can create a road map for these services. Not all services will apply to all patient populations nor to all micro-regional contexts. But by combining the rigor of the Patient Pathways analysis with the Services Framework (Figure 5.11), an Around-the-Patient Innovator can deploy a structured approach that aligns internal functions, partners, and its performance monitoring and rewards systems.

THE QUESTIONS THAT AROUND-THE-PATIENT INNOVATORS ASK AND WHY THEY ASK THEM

Around-the-Patient Innovators invest in real-world data assets and advanced analytic capabilities. They also understand the specific benefits and inadequacies of current population and patient management approaches; they invest in infrastructure that supports their partnering models with large provider systems and payers; they hone their ability to integrate technologies and services flexibly around a patient in a variety of geographies and contexts; and they seek strength in collaborative and joint service management relationships with technology and health services providers. To do these things successfully, an aspiring Around-the-Patient Innovator needs to persistently ask the following kinds of questions:

1. What is the *full scope of activities required to achieve the best possible outcomes* for (a) the patient and his or her family; (b) the health providers, based on the metrics and incentives they require; and (c) the risk bearer (may be the health provider in some contexts) and how the risk bearer sees avoidable and controllable costs falling and increasing in predictability?

   This question covers therapeutic interventions (e.g., drugs and devices), diet, exercise, key health status attributes indicating response, positive progression, negative trends, etc.—all aspects required to achieve an outcome or positively contribute to the health status of the patient.

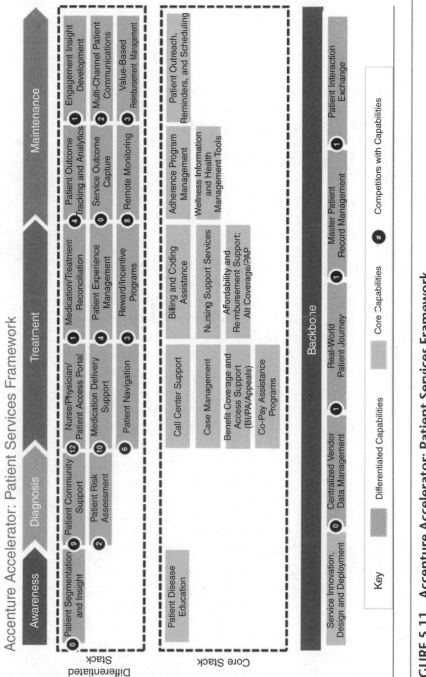

FIGURE 5.11 Accenture Accelerator: Patient Services Framework

Source: Accenture research.

2. How is the *system performing from the perspective of each critical party* in the health ecosystem surrounding the patient (e.g., patient, primary caregiver, care provider institution, health payer, patient's family, etc.)? Where are there gaps or failure points? Who holds the responsibility or access to the patient at each of those points? Who is the natural partner to integrate the elements together? Where there is no natural partner, can one be defined and deployed to accomplish this? Do current financial incentive and reimbursement approaches align the different participants to meaningful outcomes and value? How is value created being appropriately shared across the participants?

3. How do we *achieve superior economics and outcomes* from any new system solution and how can the benefits of that accrue to new parties providing services and bearing risk for the outcomes of the entire process or key elements? Often the challenge is not achieving a superior outcome but doing so in a manner where there is a basis of benefit being received for those making the investment or doing so in a manner that does fall within any compliance limitations (e.g., laws governing inducements, and so on). Accomplishing this often requires questioning not only the structure of roles, but also the mechanism of their payments and the responsibility or risk for specific outcomes they are assuming.

4. Who are the *partners and collaborators that can provide this solution with the highest confidence* and greatest flexibility to integrate to a wide array of care and home settings, across geographies, across national boundaries?

5. How can this *solution be framed or implemented as a multiyear contract and service* such that local investments and implementation of the Around-the-Patient solution can be justified? How can this be established as a service or solution that can be improved over time— as a live and dynamic solution that can build upon the improvements initially realized and sustained or improved over time?

6. How will we *ensure that the solutions we develop have some "proprietariness"*? What are the ways of working and platform elements that make this a sustainable and justifiable, differentiated new operating model? Is advantage created through deeper knowledge and first-move advantages or is there a more sustainable source?

7. How should we *organize company functions* to drive the new product-and-service orientation?

8. How will we *drive the right behaviors* through every aspect of the organization to ensure that the patient orientation becomes an inherent part of the culture and not simply a commercial function?

These questions are about the operating model, the mindsets of leadership, the core values of the organization, the optimum operating model working across the individual silos that existed in the product orientated environment, the relentlessness of its demand for insights into the disease of the patient, and solutions from research through development, supply chain, and commercial operations (sales force, marketing, marketing analytics) that are coordinated to improve all outcomes. A commitment to this model is not simply a matter for the commercial organization; rather, it implies a level of patient and value centricity for the company overall—from early research through to commercialization and life-cycle management.

For example, if value will be realized through treatment strategies that target the highest responding patients in a real-world setting, there may be a need for advanced diagnostics and analytics to be brought to bear through the research and clinical development phases. Insights from these analyses must be available at the point of registration, approval, and launch. Similarly, the availability of specific patient engagement platforms that measure adherence (whether patients are doing what the doctor tells them to do), treatment effectiveness, and disease progression may have a timetable comparable to the completion of phase III clinical trials and therefore need to be identified, specified, and developed within or coincident with those trials. Finally, the need for real-world results to converge with clinical trial outcomes further reinforces the need to deploy critical tools and services in the R&D phase versus these being add-ons or post-approval commercial strategies.

Similarly we are seeing the emergence of new roles for key functions—medical affairs being among the most central. Medical affairs is increasingly responsible for setting the company's real-world data strategy, partnerships, and aspects of the company's overall operating model and risk plans for this area. This is placing them at an active interface with R&D, IT, legal, regulatory, and commercial.

These shifts will force an overall change in the funding of and resource allocation approach for innovation funds within the company. Historically, research and development (R&D) would have been thought of in two ways: (1) allocation of human, facilities, capital, and expense dollars for internal R&D, and (2) allocation of business development and licensing (BD&L) funds for external transactions—licensing or acquisitions—to augment the internal pipeline for new therapeutic or product technologies. The Around-the-Patient Innovators need a wider view on this—considering internal real-world data management and analytic capabilities, complementary technologies (e.g., algorithms, therapeutic delivery, remote monitoring), and co-development agreements with technology or care infrastructure partners—to name but a few of the categories that are rising in importance.

THE AROUND-THE-PATIENT OPERATING MODEL: INNOVATING THE THERAPY AND PATIENT CARE

The top performing Around-the-Patient companies are science driven, innovative, and increasingly skilled at adapting their operating models to different therapeutic areas, patient journeys, and micro-regions. Whereas the Lean Innovators were relentless cost managers looking for innovative therapeutic arbitrage opportunities, the Around-the-Patient Innovators are driving into new areas of disease biology, reshaping the market, and addressing fundamental inadequacies of current therapies and care management approaches. Consequently, Around-the-Patient organizations focus on the more mature markets where healthcare spending is high, needs are high, and adoption of meaningful innovations is considered an imperative and a right. That is not to say that these markets are not focused on reducing the cost of care, improving population outcomes, and optimizing acute care resource efficiency and utilization. In fact, these are the very same markets where healthcare reform is most advanced—it is just that the capacity to fund care remains substantially higher in the recently emerged or emerging markets of Asia, Eastern Europe, and the Gulf Region. (See Figure 5.12.)

Around-the-Patient Innovators appreciate, invest in, and acquire advanced capabilities for (1) gaining rich insights into the current standard of care, (2) potential device and digital interventions that could transform care, and (3) partnerships and collaborations that could enable them to access emerging capabilities. All this is done in the context of a science-driven enterprise—where fundamental advances underpin the broader value proposition that is "around the patient." They are true

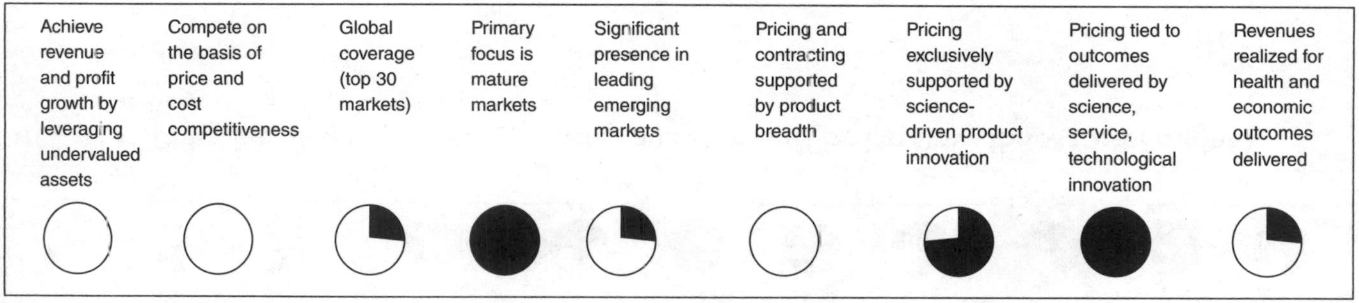

FIGURE 5.12 Market Positioning (What Unique Position in the Market Does the Company Want to Occupy?)

Source: Accenture analysis.

Figure Key: The circles in the graphic, known as "Harvey Balls," are used to qualitatively provide comparisons across categories and items. They indicate the extent to which any given component (or category) is complete, meaningful, representative, or fulfilled. A blank circle indicates that the criteria are not met; a circle that is completely filled in indicates that the criteria are fully met.

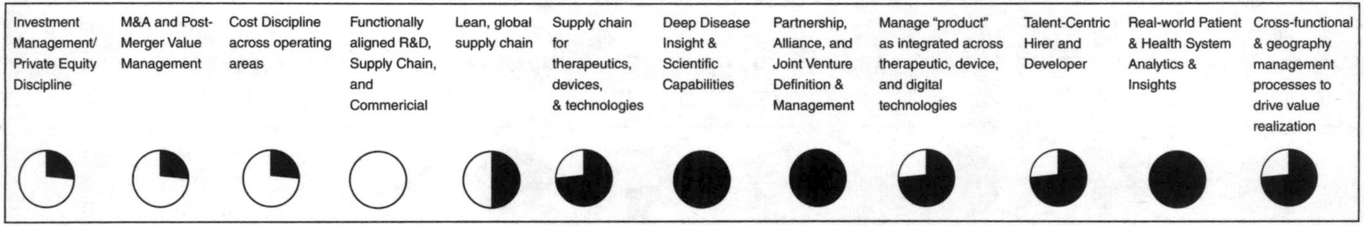

FIGURE 5.13 Differentiating Capabilities (Critical Capabilities Needed to Drive the Market Position)

Source: Accenture analysis.

innovators who are willing to invest, trial, and fail fast. With success they easily "ante up," making financial investments or doing direct acquisitions.[13] They are fundamentally different from the Lean Innovators that use experience, precedent, and applied financial analyses to drive options and decisions. (See Figure 5.13.)

Around-the-Patient Innovators are generally not "pure plays" in that they have diverse portfolios with "tail" or later life legacy products that largely will be managed as "volume" businesses. This is a conundrum for sure. They are managing in two or more worlds. They need to ensure the effectiveness and profitability of the management of legacy innovator products while transforming the main line of the company to being a value-centric innovator.

We noted earlier that one of the emerging truisms of the digital business model era is that companies will not be able to be successful based on deploying the best practices of others or the past. Digitally enabled or entirely digital operating models are predicated on ever-improving responsiveness to customers and consumers, an increasing ability to anticipate and predict needs and requirements, and ever-improving economics of service value (top-line) and service provision (bottom–line). That is the mantra of the Around-the-Patient Innovators where performance comes directly from clearly targeting a profitable future state and aligning performance systems to that destination.

Since Around-the-Patient Innovators get few opportunities to launch new products and transform whole therapeutic areas, they need to use major new product launches and acquisitions to game-change the external environment and broadly realign internally to this new operating paradigm and norms. For all of the companies in this class this will include being real-world evidence driven, executing externally through a rich partner network, and aligning internal incentives to the patient health ad health system economic outcomes realized. Not doing this creates a high vulnerability to the Lean Innovators, the better operators of the volume world. Doing this with conviction, and with a true throw-weight of investment, strategic, partnerships, and new talent acquisition can reshape capabilities, the external adoption of meaningful innovations, and their fundamental roles in the healthcare system. (See Figure 5.14.)

Growth and profitability will continue to be key measures of success and performance for the Around-the-Patient Innovators. However, how this is realized needs to be measured differently and explicitly part of the

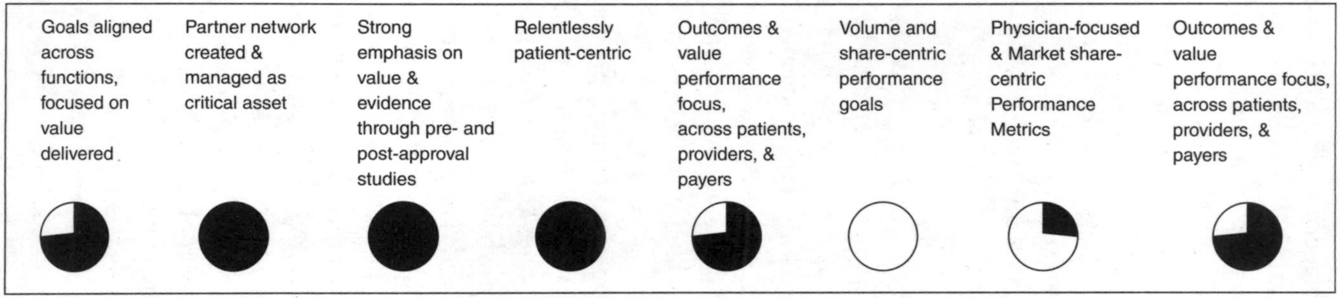

FIGURE 5.14 Performance Anatomy (How to Organize for Success)

Source: Accenture analysis.

performance systems and balanced scorecard. Increasingly, the proportion of revenues coming from value-based contracts and value-linked pricing will be material to near-term and longer-term performance and market position. The quality and breadth of relationships with key agencies, health authorities, and risk-bearing provider systems will define market position and the foundation for performance. Finally, the partners that have been assembled to provide access to key devices, sensors, data, advanced analytics, and digital services will be assets for innovation and value realization. Together, these form a collectively exhaustive set of key performance measures for the top team and top talent throughout the company.

AROUND-THE-PATIENT: NEW COMMERCIAL MODEL OR VALUE VANGUARD?

We've heard a lot of debate about whether integrating device technologies, services, and digital infrastructure truly represents a new business and operating model or whether it really is only the next-generation commercial model for a set of very wealthy companies. The answer can be found through our fundamental questions: "What value is being paid for?" and "Who is paying for that value?" The "what" is now demonstrable clinical outcomes. The "who" is being redefined by the meta- and micro-regional healthcare reforms that are creating new structures and placing more risk on healthcare providers. New market demands and new payers all imply that new business and operating models will be required. There should be no debate. The more disrupted the legacy models are, the more differentiated the new ones need to be. Around-the-Patient Innovators are a new value vanguard.

In the next chapter, we will develop a view on how the Around-the-Patient Innovator model might evolve into a fully integrated care management approach: the Value Innovator. These two operating models are not at odds with each other—in fact they may co-exist under some circumstances. They both reflect the direction of investments and market evolution. The pace of change will often prove to be the ultimate determinant of which model makes sense for what regions, therapeutic areas, or large health system customers.

Chapter 6

Value Innovators

Predicated on improving patient outcomes, this business model bets on improving the efficiency of the health system overall. Businesses using it are rapidly developing deep expertise in creating therapeutic packages, utilizing a digital infrastructure that integrates drugs, devices, and services with clinical processes.

While Around-the-Patient Innovators offer digital clinical and engagement services complementing the therapeutics or devices they make, Value Innovators have moved further toward a pure services approach, improving patient and clinical outcomes on a broader scale. They go to market as a single, integrated offering that includes personal and digital services, integrated analytics, and product elements. And they are willing to tie their revenues or reimbursement to their ability to achieve patient outcomes and health system efficiencies. Their customers may include regional health authorities, risk-bearing health systems, private payers, or private employers.

Some companies will use this model as their primary go-to-market approach where an entire micro-geographic or national market has become value- and performance-based. Others will view it as specific *to a therapeutic area or to the characteristics of a micro-region, sustaining an Around-the-Patient model in their legacy markets.*

The Value Innovator model overrides former product strategies (or layered product/service strategies) into a strategy about value creation. Most of the Value Innovators we're seeing today have a "product-centric" heritage; however, they are largely leaving that heritage behind.

*   *   *

The way to gain insight on a marketplace is to figure out, first, what's really impacting your customers. The more you know about the context in which your customers are using your product or service, the better you'll be able to define or redefine your offering to be relevant as a solution versus a cost, and your relationship as a partner and not a vendor.

That's why, increasingly, healthcare providers and payers are trying to identify the two, three, or four levers that really influence the health of any given patient population. Then, with that information in hand, they're conducting in-depth analyses to ensure that individual patients receive care that is consistent and aligns with the health drivers of their corresponding population.

And if they aspire to the Value Innovator model, they use those analyses to focus on the health outcomes of *populations*, and to develop *system solutions*. Their strategies hinge on value creation for populations and for the system because they know that their compensation will be based on their ability to prove that value; they set it up that way.

A MINDSET SHIFT ("HEALTH" AS OPPOSED TO "DISEASE")

Why is this a "new" thing? One reason is that healthcare markets have typically been divided and classified in three ways: therapeutic areas (e.g., cardiovascular diseases, or hypertension, also known as "disease states[1]"); geographic regions; and location of service (e.g., acute hospital setting, ambulatory or outpatient setting, long-term care facilities, home healthcare, and so on).

Historically, slicing the market in this way made it easier to establish and maintain certain standards of care. However, doing so also led healthcare companies to develop narrowly focused solutions for specific diseases in well-defined therapeutic areas, pushing a broader, more holistic view of the patient to the side. Health providers focused on selecting treatments for individual patients based on institutional and externally developed clinical care guidelines. Then, as we've discussed, they were paid on the basis of the procedures that were done and on how frequently certain technologies were used in their hospitals, labs, and other healthcare facilities. Given the payment schema, providers focused on optimizing the "coding" for their activities or within their diagnosis-related group (DRG).[2] Figure 6.1 shows a list of sample DRG codes, illustrating how they are focused on actions taken with no linkage to outcomes achieved.

Life science companies developed their products for and sold their products into this landscape. Predictably, strategically, their overall goal

MS-DRG	MDC	TYPE	MS-DRG Title
001	PRE	SURG	Heart transplant or implant of heart assist system w MCC
002	PRE	SURG	Heart transplant or implant of heart assist system w/o MCC
003	PRE	SURG	ECMO or trach w MV 90+ hrs or PDX exc face, mouth & neck w maj O.R.
004	PRE	SURG	Trach w MV96+ hrs or PDX exc face, mouth & neck w/o maj O.R.
005	PRE	SURG	Liver transplant w MCC or intestinal transplant
006	PRE	SURG	Liver transplant w/o MCC
007	PRE	SURG	Lung transplant
008	PRE	SURG	Simultaneous pancreas/kidney transplant
009	PRE	SURG	Bone marrow transplant
010	PRE	SURG	Pancreas transplant
011	PRE	SURG	Tracheostomy for face, mouth & neck diagnoses w MCC
012	PRE	SURG	Tracheostomy for face, mouth & neck diagnoses w CC
013	PRE	SURG	Tracheostomy for face, mouth & neck diagnoses w/o CC/MCC
020	01	SURG	Intracranial vascular procedures w PDX hemorrhage w MCC
021	01	SURG	Intracranial vascular procedures w PDX hemorrhage w CC
022	01	SURG	Intracranial vascular procedures w PDX hemorrhage w/o CC/MCC
023	01	SURG	Cranio w major dev impl/acute complex CNS PDX w MCC or chemo implant
024	01	SURG	Cranio w major dev impl/acute complex CNS PDX w MCC
025	01	SURG	Craniotomy & endovascular intracranial procedures w MCC
026	01	SURG	Craniotomy & endovascular intracranial procedures w CC
027	01	SURG	Craniotomy & endovascular intracranial procedures w/o CC/MCC
028	01	SURG	Spinal procedures w MCC

FIGURE 6.1   Sample DRG Codes

Sources: https://www.cms.gov/Research-Statistics-Data-and-Systems/Statistics-Trends-and-Reports/MedicareFeeforSvcPartsAB/downloads/DRGdesc08.pdf and https://www.cms.gov/Medicare/Medicare-Fee-for-Service-Payment/AcuteInpatientPPS/Acute-Inpatient-Files-for-Download-Items/CMS1247844.html.

was to maximize the places where their products might be used or prescribed, within the specific limitations of what was allowed by a given product's FDA approval, and with consideration for local conventions of clinical appropriateness and compassionate use.[3]

Now, however, healthcare finally has the opportunity to take more of a big-picture, "system" view. For an analogy, consider: The average consumer might still think of Michelin as a company that makes tires at the premium end of the market. But Michelin does not see itself that way. Michelin takes a system view now, and sees itself as a company that has transformed over the years into a transportation-focused company selling "miles" and not rubber.[4] Similarly, companies such as General Electric Company (GE) provide propulsion solutions to airplane builders and others needing aircraft engines with different performance characteristics as part of a "system." For healthcare, this transition takes the form of an emphasis on health as opposed to disease, outcomes instead of inputs, and value in lieu of volume. The lack of data was always cited as the inhibitor to change in the healthcare environment; that's no longer a valid excuse.

Recent healthcare reform measures have exemplified that transition, focusing on patient outcomes and cost control and driving change across the board. And as reforms gained traction in the United States, large private payers, public payers, and risk-bearing provider systems began to respond. *Population health,*[5] as a field of study, and as a strategic consideration in most major healthcare organizations, began to take shape.

Population health is about a) leveraging the knowledge we have about a disease, b) defining the therapies and interventions we have available for that disease and population of patients, and, critically, c) setting specific outcome targets. Usually these targets are expressed in terms of health outcomes, economic outcomes, and quality outcomes. Population health approaches are becoming more universal—with a focus on initiatives in Europe and the United States. Ultimately a population health approach to healthcare may provide a powerful guiding model for global healthcare.

Consistent with these policy changes and a greater demand for value and demonstrated effectiveness, the German "sickness funds," Techniker Krankenkasse, AOK Nordost, and KKH-Allianz, have recently contracted with outside partners to deliver disease management and remote monitoring programs for patients with some of the highest cost and most frequently rehospitalized patient populations—chronic obstructive pulmonary disease (COPD), congestive heart failure (CHF), and diabetes. In France, CNAMTS (Caisse Nationale de l'Assurance Maladie des Travailleurs Salariés) awarded the private health services company Healthways a four-year contract in 2011 to run the SOPHIA care management program for 600,000 patients with diabetes and asthma.

Because population health is relatively early in its implementation and adoption, the conundrum facing the healthcare system is that neither the goals nor outcomes for populations are universally established. What's more, not all health providers operate in environments where population targets and reimbursement models are in place. As a result, we're seeing a highly heterogeneous environment for targets, goals, and reimbursement. Our broad view is that this will evolve and converge over time. The wealth of publications describing alternative methodologies is increasing. The number of companies that are offering large-scale technology platforms supporting population health analytics is increasing (e.g., HealthCatalyst; IBM's Watson Health and their Phytel business as two examples of companies that are deploying highly advanced platforms and that are expanding beyond their originally U.S.-only markets).

Take a disease like heart failure.[6] Heart failure occurs when fluid builds up on the lungs, reducing overall capacity of the heart to power blood flows through the body, ultimately leading to profound activity restrictions and early death. It is growing in the number of patients who suffer from the disease, in large part because we have been more successful in keeping patients with advanced diabetes and acute cardiovascular diseases alive.[7] Heart failure patients also represent one of the highest cost populations to care for—from the perspectives of both healthcare providers and healthcare payers.[8] (See Figure 6.2.)

Heart failure patients need close monitoring and they need to take their key medications religiously. They also, generally speaking, need to reduce their salt intake, and maintain a regular though modest activity level. Many have a diagnostic or interventional device (e.g., cardiac pacemaker/defibrillator). No single device or therapeutic will keep the patient's health stable and them engaged in normal activities—doing so is fundamentally a "systems challenge" where these different aspects of care, lifestyle, and so on need to be carefully integrated and coordinated. It is also a disease where most of the "work" occurs away from formally designated health facilities and purview of a personal care physician or advanced heart failure nurse. (See Figure 6.3.)

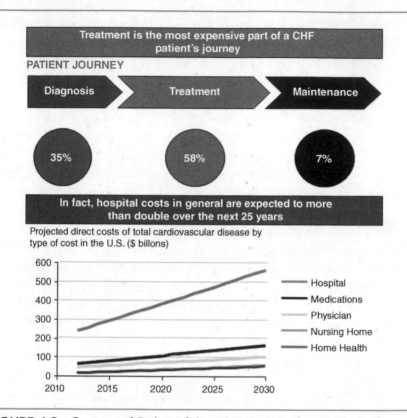

FIGURE 6.2   Costs and Point of Cost Incurrence for Heart Failure
Based on: American Heart Association: "Circulation—Cardiovascular Quality &
Outcomes"; European Society of Cardiology: "What Are the Costs of Heart Failure?"
Accenture analysis.

For most care providers, heart failure presents many avoidable costs.
With the right care coordination and interventions at the right time, a
substantial number of congestive heart failure (CHF) patients will be
better off than they would without these interventions and oversights.[9] So
this is an area where care providers and health financial risk bearers pay
attention. Most positively, when the right things are done—by the health
providers, home care providers, patients, and so on—patients do live a
longer, higher quality life.

So device or therapeutics manufacturers with a diagnostic or interventional product that is focused on heart failure patients will need to
be attentive to the overall care management ecosystem, recognizing

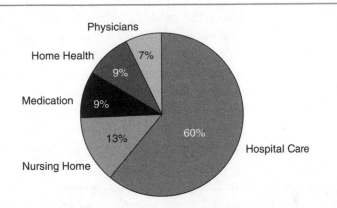

FIGURE 6.3   Inpatient Services Constitute the Bulk of Costs
Based on: American Heart Association: "Circulation—Cardiovascular Quality & Outcomes"; European Society of Cardiology: "What Are the Costs of Heart Failure?" Accenture analysis.

that success in treatment by a device or therapeutic is bound to the overall success of the care management process itself. If the company's strategy focuses on outcomes and outcomes-based reimbursement—even outcomes-supported pricing—then the integrity of the overall care management process will influence their ability to see beneficial outcomes.

Historically, this would have posed an irresolvable conundrum—having a potential transformative therapy but being unable to realize results because of inadequacies or failure-points within the healthcare and home care system around the patient. Today, the idea of such an irresolvable conundrum shouldn't be acceptable. Providers and payers have accessible, efficient, and effective ways to monitor patient status in remote settings. And services that are delivered via telephone, home nursing, and mobile platforms are already advanced, and becoming moreso by the day.

VALUE INNOVATORS: THE "LIVING" SERVICE PROVIDERS

Everyone knows that most of what is needed to manage a disease state occurs away from health professionals and formal health facilities. Consider our heart failure example. Salt intake, diet, a prescribed level of physical activity, and close monitoring of blood pressure and weight are all things that can be done in the patient's own home without the direct presence of a healthcare professional. Under recent care models, population health outcomes and risk bearing can be determined by actions and activities outside of these professionals' control. And so the ability to influence patient health outside of the traditional domains of healthcare will be especially important for closing the treatment gaps that exist in the care of patients with chronic illnesses, like those of diabetes discussed above as well as congestive heart failure and chronic obstructive pulmonary disorder.

The Value Innovator model has emerged in response to this need. Value Innovators are developing full-spectrum solutions—these organizations are frequently in contact with their patient/customers; they are aware of the greater patient and healthcare context; and they are dynamic: willing and able to change their offerings to fit changing needs and take advantage of new technologies and new findings. In other words, the Value Innovator model calls for an organization to look at populations of patients and seek to understand the balance of products, interventions, and patient care services that could provide the optimal therapeutic outcomes to patients and value to the healthcare system overall.

Value Innovators thus go an extra step beyond Around-the-Patient Innovators by focusing on population health to align with providers and payers on targeted patient outcomes as the core of their business model— as a services model. Perhaps most importantly, they are willing to tie their payment—whether done on a per patient per month or population basis—to their ability to achieve those outcomes. So while the Around-the-Patient Innovators are linking prices to the outcomes realized, they are still fundamentally product-focused companies versus looking at the service as the business and revenue model.

Take a look once more at the Value Curve (Figure 6.4). Lean Innovators focus on a cost- and financial-performance optimized version of the A point on the curve, and can also move from A toward B. They look at the opportunities to acquire and commercialize products based on the financial value they can deliver in their optimized tax and financial performance optimized structure. Around-the-Patient Innovators, by contrast, are looking at the patient journey, and moving from B to C on the curve.

The final frontier, area D, is difficult for many life science companies to enter, given legal limits on their ability to engage directly with patients and avoiding levels of investment within the healthcare provider system that

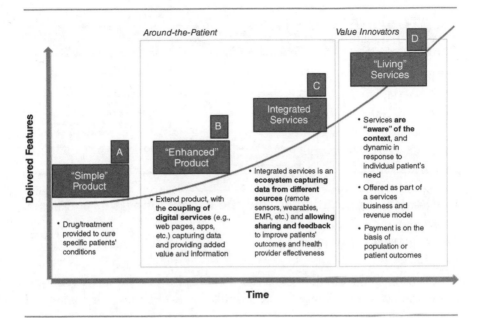

FIGURE 6.4   Value Curve
Source: Accenture analysis.

would qualify as a potential inducement to prescribe or use their products.[10] Nonetheless, what differentiates the Value Innovator model from the Around-the-Patient model is its ability to engage fully in area C, and reach toward area D—through its focus on population health to align all of its activities around targeted patient outcomes and then be reimbursed for hitting or improving those outcome targets. Value Innovators, as we've said, take a *system view*.

Value Innovators will be nimble entities, defined by their ability to use digital technologies to generate and respond to insights very quickly. Today many life science companies are still driven by data management and lagging analytic insights. Value Innovators innovate more broadly. They will create ecosystems of care rather than simply products. They will be in a market with a far faster "clock-speed" than therapeutics companies were traditionally.

Consider the chart shown in Figure 6.5. Around-the-Patient Innovators, located in the middle of the chart, create a set of services that complement the therapeutic area that aids health providers or payers in the management of a population or individual patient's care. Value

Patient Engagement	Patient Services	Patient Care Management
Mobile apps from providing disease and therapy specific tools; care coordination linkages between patient and provider	Mobile apps and provider facing tools (e.g., patient treament selection algorithms) that enhance the ability to identify high-responder patients and collect patient outcomes in a real-world data registry-type of model	Fully integrated model wherein the company partners with risk-bearing health providers, payers, and authorities to advance the health status of individual patients and a well-defined population, usually contracted as a services and outcomes linked revenue model
e.g., adherence reminders and activity trackers in diabetes	*e.g., advanced treatment of neurodegenerative diseases and novel oncology treatments*	*e.g., for heart failure, or chronic obstructive pulmonary disease*

FIGURE 6.5   Contrasting Around-the-Patient Innovators and Value Innovators

Source: Accenture analysis.

Innovators, by contrast, are creating new businesses that are collaboratively taking responsibility for the population and patient outcomes and having their reimbursement and incentives tied to this outcome. They are managing a set of care services that contribute significantly, measurably, and unambiguously to the outcomes realized—providing the sets of services denoted by the Patient Care Management description below.

Imagine a scenario where a medical device company marketing an acute cardiovascular device approaches the largest customers in its market—hospitals, health authority, and community providers—with a risk-shared value proposition. The contract requires that the provider use certain predictive analytics tools to identify the treatment approach patients will benefit from most and include specific monitoring for patient response. The contract in turn commits to a certain set of readmission rates—lower than current rates—that are a major driver of costs in the healthcare system as payers reimburse a set cost for a procedure. This is where the Value Innovator model expects to deliver.

One pilot program in Sweden focused on addressing heart failure offers a good example.[11] The population in Stockholm has grown significantly in recent years, putting pressure on the provider system to provide better services for individuals with heart failure. And the New Karolinska Solna University Hospital (NKS) is scheduled to open in 2016 (representing a massive investment in healthcare infrastructure in Stockholm). The NKS has been designed with a greater focus on the patients' needs, faster provision of care, and increased patient safety with single rooms for all inpatients. However, overall bed capacity will be reduced, requiring much higher levels of efficiency in the overall healthcare delivery system of the region—namely shorten length of stay, reduce avoidable readmissions, better coordinate care across providers to aid efficiencies and non-redundant treatment (e.g., single imaging studies, non-overlapping lab diagnostic testing, and so on), and shifting care to lower-cost, non-acute settings—including the patient's own home.

Anticipating those needs, the Stockholm County Council, together with Karolinska University Hospital and Boston Scientific Corporation, launched a pilot program with a set of patients in 2014 "to identify and prioritize gaps in care delivery to patients with congestive heart failure that require innovative solutions."[12]

The opportunity for Boston Scientific is to advance a Patient Care Services approach that transcends its traditional device-only patient population. Working with Karolinska University Hospital, Boston Scientific is striving to build a reference model for value-based care, and at the same time, develop the basis for a new way of working.

A set of services monitors the health status of patients in the pilot when they are at home—capturing additional critical information to guide that specific individual's care. Patients are actively engaged and monitored throughout to encourage following the required diet and exercise modifications. Predefined care management, clinical outcome, and financial goals ensure that all parties involved are aligned in roles and economics.

Risk and outcomes—as the scenario plays out—will be managed by predictive models, which are powered by machine-learning algorithms that will improve their accuracy rates over time. Today, that "future state" is not within the domain of most typical health providers, manufacturers, or payers. But as the focus on value and financial incentives for outcomes formally grows, healthcare stakeholders will partner for improved patient outcomes driven by holistic products and services (see Figure 6.6).

BETTER OPERATORS: EXAMPLES OF EMERGING VALUE INNOVATORS

Boston Scientific is not the only example of an organization formally launching Value Innovator services or progressing toward a Value Innovation model.

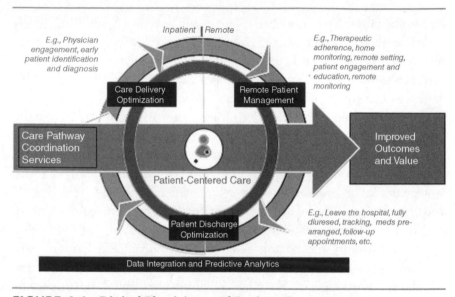

FIGURE 6.6   Digital Physician and Patient Engagement
Source: Accenture analysis.

Medtronic, for example, publicly announced the formation of its Medtronic Hospital Solutions in the fall of 2013 to develop partnerships with hospitals to improve efficiencies, reduce costs, and improve patient access and outcomes. The company has formally targeted an increasing proportion of their total global revenues to come from these new services businesses that are tied to the success of its health system customers and the health of its patient populations in acute cardiovascular diseases and diabetes.

To support this broader strategy, Medtronic engaged in a series of acquisitions to support these services, including Cardicom (2013)[13] and Corventis, Inc. (2014), which supported Medtronic's mission of looking outside of devices for improved health outcomes through passive remote patient monitoring services.[14] This monitoring allows Medtronic to collect patient data and intervene when results fall outside the range of normal deviations. In addition to supporting patients, the approach allows Medtronic to prove the impact and value of its devices to payers and physicians.

Remote patient monitoring is especially valuable in Medtronic's main heart failure business as rapid weight gain, caused by fluid retention, is a leading indicator of future health issues. Catching it early can prevent a readmission to the clinic or emergency department. This has become increasingly important to health system clients as heart failure readmissions have step penalties since the start of the Affordable Care Act.

Medtronic is also actively encouraging patients to collaboratively manage their own care and enables this through its CareLink® product. CareLink® allows patients to connect with their care team and family to download data from their devices and proactively share this data. Medtronic is also actively exploring ways to bring the patient into remote monitoring notifications.[15]

In addition to these changes occurring within the healthcare ecosystem, new and complementary trends are facilitating the development of Value Innovators. Companies such as Apple and Google are interconnecting devices and sensors at scale and with functional economics. These global digital organizations are creating foundation capabilities to bring services to market at scale. EMR companies such as Epic, Cerner, and athena-health are becoming the new standards of electronic health information, increasingly integrating decision support tools and advanced analytics capabilities. Newly formed entities such as Watson Health, Optum, and Accenture's own Predictive Health Intelligence and Intelligent Patient analytics services are creating global infrastructure for highly advanced analytics that are the core of these services. The wealth of venture and private equity backed entities making focused tools and applications play well into this system, allowing for differentiated models by region but around the same core service. (The next chapter focuses on these "Digital Gone Healthcare" businesses.)

HOW TO SUCCEED AS A VALUE INNOVATOR

The sicker the patients, the more chronic the disease, and the greater the cost burden the disease places on the health system, the higher the likelihood that a value-based economic model can be successfully defined. The more clinical outcomes require coordinating the patient's care outside of a formal healthcare facility and healthcare professionals, the higher the likelihood that there is a services-based approach that can deliver the outcomes more effectively than a medicine or device alone. Here the management of the patient's health may require higher engagement of the patient, his family, or his caregivers than a fully integrated approach, with connections across the patient's care provider, home, and work. Examples of these sorts of diseases include heart failure, other acute cardiovascular diseases, chronic obstructive pulmonary disorder, and severe asthma, to name just a few. Increasingly this is how healthcare will be delivered. Given the relatively high expense of formal healthcare facilities, this is also how we are going to be able to take care of the sickest patients, keep them healthier, but do it affordably.

These are early days, and many of the companies that have aspired to do this are at the pilot stage. In fact, most, if not all, pharmaceutical companies that engage in Around-the-Patient initiatives include in their strategic road map a desire to show a value proposition to payer and health systems but few have successfully gotten there. In order to do so, they must face and overcome the following three barriers:

1. Transitioning to a Value Innovation requires leadership support of full impact assessment. For some players, notably those working in the hepatitis C (HCV) space, real-world efficacy may be less than clinical trial success unless comparable controls and oversight for patient medical adherence and engagement are in place.

2. Accessing real-world clinical data, on an ongoing basis, whether considered fully identifiable or deidentified[16] must be done within specific legal frameworks and technical protocols. Working with patient data and defining specific health outcomes is complicated. Increasingly, though, this is getting facilitated by risk-bearing health providers seeking new insights into how to advance population health goals and a growing market for intermediary firms who can stand as the industry "neutrals" for handling personal health and other identifiable personal data when done in a context and model for the patient's and health systems benefit.

3. For many conditions, value-based innovation requires a longer-term horizon for evaluating returns and the multiyear services contract may be seen as investment. So whereas product sales can be seen as month-over-month, and specific point sales seen as year-over-year for "same institutions," the value-based services contract may be multi-year and require improvements over the baseline health status of a population and then year-over-year improvements in the health of the population.

SUITES OF SOLUTIONS

The Value Innovators are driving to become fully integrated and dynamic service organizations that are responsible, in formal partnership with health providers and payers, for the health and economic outcomes of patient populations. Their focus on population health outcomes, and explicit linking of financial incentives to multiyear outcomes, differentiates them from Around-the-Patient Innovators. There is nothing, however, that could preclude an Around-the-Patient Innovator from moving to a position as a full Value Innovator as they saw the entire market turning toward value-based pricing and some value- and performance-based contracts for population outcomes. While the Value Innovators are able to do this today in focused micromarkets, the current Around-the-Patient Innovators may find them the natural partners or acquisition targets of the future.

Given the U.S. trends in healthcare, which are similar to what Europe has recently gone through, we expect to see a continued push and requirement for Value Innovation in pharmaceuticals and medical devices through partnerships with payers and provider networks both domestically and globally. It is already well underway in Europe with the early results confirming the overall promise.

What remains unclear is whether Value Innovators will begin looking holistically at patient health not only by populations and/or disease areas (i.e., cardiovascular) but also to provide solutions for the *suite* of health problems patients face (i.e., cardiovascular, diabetes, and hypertension). It's rare that a patient will suffer from one ailment alone, and taking that step would truly address the patient's health needs holistically.

THE VALUE INNOVATOR OPERATING MODEL IS INTEGRATED, DIGITAL, AND SERVICES- AND OUTCOMES-CENTRIC

The top performing Value Innovators are technology driven and very focused on the needs of their health system provider partners. Their legacy has not been as patient-centric as the Around-the-Patient innovators, but this is beginning to change with their emphasis on patient care management services as the business and operating model. In fact, most of the Value Innovators would benefit from the new analytics tools and methodologies for interpreting patient journeys, critical moments of interest, and patient engagement solutions being developed and deployed by the Around-the-Patient Innovators.

Still, the Value Innovators are global, with significant presence in the leading global markets. Whereas the Lean Innovators were relentless cost managers looking for innovative therapeutic arbitrage opportunities, the Value Innovators are driving into new integrated services and, guided by the evolution of micro-regional health systems, addressing fundamental inadequacies of current therapies and care management approaches. These are the micro-regions, where healthcare reform is most advanced and most focused on reducing the cost of care, improving population outcomes, and optimizing acute care resource efficiency and utilization. (See Figure 6.7.)

Thus far, it seems that organic development of these new services-at-population-scale capabilities is as successful as those that are acquired and integrated into a new platform capability. In ways that are quite differentiated from the Lean Innovators or Around-the-Patient Innovators, the Value Innovators have always had both physician leadership and clinical administrator relationships, sometimes going back decades. So the overall stronger determinant of success is health authority access and health system relationships, this building on some of their legacy capabilities. That combined with the internal resolve to compete through services and a view that broad multiyear agreements are the foundation for future innovation and growth.

Value Innovators are similar to the Around-the-Patient innovators in that they are increasingly depending on advanced capabilities for (1) gaining rich insights into the current standard of care, (2) potential device and digital interventions that can meaningfully and predictably improve the health of a targeted population, and (3) partnerships and collaborations that could enable them to access emerging capabilities. Most of these companies were born as technology- and disease state–centric device companies. This has been a more cost-competitive business for years as they were the target of hospital purchasing-spend initiatives and payer cost-reduction strategies over the past decade or more.[17] As such, their investments are long considered and implementations considerably more "lean" than their Around-the-Patient counterparts. In fact, just one of the Around-the-Patient Innovator investments in advanced patient analytics exceeds the public total of all of the Value Innovators in patient care management services.[18] Still they share many of the same

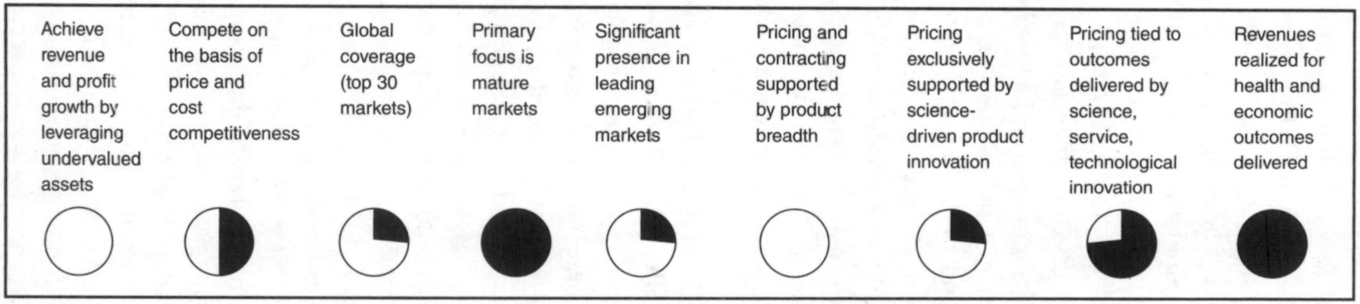

Achieve revenue and profit growth by leveraging undervalued assets	Compete on the basis of price and cost competitiveness	Global coverage (top 30 markets)	Primary focus is mature markets	Significant presence in leading emerging markets	Pricing and contracting supported by product breadth	Pricing exclusively supported by science-driven product innovation	Pricing tied to outcomes delivered by science, service, technological innovation	Revenues realized for health and economic outcomes delivered
○	◐	◔	●	◔	○	◔	◕	●

FIGURE 6.7 Market Positioning (What Unique Position in the Market Does the Company Want to Occupy?)

Source: Accenture analysis.

Figure Key: The circles in the graphic, known as "Harvey Balls," provide qualitative comparisons across categories and items. They indicate the extent to which any given component (or category) is complete, meaningful, representative, or fulfilled. A blank circle indicates that the criteria are not met; a circle that is completely filled in indicates that the criteria are fully met.

differentiating capabilities and priorities for new capability building of the Around-the-Patient Innovators, as they are all increasingly value-centric in their business and operating models. Finally, they need to move from being health provider–centric to a balance of patient and health system consistent with the triple-aim and other value-based frameworks that speak to value outcomes for a population, costs for the system, and engagement and benefits to the patient. (See Figure 6.8.)

The Value Innovators are overall very focused. They may have multiple products and play across multiple disease categories, but they are often looking for product and business capability synergies. Whereas the Lean Innovators are looking to maintain generic portfolio breadth and opportunistic innovator acquisitions, and the Around-the-Patient Innovators are looking for the next large-market specialty therapeutic, the Value Innovators are often evaluating how new products extend their current solutions or take them into very close product adjacencies.[19] As they see markets evolve toward value-based and performance-based models, they are scaling up their Value Innovator services in parallel and with increasing conviction.

For all of the companies in this class this will include being real-world evidence driven, executing externally with a narrow set of close partners, and aligning internal incentives to the patient health and health system economic outcomes realized. These companies are leaner than the Around-the-Patient Innovators and better operators in the demand, value-based micro-regions that have undergone healthcare reform. In short, their performance "centering" is well positioned for the changing, value-centric world we are accelerating toward. (See Figure 6.9.)

Growth and profitability will continue to be key measures of success and performance. Whereas the Lean Innovators are gaining these improvements by adding on niche innovator products, and the Around-the-Patient Innovators are defending their legacy margins even while they transform into better value-operators, the Value Innovators are seeing superior growth and profit potential in their broader services businesses. It is aiding them in getting out of a narrow business definition and set of negatively spiraling economics. They now need to explicitly focus on how these new services are considered the new core business, and how their very product-centric performance systems and balanced score-cards should be adjusted to catalyze them forward. Already some of these companies are reporting that services are becoming an increasingly

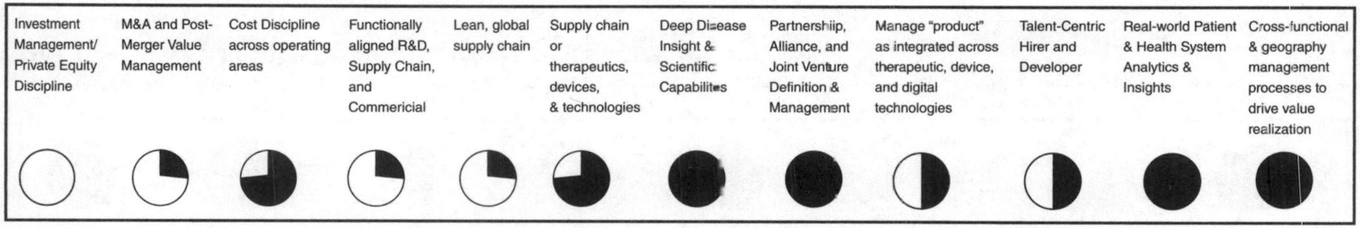

FIGURE 6.8 Differentiating Capabilities (Critical Capabilities Needed to Drive the Market Position)

Source: Accenture analysis.

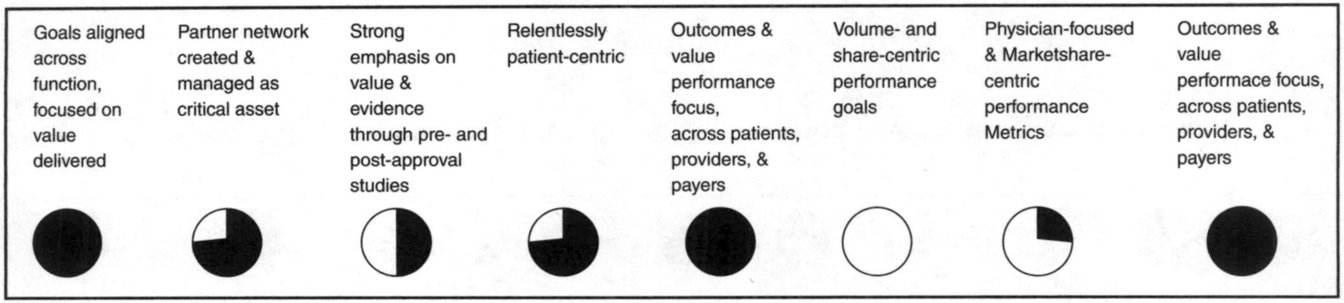

| Goals aligned across function, focused on value delivered | Partner network created & managed as critical asset | Strong emphasis on value & evidence through pre- and post-approval studies | Relentlessly patient-centric | Outcomes & value performance focus, across patients, providers, & payers | Volume- and share-centric performance goals | Physician-focused & Marketshare-centric performance Metrics | Outcomes & value performace focus, across patients, providers, & payers |

FIGURE 6.9 Performance Anatomy (How to Organize for Success)

Source: Accenture analysis.

important and material portion of their total revenues and earnings growth.[20]

Still, it will be quality and breadth of relationships with key agencies, health authorities, and risk-bearing provider systems that will define market position and be their foundation for performance. So too will the critical relationships and partnerships they are assembling. Together, these form a collectively exhaustive set of key performance measures for the top team and top talent throughout the company.

THE VALUE INNOVATOR: VALUE PARTNER AND SERVICES PROVIDER

Value Innovators arrive with critical relationships with leading health systems. They are credible from the outset. They have come through a period where costs have already mattered and where pricing was becoming increasingly competitive. They are prepared to transform from product and product-centric companies to a focus on services that transform the health of populations and the performance of health systems. Their challenge will be overcoming their own past success as great product and device marketers, and instead see themselves as distinctive partners and service providers at scale—ever focused on integrating multiple solutions to drive measureable and ever improving value for patients and the health systems.

Chapter 7

The New Health Digitals

The leaders of other industry sectors, including digital consumer technologies and services, and global scale digital cloud services, have arrived (along with some opportunistic start-ups) to create a new segment in the healthcare industry, to collaborate (and compete) with value innovators, and to change where and how patients receive care.

Spotting the opportunity to disrupt traditional processes and fundamentally reinvent ways of working and living (as they have elsewhere), several very well known digital companies (Apple, Google, and Samsung among them) have entered the healthcare space. We call them "Digital Gone Healthcare" businesses. Complementing and competing with these companies are legacy "Healthcare Gone Digital" businesses, led by IBM, QualComm, GE, and Philips.

New "Start-Up Digital" companies are also entering the space, for the dual purpose of connecting patients to providers and making their communications more meaningful by capturing and transmitting patient data in real time.

Together, these companies represent the "New Health Digitals" model. This model is enabling increasing numbers of patients to take control of their health, creating the foundations for the emerging business models, and redefining what we may even mean by "healthcare" as a service. If early indications are correct, this model will underpin a new set of health and wellness economics. Healthcare stakeholders will need to be strategically prepared for this model's arrival, and, similarly, the companies utilizing it will need to think long-term as their initial positions take shape, or they will quickly become obsolete.

* * *

Almost all healthcare professionals now have a smart device that they can use to access the full compendium of healthcare diagnostic and treatment option information wherever and whenever they choose, using applications such as ePocrates and UptoDate. Almost all healthcare professionals also use EMR systems to capture and store patient data, schedule appointments and procedures, check health system protocols, send prescriptions to pharmacies, and monitor potential drug-to-drug interactions. In addition, physicians and other healthcare professionals are also increasingly networked—many are making decisions collaboratively as a matter of course, rather than making decisions by themselves, or having to reach outside of their normal channels to contact another caregiver for input.[1]

In most of these cases providers are purchasing these digital applications—sometimes from consumer-focused technology companies such as Apple, Samsung, and Google. Those companies, which we call "Digital Gone Healthcare" businesses, have identified great potential in disrupting healthcare markets and are wasting no time pursuing those opportunities.

But many healthcare organizations, "Healthcare Gone Digital" entities, are also beginning to develop and provide digital enablers to patients and caregivers. These companies—Philips Medical, GE, IBM Watson Health—started in healthcare, usually as technology companies, and were early to recognize the ongoing and impending changes to the healthcare system. They've targeted maintaining their legacy product-centric businesses even while they create entirely digital new businesses.

At the same time, an increasing number of "Start-Up Digital" companies are also appearing on the scene, created for the purpose of using digital solutions to meet needs, fill gaps, and, if possible, create new markets in the healthcare ecosystem.

These three types of organizations are converging on and disrupting healthcare from all angles; we can describe what they're doing, and envision the implications, but the ultimate potential may very well be beyond what we can fathom.

DIGITAL GONE HEALTHCARE

A whole range of technology companies, including global and multisector powerhouses such as Apple, Google, Amazon, and Samsung, have determined that the healthcare market presents a strategic opportunity for their capabilities and unique skillsets. These are already among the world's wealthiest enterprises. Each dwarfs the largest healthcare providers, payers, pharmaceutical companies, and device manufacturers. They see the 11 to 17 percent expenditure of mature economies' gross domestic product on healthcare as a target for their highly distinctive and evolved capabilities.[2]

In fact, the absolute dollars spent, and the pace of R&D spending increase of the largest digital gone healthcare companies is accelerating, and comparable to that of the largest pharmaceutical companies on a percentage-of-revenues basis—and healthcare is a top priority focus.[3,4] The R&D budgets of the major pharmaceutical companies range between $8 and $10 billion each, annually, with two-thirds of that spending going to the clinical trials of experimental therapeutics that are required for regulatory approvals. This breakdown is unique to pharmaceutical companies, but it also means that fundamental and translational research is considerably smaller as a percentage of total revenues for these companies—between 5 and 6 percent. By contrast, Google itself spends 13 percent or more on R&D as a percentage of revenues— more than $11 billion annually based on its current $2.7 billion in quarterly R&D spending.[5] (See Figure 7.1 for a review of Apple's R&D spending.)

The digital gone healthcare companies do not report their spending separately by sector.[6] Yet, Calico (California Life Company), a Google investment to research the biology of human longevity, and a wholly owned subsidiary of Alphabet Inc., received $240 million from Google in 2014 with another $490 million committed for 2015.[7] Meanwhile, Google's investment arm, Google Ventures, increased its investment in

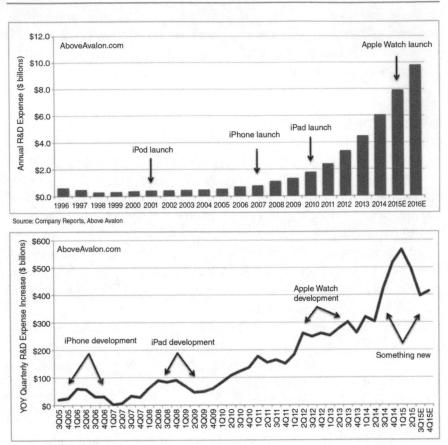

FIGURE 7.1   Apple's R&D Spending

Source: Company reports, Above Avalon.com. www.aboveavalon.com/notes/2015/5/3/significant-rd-increase-suggests-apple-is-working-on-something-big.

health and life sciences companies from 9 percent of its portfolio in 2013 to 36 percent in 2014, a total of $576 million.[8]

The investment is there, if the distinction is not, and that makes sense. In fact, it is the foundation of these companies' disruptions to healthcare. Already consumers and advanced analytics experts, digital gone healthcare businesses have deep experience in bringing technology to very human problems and opportunities—they have already reinvented the ways in which we work, communicate, and transact. What's adding another sector to the mix? Why *wouldn't* it make sense for Apple to partner with Epic, the largest EMR provider, to enable patients to access their own data.[9] Why *wouldn't* it make sense for physicians to access their institution's EMRs through their tablet or large-screen smart phone (as we noted at the top of this chapter, close to 100 percent of physicians now have a smart phone and use it for professional purposes, with 85 percent of physicians in the United States on an Apple iOS device).[10]

What's more, consumers already trust them; they have strong track records in delivering on their capabilities. Now, they are mustering their forces to anticipate the needs of those same consumers—now as providers and patients—and fulfill those needs before they are even formally expressed, fitting themselves into newly forming value chains (and ensuring shared risk) as new healthcare markets develop.

Apple, for example, has released several application development kits and apps—HealthKit, Activity, ResearchKit, and Health—which collectively monitor a user's daily health activities and serve as a central hub for app development and data aggregation and exchange. Google has Google Fit and its ambitious Baseline study. The former collects and presents data in the form of a user friendly dashboard while the latter is an attempt to map the biology of a healthy human being, establishing a benchmark against which patients can be compared and with which doctors can better predict the onset of disease.

Apple leverages the combination of its wireless infrastructure to allow patients to access their personal health records and share these with their primary care physician and healthcare team. In addition, Apple has ventured into supporting the management of specific diseases, such as diabetes, which requires a combination of therapy, diet, and exercise; and attentiveness to overall fitness and personal health.[11] Any one application or personal technology solution geared toward managing diabetes can draw on elements of others' solutions to improve the entire ecosystem. This is the nature of cloud infrastructure, networked businesses, and platform pervasiveness; it will be a given for future generations, but it wasn't possible even a few years ago.

Even the digital technology, services, and retailing giant Amazon is leveraging its efficient global technology infrastructure for health and life-sciences related solutions, creating what it is calling an "ecosystem" of partners that can leverage its Amazon Web Services (AWS) cloud infrastructure to complete tasks in a fraction of the time and expense that would have been required even three to five years ago (if they could have been completed at all).[12]

For example, AWS has enabled the integration of healthcare provider and real-world data. With the help of Amazon Web Services, Orion Health built Cal Index, one of the largest health information exchanges in the United States. If several life science companies are looking to combine their clinical trial data with real-world data, the cloud can make it happen. Amazon's Health Cloud can also make it much easier to track how clinical trial patients do in the real-world setting after the trial is over and compare that data to other data from people who fit the same profiles and take the same medicines, but did not participate in the trial. Results in clinical trials are often superior, given strong adherence support and intervention, but just how much better remains unclear.

The cloud also makes it relatively easy to deidentify and share data between healthcare organizations. That benefit is especially powerful in rare or so-called "orphan" diseases, where the population size is often too small to find statistically significant results for any single health system.

HEALTHCARE GONE DIGITAL

Legacy healthcare technology companies traditionally made hospital-centered diagnostic, imaging, internal patient monitoring platforms, and information management systems. But these organizations, too, have been experiencing and seeing the changes to the healthcare system. And as a result, they are now trying to bridge from their positions in the hospital and outpatient settings toward the broader home and remote contexts where more care will be delivered and health maintained or improved.[13]

Philips Medical, for example, is expanding its hospital-based device integration network into a broader platform that can extend to other health facilities and into the patient's own home. In doing so, Philips Medical is essentially moving in the opposite direction as Apple, in that it is growing from the hospitals where it currently operates into the non-acute and home settings (Apple's original home turf) where the patient will increasingly receive more care. Philips has also put together a novel collaboration with Salesforce.com in an effort to connect its operating infrastructure and remote monitoring to patient and physician engagement approaches. Salesforce.com is a cloud services provider of customer relationship management tools used by most major sales forces to plan and maintain contacts with current and prospective customers. As an example, in September 2015, Philips, Salesforce and Netherlands-based Radboud University Medical Center deployed a mobile diabetes monitoring system to enhance self-management and continuity of care for those with chronic disease conditions.[14] So Philips is combining its highly robust and secure clinical data management infrastructure with the rather ubiquitous digital marketing cloud of Salesforce.com to create a new integrated capability. Again, the notion is that as patients move from a traditional acute intervention setting to a home or other remote location, the company will be able to follow—better coordinating, managing, and monitoring patient care.

GE—a conglomerate with a strong historic heavy presence in inpatient healthcare (MRI, ultrasound, etc.)—and Intel (one of the world's largest semiconductor chip makers) have similarly established a partnership, CareInnovations™,[15] to provide telecare services to advance the remote monitoring, remote management, and enable patients and their families and caretakers to engage in remote care.[16]

IBM's Watson Health and Johnson & Johnson (J&J) offer another example. The two companies are collaborating to help patients prepare for and recover from orthopedic surgeries.[17] Their objective is to provide patients with an expert advisor through a mobile app or web portal that is technology enabled, aiding the patient to better understand when treatment should be sought and what to expect. Post treatment, the same approach can help patients stay compliant with mobility restrictions and then help them set targets to ensure the best possible outcomes from their surgery.

Watson Health and Medtronic are similarly working together to improve diabetes care management, using the data from real-time blood glucose monitoring and an automated glucose pump to optimize the care for each specific patient. In effect, they aim to provide a "clinical expert" of sorts that is with the patient at all times.[18]

The cloud-based EMR company AthenaHealth.com is taking a further differentiated approach by providing a set of tools to manage clinical data and scheduling comparable to premises EMRs such as Epic and Cerner, but get paid for improving the financial performance of its customers' clinical practices. Consistent with that move, it has acquired and integrated risk management tools and decision support applications such as ePocrates.[19] They are now taking the physician office and risk management capabilities into the acute healthcare setting through the licensing of hospital information technologies from Beth Israel Deaconess in Boston.

Finally, take Qualcomm Life. This company is a separate digital technology "platform as a service" subsidiary of the technology company Qualcomm.[20] Qualcomm Life was created through a combination of internally developed technologies and acquired services (e.g., the Healthy-Circles patient engagement platform[21]). It recently expanded through the acquisition of Capsule Technologie, a firm with expertise in connectivity and data management of hospital and health facilities located devices. This provides QualComm Life with end-to-end healthcare ecosystem capabilities, leveraging their position in remote and mobile devices with those in formal healthcare facilities, to follow the patient across the course of a disease and for each aspect of care management and engagement.[22] Qualcomm Life, Inc., is collaborating with Davita Healthcare Partners and P2Link to develop chronic care management solutions using Qualcomm Life's 2net™ Device Connectivity Platform and Healthy-Circles™ Care Coordination Platform to enable continuous care and proactive management of at-risk populations.[23] Their model will be pay-for-performance services, leveraging proprietary predictive models and an in-house clinical call center. They are targeting reducing the cost of care for HF and COPD patients by 10 to 15 percent, aiding payers and providers as they transition to a value-based reimbursement system.

The Healthcare Gone Digital businesses are doing important work. Taking the sickest patients with the highest needs, driving a disproportionate share of the avoidable costs, and providing a practical alternative that is implementable today. They are capable, and they have medical device grade infrastructure and histories of deploying solutions of great complexity and robustness.

What these companies are doing is complicated in terms of market and partner dynamics, as they are working within an existing market to change it and its defined customer base. Existing health and life science companies that are moving into the digital space arrive with strong provider relationships, highly precise capabilities, and confidence in their respective domains. However, they also carry legacy cost structures from their former operations that may limit their ability to succeed in the new digital environment.

It remains to be seen whether it will be easier to move from the highly expensive and expert hospital setting into the remote and home settings, or to move from the position of already being in the home and pocket of the patient into a critical role as care and health partner.

START-UP DIGITALS

With their clear advantages as large digital players entering the healthcare space, it might seem as though the Digital Gone Healthcare and Healthcare Gone Digital organizations would deter start-ups from trying to stake their own claims. (As Figure 7.2 shows, funding of digital health initiatives is growing at a rate of 2.5 to 4 times per year.)

But that has not been the case. Start-ups often look for specific niches: geographic areas, certain disease- or condition-specific markets, creating value for caregivers and patients, and sometimes skirting traditional reimbursement paths entirely in favor of more straightforward, "retail" transactions.

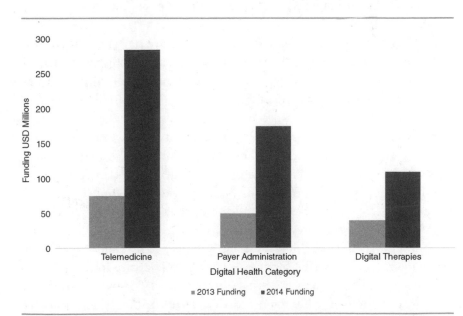

FIGURE 7.2   Fastest-Growing Categories of Digital Health, 2014
Source: Rock Health: Rock Reports (http://rockhealth.com/resources/rock-reports/), Digital Health Funding: Year in Review 2014.

Pager, Propeller Health, Preventice Solutions, and Heal are just a few of a fast-growing number of brand new entities (as of this writing) that were "born" to infuse healthcare delivery with new digital strengths. Preventice, for example, is a combination with a medical device, advanced algorithms co-developed with the Mayo Clinic, an engagement app, and cloud infrastructure to enable advanced remote cardiac monitoring. While it was a primarily venture-backed entity up until recently, it is now attracting partnerships with current market leaders, such as Boston Scientific. Joe Fitzgerald, executive vice president and president, Rhythm Management, Boston Scientific, commented that the healthcare system needs "solutions that identify relevant clinical insights from large volumes of patient data and integrate those insights to improve clinical decision making," noting that Preventice's model could "improve patient outcomes and reduce healthcare costs."[24]

DIGITAL ECONOMICS IN HEALTHCARE

All types of health digitals bring fundamentally new economics into the market.

The Digital Gone Healthcare companies that are newer to the healthcare arena (Apple, Google, and Amazon) have traditionally made money by creating broadly accessible, virtual (and commercial) infrastructures that make markets. The app store would be one example—a virtual "location" where developers, content companies, and others can access consumers through a robust, secure, and attractive ecosystem of devices, mobile platforms, data services, and applications. These players make products accessible to potential customers and generally claim 30 percent of sales revenues when transactions occur.[25] And they are bringing that same approach to healthcare. In addition, they are making these new cloud-based infrastructures available to other companies for deploying their programs. To do so, they are using a variety of revenue models—fee per patient, fee for specific services, and so on. They are focused on the patient, expanding from their strongholds of extended networks and loyal consumer relationships. For them, individual health, monitoring, and care management applications involve few incremental resources and provide their partners (providers/doctors) with a framework for approaching patients at a modest cost. This is the same approach, with its digital scale advantages and digital economics, which has displaced and disrupted most other consumer and consumer-facing markets.

Existing health and life science companies that are moving into the digital space have a greater challenge. While they arrive with strong provider relationships, highly precise capabilities, and confidence in their respective domains, they also carry legacy cost structures from their former operations that may limit their ability to succeed in the new digital environment. Unlike the Digitals Gone Healthcare, these companies reach patients only when they have a contract for services. It is one of those rare circumstances where incumbency may be a burden, and where the aspiring disruptor is advantaged.

IMPLICATIONS NOW, SOON, LATER ON

Think back to the time when people always went to record and CD stores to purchase music, when we always rented videos at retail stores, and when we considered that making a trip to a mall or shopping center was our primary option for buying holiday presents. We lived in a physical world that required us to conduct active research, and invest time and effort into trips here and there to procure what we needed and wanted. Doing so could take hours to weeks. Now it takes seconds to minutes. We can have what we want streamed, downloaded, or shipped to us in a day (or even in a few hours, for certain items, in several major metropolitan areas). The CD store and video purveyors are, for the most part, no longer there.

No sector of our economy will remain the same after the forces of digital disruption converge and the capabilities of the New Health Digitals are brought to bear on existing industries. Uber, albeit with setbacks, quickly appears to be well on the road to becoming the largest personal transportation company in the world—and, as we write, is attempting to challenge UPS and FedEx on local package delivery. All this and it owns neither planes, trucks, nor cars. Three or four years ago, Uber was a concept; now it's a broadly used verb. Similarly, AirBnB may eclipse the largest hotel chain in beds provided per night—and it owns no real estate. Hulu and Netflix, with no infrastructure, are streaming more content to viewers each day than any network or cable provider does; they are also increasingly producing their own original content with no studios—

disrupting cable infrastructure providers and content production companies simultaneously.

These companies are inventing and deploying new operating models and fundamentally different operating economics in several different sectors. We expect healthcare and diagnostics to take a similar path, as the technology is there to enable the same sort of shift. Why wouldn't care management programs embrace the idea of capturing your weight and blood pressure data from a wireless device in your home, or off your smart watch, or from a connection in your texts to your doctor when you are discussing the pain in your leg or semi-chronic fatigue? Salesforce. com, the cloud computing company that has in recent years become a leader in customer relationship management, is betting they would. Salesforce.com recently announced the creation of the Salesforce Health Cloud. This patient relationship management solution will integrate patient data from a variety of sources—such as EMRs, medical devices, and wearables—to give care coordinators a comprehensive understanding of their patients. With alerts to refill medications and keep appointments as well as messaging to facilitate conversations between patients and their caregivers, the Salesforce Health Cloud represents a comprehensive, digitally enabled, and value-driven innovation firmly grounded in the patient journey. Salesforce.com is not the first to venture into this space, and it certainly won't be the last.

Similarly, why would a healthcare company need to own all of the components of the infrastructure it needs to treat patients, or to produce products? Maybe it won't.

In the coming few years, could we see pharmacies printing the medication a patient needs, in the right combinations and specific dosages, right at their local pharmacy?

In the coming few years, could a provider of healthcare services that employs no physicians nor operates any healthcare facilities emerge as the *largest* provider? It is entirely possible, and the mindset to picture it is the same type of mindset that is driving the changes we are seeing. Can you think of any patient who wouldn't be willing to consume healthcare in a different way if it meant taking one easily swallowed pill, customized to treat most or all of their specific needs, rather than taking a dozen pills or more of different sizes and shapes throughout the day? Can you think of any patient who wouldn't be willing to consume healthcare in a different way if it meant they could avoid traffic, avoid searching for parking, and avoid sitting in the waiting room for a predictably delayed appointment time?

WORKING WITH THE NEW HEALTH DIGITALS

To achieve the focus on outcomes and value that the sector aspires to, and is moving toward, healthcare *needs* to be interconnected, predictive, preventative, engaging, motivating, and collaborative. These new health digitals clearly have the potential to interconnect the entire continuum of care—all formal health facilities, remote settings, offices, and homes. They can connect patients with physicians, patients with each other,[26] patients with their family members, and physicians with each other.[27] Their infrastructures—technical, devices, and platform services—are rapidly becoming common.

But it will be up to each player in the healthcare ecosystem to determine how—and how much—to engage. To make those decisions, they should be asking questions such as: How can digital technologies help us achieve the outcomes we seek? How will we incorporate digital disruption into their current offerings? How might our competitors get ahead—both direct competitors (Healthcare Gone Digital) and indirect competitors (Digital Gone Healthcare)? What capabilities do we need, and should we build, acquire, or collaborate to gain them?

To help develop answers, we suggest using the following five considerations as backdrop for discussion and debate about strategy:

1. *New solutions for driving value in healthcare require the interconnectivity of devices and people.*[28] This will be true of health insurers, healthcare providers, life science companies, patients, consumers, and family caregivers.
2. *These new solutions will require radical new models of partnering, venturing, and collaborating.* No one player has all the physician, consumer, patient, family, and health retailer contact points to stand alone. For example, healthcare providers may need to work with networks of retail urgent care centers to move patients to convenient and low-cost sites for emergency care. Medical device companies may be working with large regional provider systems and governments to ensure that technologies and tools are being integrated for the purpose of innovation, profitable growth, and the achievement of better health

outcomes. Healthcare providers could be working closely with health insurers to implement broad population management programs that combine positive incentives for physicians and patients. Pharmaceutical companies can provide partnered tools and services that will enable risk-bearing providers to successfully treat only those who will truly benefit from their interventions.[29]

3. *New Health Digitals must scale to meet economic expectations.* Expect the New Health Digitals to launch initiatives at scale—beyond the historic pilots in individual health systems and disease states we have seen traditionally. New Health Digitals will focus on whole populations of patients, diseases, and countries. Justifying the scope of investment, often in the tens to hundreds of millions of dollars, requires global cross-disease scale.

4. *Consumers, Patients, and Physicians will embrace the New Health Digitals.* Healthcare is a world filled with queues, documentation, and bureaucracy. In such a world, consumers, patients, and physicians will welcome the New Health Digitals. They understand that the New Health Digitals will simplify their lives and allow them to improve their care and health. This means that new solutions may move in quickly and provide fundamentally new sources of value.

5. *Immediate action is required to respond to and adopt New Health Digital strategies.* While the New Health Digitals undoubtedly plan for the long term,[30] most of their business models emphasize year-over-year and semicontinuous innovation. If you are waiting for new functionality and evidence, you may have missed your opportunity. If you want time to "get the model right," someone else may be offering the value you targeted. This is not about trial and error; rather it is about partnerships rapidly deployed that prove out approaches. It is about refining as you go, focusing on scale and long-term economics, and being the new standard.

HEALTH DIGITALS POSITIONING, CAPABILITIES, AND ANATOMY

The Health Digitals, with the exception of the start-up entries, have the most significant presence in all global markets of any of the models and companies discussed. Whereas the Lean Innovators were relentless cost managers looking for innovative therapeutic arbitrage opportunities, the Around-the-Patient Innovators were looking to ensure value in their therapeutics, and the Value Innovators were driving value through new integrated services, the Health Digitals compete through ubiquity. Their devices are in every pocket or purse.[31] Their operating platforms have a global scale and transcend sectors and uses. Their services support basic intra-family and intra-organization communications. They are providing the digital infrastructure to whole cities.[32] They are deeply technical and scientific.[33] Whereas these once were consumer-focused companies, they are now the underlying technology of most major corporations, non-profits, governments, families, and social circles.

Finally, they have a history of, and expectation for, disruption. The industries of the past—photography, recorded music, books, to name only a few—have been entirely displaced by new devices, new distribution, and new payment approaches. They have understood the concepts of pricing to value from their origins. It is how they disrupted—new ways of working and new sources of value in traditional activities that people were willing to pay for. And their operating economics were superior to those they disrupted, allowing them to outpace the legacy firms in new investment and services expansions. (See Figure 7.3.)

These Health Digitals solve for "systems" in that they are not looking at apps or devices in isolation. Rather they are thinking about end-states they would like to create, the current elements of the technology ecosystem that can support building toward this, and what new elements need to be put into place. They are also persistently assessing what it will take to achieve "population scale" and create the basis of a new market or a catalyst for double-digit growth or advantaged economics in a current one.[34]

In many respects, they have an unusual vantage point in not producing the end solutions, instead bringing together all the enabling technologies, tools, and infrastructure, and allowing others to complete the picture. For example, Apple's ResearchKit does not collect or store patient data but rather provides a set of tools, standards, and application programming interfaces that enable a health provider or life sciences company to do this themselves but within Apple's ecosystem of iOS devices. The risks of ultimate failure or success rest on the organization or firm deploying the point solution. The value that Apple or Google needs is in the broad adoption of their approaches and that some small proportion of these initiatives become the "killer app" or somehow essential to how we work and live.

These organizations have highly evolved operational capabilities. Apple's supply chain is often referenced as a key capability of the

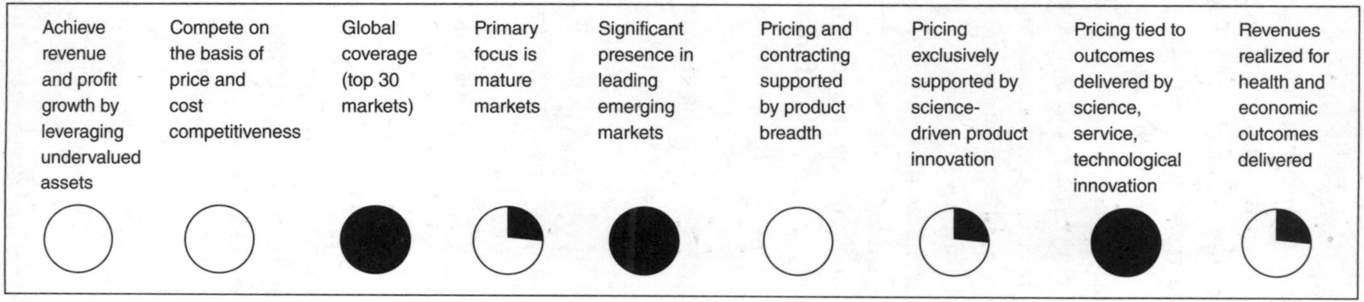

FIGURE 7.3 Market Positioning (What Unique Position in the Market Does the Company Want to Occupy?)

Source: Accenture analysis.

Figure Key: The circles in the graphic, known as "Harvey Balls," provide qualitative comparisons across categories and items. They indicate the extent to which any given component (or category) is complete, meaningful, representative, or fulfilled. A blank circle indicates that the criteria are not met; a circle that is completely filled in indicates that the criteria are fully met.

company, allowing them to do large scale and carefully orchestrated global launches of millions of devices. The facilities that host data are among the largest such operations in the world, with top security, reliability, and energy management systems. So their global, pan-industry, and population-scale view is underpinned by the top performing global operations in the world. Remember, these organizations' operations are so vast they dwarf the largest life science companies, especially in their data, analytic, and digital infrastructure. (See Figure 7.4.)

The Digital Gone Healthcare companies have been strongly consumer- and customer-focused in their origins. They have well-publicized codes of conduct emphasizing the primacy of their consumers (e.g., Google's "Do no evil"[35]) that guide their internal decisions, the businesses they go into, the goals of their engineering teams, and the overall go-to-market approach. They are defined by the superiority of the technologies they advance and the changes these bring to their consumers' and customers' lives. As such they have tightly coupled internal functions, decision processes that are well defined and understood (tightly centralized, e.g., Apple and Samsung; or intentionally decentralized, e.g., Google), and key external partnerships around technologies and creating new end-markets. The scale and scope of their initiatives require tightly managed resources, highly advanced financial and supply chain management capabilities, and aligned supplier investments and capacity. This relationship is so tight that, as New Health Digitals, their valuations and those of their suppliers are tightly correlated.[36] This is far more than a beneficial ecosystem of suppliers, but rather a vertically and horizontally integrated *zaibatsu*.[37] (See Figure 7.5.)

Year-over-year growth, total numbers of consumers within the platform, and the increasing profitability of those customers across multiple services will continue to be key measures of success and performance. While public markets command quarter-by-quarter and year-over-year financial targets, these organizations also take the long view, putting into place today elements of future businesses. It is likely now that Amazon is reporting AWS separately (operator of Health Cloud, Research Cloud, and other health and life sciences services), and that Alphabet will be reporting Google and unrelated operations (e.g., therapeutics, life sciences ventures, health, and devices) separately, and that IBM has separated out Watson and Watson Health, we will see an even greater emphasis on large scale investment, acquisitions, and growth.

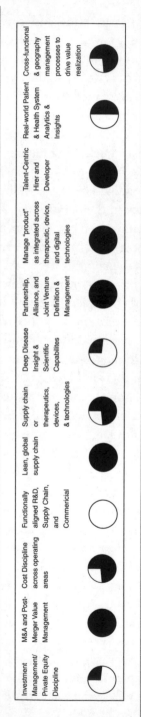

FIGURE 7.4 Differentiating Capabilities (Critical Capabilities Needed to Drive the Market Position)

Source: Accenture analysis.

154

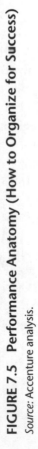

FIGURE 7.5 Performance Anatomy (How to Organize for Success)

Source: Accenture analysis.

THE HEALTH DIGITALS: DISRUPTIONS AND NEW FOUNDATIONS

The New Health Digitals are technologically and digitally savvy players who are at once key partners and potential disruptors. The Digital Gone Healthcare businesses offer new digital-era economics coming from consumer devices, national-level infrastructure technologies, and new cloud services. They are already bringing the consumer as personal health manager and as patient back into the center of healthcare. The Healthcare Gone Digital businesses have digital infrastructure in place within healthcare systems and deep relationships with health providers. They are crossing into care integration, acute patient remote monitoring, diagnosis as a process, and predictive analytics. They will clearly contribute to the efficiency of the healthcare system in the short run as they bring their capabilities to bear on the outcomes and cost of the most expensive acute patients.

But we may not yet even be able to estimate their potential. Consider Aprecia Pharmaceuticals Company, which announced in August 2015 that it had obtained FDA clearance for a 3D-printed version of its drug Spritam—an anticonvulsant used to treat epilepsy.[38] The essential benefit to this particular application seems to be ease of swallowing. But the novel and proprietary 3D-printing method, which Aprecia calls ZipDose©, may in fact signal the beginning of customizable medication.[39] Imagine for a moment the ability of an Amazon or Google, partnered with a CVS Health or Walgreens, to create a new value chain beginning with the remote diagnosis of the patient, to automated ePrescribing consistent with guidelines and evidence presented, to local 3D-printing of the therapeutic at a pharmacy a few blocks away, and delivery to the patient within the hour. We have the infrastructure, the advanced analytics, the production technology, and the delivery infrastructure—what is missing?

BUILDING NEW ORGANIZATIONS

Chapter 8

Toward a New Model of Collaboration and Competition

All new healthcare business and operating models must rapidly embrace technologies that are fundamentally collaborative; building ecosystems of value-enabling partnerships is both strategic and an operating imperative. The catch is that the nature of collaboration in this context also breaks new ground for many businesses in the sector.

When a pharmaceutical or medical device company expands its product offerings to include therapeutic and digital attributes, it will also need to forge unprecedented partnerships with organizations that might have never before been on its radar. Only by doing so will it be able to work with, and within, a finely tuned ecosystem of real-world data, analytics, sensors, devices, and digital apps. Only by doing so will it develop a digital business foundation that can keep pace with disruptive change, align with a global digital infrastructure so that it can operate at a population level, and leverage digital economics.

In the digital world, collaboration and competition sometimes do not seem far apart, but in this new world, partnerships, collaborations, joint ventures, and population-scale pilots with competitors and other health-care stakeholders will predominate. These unlikely partnerships will reinvent the entire value chain of the healthcare industry, from R&D to supply chains, to care.

No single company will be successful with a go-it-alone approach. But the double-edge is that few relationships will be exclusive; that is the nature of digital and cloud-centered operating models. Protections of proprietary approaches will come from achieving scale rapidly, accelerating and applying meaningful insights, and setting the pace for delivering value.

* * *

The healthcare system is still governed through regulations that limit interactions among health providers, health payers, and manufacturers.[1] Many of these regulations were defined during a period of time when healthcare providers solely delivered care, manufacturers marketed only their own products, and health payers reimbursed according to procedures performed. They kept healthcare players at arm's length from one another in order to prevent market influence from swaying decisions and directing the flow of funds and to keep the focus on clinical evidence.

But health providers today are increasingly managing both clinical and financial outcome goals. Health payers are assuming responsibility for care[2] and clinical outcomes. And manufacturers may have the prices of their products driven by validated outcomes, or they may be bearing risk for achieving an outcome. Increasingly, all healthcare participants have the same information and the same analytic needs.

The scope of capabilities and changes needed to identify, design to, and realize value is beyond any one company. And so Around-the-Patient Innovators and Value Innovators are putting together critical partnerships and relationships with regional health systems, with advanced technology companies enabling care in remote and home settings, and with the New Health Digitals.

These new forms of collaborations directly enable new business and operating models. They also call for aligned investments in new technologies and the joint shaping of new uses and markets. And this means that even as these organizations break new ground together, they are also changing the nature of competition. In digital business models and digital medicine, advantage gets created with scale. With scale comes influence, as any given solution may become the new standard. With broader use of a platform, actionable insights accelerate. So digital economics are prevailing early on, creating an advantage for those that move early to collaborate, and making it difficult in some situations for later entrants to justify the investments and access the partnerships that may be required to catch up.

CRITICAL INNOVATIONS FROM "WITHOUT"

Adjusting to the fact that more innovations will likely come from outside their organizations and companies than inside is easier to accept in theory than it is in practice. And yet doing so is a competitive necessity. Many if not most of the leading companies today are innovators, but the market innovates several-fold more than any single company.

Consider the evolution of research and development (R&D) in pharmaceutical companies as an analogy. Think back to what it looked like in the 1990s. Since then, it has been completely transformed from an inwardly focused, horizontally integrated, and largely unproductive[3] set of functions to an externally sourced, highly productive, and highly collaborative system. Before this transformation, many life sciences and R&D organizations attempted "going it alone" in their efforts to understand the pathophysiology of a disease and identify new therapies to bring to market. Now, however, R&D is increasingly taking place in clusters—areas where there is an unusually high concentration of academic research and pharmaceutical enterprise activity, such as Cambridge, Massachusetts and San Francisco, California in the United States, and Basel, Switzerland.[4]

These regions are now large engines of innovation, where ideas are moved from basic scientific insights discovered in academic centers to full clinical development and commercialization in a combination of biopharmaceutical and larger pharma partnerships. The initial basic research is often government funded. When research begins to show promise, entrepreneurial angel funds often provide money to create companies that will advance early phase programs to meaningful milestones. From there, if successful, venture capital–backed firms transform the idea into a marketable therapeutic, launching it into the marketplace as an initial public offering or letting it be acquired by a larger biopharmaceutical company. It is a highly productive, interdependent, and collaborative model. It is unlikely any one company could bring together the same sets of differentiated capabilities, talent, financing, and cultures required for innovation by itself.

Now think of the demand for new forms of innovation to deliver outcomes and value in a "volume" world. All value-based business models will be digitally enabled and powered and moving at digital speed, with increasingly digitally driven economics. And they will need a critical network of partners and (sometimes unlikely) collaborators in order to innovate at the pace of the market.

VALUE INNOVATING WITH YOUR CUSTOMERS

Biopharmaceutical and medical device companies used to view health providers as customers where the goals were to build loyalty and increase their relative share of products purchased. Health authorities and private payers viewed pharmaceutical and device companies as purveyors of products that could drive up their costs.[5] Health providers often viewed them similarly, but also felt a responsibility to consider prescribing the latest approved therapies and gaining experience with them, given their promise. All parties were captured in a volume paradigm.

However, with the move to value—a focus on patient outcomes, and the goal of advancing the health status of a population with greater efficiency— there is new purpose in collaborating with one's "customers." Health providers, health authorities, health payers, biopharmaceutical and medical device companies all have aligned interests on which to build.[6]

Consider several examples, beginning with Novartis. In August 2015, Novartis put together an outcomes-based program with the National Health Service–Wales[7] that is brand or product neutral, focused on the total patient (e.g., heart failure with the diabetes that is associated with it 70 percent of the time), and comprehensive in systems focus and interventions. It is explicitly:

1. *Multi-interventional*, addressing risk factors, clinical and operational pathways, performance management, skills building, mindsets, and behavioral changes and other relevant factors.

2. *Multi-morbidity focused*, adopting a "whole patient," multi-factorial perspective.
3. *Multi-drug*—not confined to any one medicinal product or medical device.

This program is comparable to the 2015 Boston Scientific collaboration with Karolinska University Hospital, Sweden we described in Chapter 6, where the goal was to develop a comprehensive approach tuned to the new value-based reimbursement and population health goals set by Stockholm County Council.

Philips, using a Healthcare-Gone-Digital approach, offers another example. Philips, in 2015, created a $500 million multicenter collaborative model with Westchester Medical Center Health Network (WMCHealth) in Valhalla, New York,[8] (after developing a comparable relationship with Georgia Regents Medical Center in 2013) to provide connectivity across the health system and into remote sites of care on the foundation of its HealthSuite[9] cloud services and technologies. These relationships seek to define and deploy new patient-centered models of care to support population health management services in an increasingly value-driven reimbursement environment.[10]

Merck & Co. developed collaborations with Regenstrief Institute[11] in 2012 and Maccabi Health Services[12] in 2014 to advance real-world analytic insights to help optimize patient treatments and outcomes. Both relationships involved accessing masses of real-world electronic medical-derived data and advancing insights within an advanced big data analytics environment.

And as a sign of what can already be considered the "next generation" of this model, Intel, in August 2015, forged a collaboration with Oregon Health & Science University (OHSU) and other academic Cancer Centers[13] focused on advancing interpretation of molecular data on cancers and other diseases to aid more precise treatment selection and treatment monitoring. As part of the collaboration, Intel assembled a secure and HIPAA[14] compliant multisite infrastructure for sharing patients' electronic medical records and molecular and genetic data.

Intel clearly sees the opportunity to advance meaningful insights into an area that is growing as fast as the Internet itself (as Figure 8.1 shows, within the next 10 years, the amount of new data created each year from

FIGURE 8.1 Four domains of Big Data in 2025

Data Phase	Astronomy	Twitter	YouTube	Genomics
Acquisition	25 zetta-bytes/year	0.5–15 billion tweets/year	500–900 million hours/year	1 zetta-bases/year
Storage	1 EB/year	1–17 PB/year	1–2 EB/year	2–40 EB/year
Analysis	In situ data reduction	Topic and sentiment mining	Limited requirements	Heterogeneous data and analysis
	Real-time processing	Metadata analysis		Variant calling, ~2 trillion central processing unit (CPU) hours
	Massive volumes			All-pairs genome alignments, ~10,000 trillion CPU hours
Distribution	Dedicated lines from antennae to server (600 TB/s)	Small units of distribution	Major component of modern user's bandwidth (10 MB/s)	Many small (10 MB/s) and fewer massive (10 TB/s) data movement

Source: Z.D. Stephens, S.Y. Lee, F. Faghri, R.H. Campbell, and C. Zhai, et al., "Big Data: Astronomical or Genomical?" *PLoS Biol* 13, no. 7 (2015): e1002195. doi:10.1371/journal.pbio.1002195.

genetic sequencing and genomic analyses will exceed the amount of data created on YouTube).[15]

These aren't nearly all.

In August 2015, Accenture advanced a similar collaboration with Duke University and the Duke Health System[16] to provide predictive insights into the efficacy of different patient treatment approaches and clinical interventions. The joint team will utilize advanced predictive analysis to identify the most effective care management interventions for optimizing patient outcomes in the shortest amount of time at the most efficient cost.

Meanwhile, the venture-backed private entity TriNetX[17] is working with a global network of health provider participants who participate in i2b2 initiative. Informatics for Integrating Biology and the Bedside (i2b2).[18] This company is enabling direct interactions for trial design, prospective recruitment into regulatory clinical trial studies, or non-interventional observational studies. It has already fostered a dynamic and collaborative network of patients and expertise that less than three years ago would have been technically infeasible, cost prohibitive, and out of consideration for competitive reasons.

Think of these examples as just one "highlight" reel. These kinds of collaborations have the potential to transform the entire healthcare value chain. The insights into patient populations that can come from rich genomic, genetic, and pathway biological data collaborations can accelerate the time it takes to identify a new therapeutic target in a devastating disease and increase the confidence in the success of the program. These same data, combined with health provider insights coming from the collaboration, can drive to a new approach to early phase clinical trial design and execution that focus on the most meaningful endpoints and real-world relevant approaches. We use the term *precision medicine* when we describe the use of genomic, genetic, phenotypical, and other real-world data sources to select a specific therapeutic and treatment approach—but "precision" is best designed into approaches, beginning with the earliest phases of biological target identification, and the design-to-regulatory clinical trials.

As digital medicine and new forms of technology and customer-centric collaborations determine how healthcare companies innovate, we will see R&D as a continuous process. It will certainly be inclusive of the traditional regulatory phases that brought forward new medicines, but increasingly the value will come from what continuous real-world insights, advanced analytics tools, and digital medical services bring to the patient and health system.

We do believe that healthcare provider and industry collaborations and initiatives will increase, just as we are seeing provider-to-provider programs scale,[19] as well as provider-to-disease association,[20] and provider-to-health payer initiatives form.[21] These trends together help ensure a growing and more rapid access to confederated data sources, technical expertise, and accelerated insights.

These are new forms of relationships. Increasingly less of the dialogue is around product share and incentives to increase loyalty. Health authorities, health payers, and health provider relationships are becoming value focused, aligned around joint responsibilities, and highly interactive. These relationships provide access to real-world data at population scale, advance new views on how to optimize care around the patient, and broadly challenge the historical paradigm of roles and capabilities in the delivery of care. Parties come to these new relationships committed to the transformation of healthcare for the benefit of the patient and health system.

DRIVING CONVERGENCE: AT THE INTERSECTION OF THERAPEUTICS, DEVICES, AND PROCESS

As less of the dialogue in senior-level meetings focuses around product share and incentives to increase loyalty, more will be about how therapeutics, devices, data, and processes intersect, and how various stakeholders will share and claim their own value from the mix.

For example, the Around-the-Patient Innovators, the Value Innovators, and the New Health Digitals appreciate the same insight: Health and healthcare are systems requiring system thinking and solutions. They further appreciate that robust systems are rarely hub and spoke but rather are mesh-like networks,[22] self-healing, with many alternative paths, and with intentional redundancies mimicking those found in nature.[23] Historically, the companies that are today deploying value-centric strategies were point solution providers. In the future, we see their solutions driving value, requiring a set of complementary technologies that can identify specific patients (through real-world data and analyses), assess a health status in a remote setting (through sensors, wearables, and other devices), and offer services to support care management (through integrated patient care management solutions).

The Digital Gone Healthcare organizations—in particular, the large platform services and advanced technologies companies among them— are in fact supporting this kind of network by creating a broad set of mutually reinforcing initiatives across health providers, therapeutics, medical devices, and health services companies. And even as they connect clinical decision support initiatives with health providers, they are also extending the networks to include retail pharmacy and employer programs. What is common across these is providing an integration of remote sensors and monitoring technologies, advanced analytics and machine learning, and new physician and patient engagement technologies.

Qualcomm Life has been highly active in both healthcare provider collaborations and with leading pharmaceutical and medical device companies. Qualcomm Life recently announced a heart failure remote care management program with DaVita HealthCare Partners.[24] They are further deploying the same technologies with partner P2Link with Emerson Hospital in Concord, Massachusetts for chronic obstructive pulmonary disease (COPD) and heart failure patients to better realize "the promise of the 'triple aim': a better care experience, improved health outcomes, and lowered costs for the 300,000 individuals to whom we provide Premium Care."[25]

For example, in early 2015 Roche and Qualcomm Life announced a strategic collaboration wherein they can provide a digital capability for "connected chronic care management and remote management solutions (that) can enhance patient care, enabling providers to asynchronously communicate with their patients in a high-tech, high-touch model minimizing risk of errors in result reporting."[26] Similarly, Novartis announced the formation of a joint venture fund, dRx Capital AG,[27] to advance investments in new digital business models, digital medicines, and critical enabling digital infrastructure for delivering value to patients and health systems.[28] In addition, Novartis is initiating new clinical trials with a set of digital tools and technologies that mirror those it can make available to patients and healthcare providers at approval and commercial launch.[29]

Roche Pharmaceuticals of Basel, Switzerland, and Foundation Medicine of Cambridge, Massachusetts, a next-generation sequencing–based medical diagnostic company and an individualized cancer treatment selection company, respectively, created a multifaceted collaborative relationship. And Daniel O'Day, chief operating officer, Roche Pharmaceuticals Division, noted in April 2015 that "molecular information is playing an ever-increasing role in the treatment and management of cancer" and that the collaboration could "optimize the development of and access to novel treatment options for cancer patients and to advance personalized healthcare in oncology."[30]

Collaborations and technologies focused on transforming models of healthcare and maintaining health impact the entire value chain—from the earliest R&D to creating the foundation for a patient-centric supply chain. R&D approaches that link directly to technologies and insights available in actual clinical settings—for example, the Roche-Genentech/ Foundation Medicine relationship, and Qualcomm Life and Novartis, to name only two described herein—ensure that value is integral to the program from the outset, that our approach is consistent with the goals of precision medicine, and the patient is always at the center. They are sources of insight, drive prioritization, and are brought into the design of clinical studies.[31]

Healthcare in this regard has much to learn from other industries, such as consumer electronics and consumer goods, which deal continuously with market volatility, but have the advantage of rich, always present data. The optimal new value- and patient-centric company with a digitally enabled and integrated operating model will be capable of predicting and translating market trends, health provider requirements, and patient needs through integrated planning, and patient-pull product supply and location priorities. To achieve this, the traditional supply chain must be transformed into a digitized value network with analytics at the core. Companies must reorient their traditional supply chain mentality and operating models to the patient, having their needs and requirements translated into new requirements for products, personal and remote devices, and location of care.[32]

We are seeing large platform services and advanced technologies companies creating a broad set of mutually reinforcing initiatives across health providers, therapeutics, medical devices, and health services companies. IBM's Watson Health, for example, has initiated clinical decision support initiatives with health providers to make complex, multifactor, clinical decisions easier.[33] It has also moved into the retail pharmacy and employer programs with a broad collaboration with CVS Health. As Dr. Troy Brennan, CVS Health chief medical officer, noted in a July 2015 *Forbes* interview, "This collaboration enables us to learn about how other sources of health information could help predict declining health or the need for an intervention for a patient with a chronic condition. For example, we can learn if information about a patient's activity levels from a tracker like a FitBit™ could help us identify their risk for declining health."[34] The collaboration's explicit goals are to provide the operating infrastructure for the health system's transition from fee-for-service medicine to value-based reimbursement.

The foundational capabilities of these health system, pharmacy benefit manager, and consumer pharmacy retail collaborations link to the medical device and biopharmaceutical collaborations put into place with Medtronic,[35] Johnson & Johnson,[36] and others. These are focused on improving the care of diabetes by creating an "Internet of things" network of remote blood glucose monitors, insulin pumps, personal activity devices, and more. Together, that network will generate insights that create a real-time, practical view of the patient journey. It will also enable a view that aligns the patient activities that are critical to achieving the best possible outcome with the activities that occur within the provider health system, creating a form of expert digital advisor and care assistant.[37]

Consider an unlikely New Health Digital company, Salesforce.com. This company, with its large-scale digital infrastructure, has launched a platform to integrate care among healthcare providers, clinicians, and patients.[38] The platform was developed through piloting with three health systems: Centura Health, Radboud University Medical Center, and University of California San Diego, together with DJO Global, Inc., a medical device and supplies company. It is further being deployed as a patient-care service, enabling the infrastructures of biopharmaceutical and medical device companies that are transforming into Around-the-Patient and Value Innovators.[39] One example of this is Philips Medical with its HealthSuite cloud services that integrate with Salesforce's Health Cloud and that now will include a heart monitoring watch, blood pressure monitors, a body analysis scale, and ear thermometer all transmitting data into the cloud for advanced integrated analytics for cardiovascular and musculoskeletal diseases. Philips further partners with Amazon AWA competitors Rackspace and Alibaba for cloud hosting its HealthSuite data.[40] This bridges the more hospital-centric offerings of Philips with a more consumer-oriented solution.[41]

Key remote sensors, remote monitoring technologies, and digital engagement infrastructure are being jointly developed, integrated, piloted, and deployed working through parallel initiatives with healthcare providers, health authorities, health payers, pharmaceutical companies, and medical device companies. This trend is changing where and how healthcare happens, and how value is realized. It is further reinventing the overall innovation and supply chains of the industry. The integrated technology solutions being considered by pharmaceutical, biopharmaceutical, and medical device companies have origins—or validation—with health systems and health authorities.

The goals of these collaborations and partnerships are consistent and two-fold: drive (1) outcomes for the patient and (2) billions of dollars in value for the healthcare system in optimized treatment selection, reduced length of stay, avoided errors, and avoided readmissions through integrated technological and digital solutions. These are the technologies that will define the new category of "digital medicines" as life sciences companies take their traditional core—their therapeutic products—and ensure value through patient care services, new contract structures, and potentially altogether new businesses.

MAPPING BIG DIGITAL: WHERE DIGITAL CONSUMER AND DIGITAL HEALTHCARE MEET

The digital factor warrants a deeper dive. We cannot conceive of a broadly deployed and large-scale solution that does not recognize what's in the pockets, purses, and homes of consumers. If remote monitoring technologies, sensors, and advanced analytics tools will provide a new definition of the value-centric company's products, then the enormous scale, ubiquity, and new digital economics of the Digital Gone Healthcare businesses represent their operating infrastructure and the foundation of their new solutions. These will involve:

Redefining patient relationships. These relationships are becoming empowered, active, and self-directing.

Creating new digital operating partnerships. The new digital collaborations de-emphasize labor market arbitrage and per unit costs in favor of building in intelligence within the supply chain, customer operations, and patient services.

Accessing but not owning many assets. A key insight of the most disruptive of large-scale digital operating models is that ownership is not required to have the same effective control and improved economics.

Collapsing margin economics through the model. Over time, the implementation of digital remote monitoring, digital engagement, and digital medicine will be consumption-based or provide unlimited access at limited incremental costs or costs that move toward zero (price for volume, versus consumption based, versus "all you can eat").

For example, when Apple Inc., Cupertino, California, announced the availability of ResearchKit and HealthKit, Stanford Cardiovascular Health announced one of the early apps seeking to enroll participants into a long-term observational clinical study. They gained more than 10,000 participants in one day. Alan Yeung, medical director of the program noted, "To get 10,000 people enrolled in a medical study normally, it would take a year and 50 medical centers around the country, that's the power of the phone."[42]

The new digital operating infrastructure and scale have never before been seen with a healthcare provider, health authority, health payer, or life science company. This all-digital infrastructure reduces the need for capital and highly specialized talent, declines in price through the years, can be paid for as consumed, and is lower cost at higher rates of utilization.[43] It further liberates operations to move toward a digitally enabled intelligent supply chain and operations.[44] Digital operating models allow greater agility, speed, and innovation at scale. These models are inherently more cost efficient as they leverage digital economics and provide more opportunities for customer and consumer interactive relationships.[45]

Digital business models, powered by digital operations, offer the opportunities for digital economics.[46] These scale rapidly at rates of growth approaching logarithmic. The disruption from Uber has already been massive with taxi and pre-book limousine business down in every major market within two years of entry.[47] That includes rapid devaluation of taxi medallions and licenses. Uber is even capable of seizing adjacencies with its asset-less transportation infrastructure such as in-region package delivery.[48] In its own postings for advanced analytic and digital talent, Uber notes that its goal is "moving real people and assets and reinventing transportation and logistics globally"[49] (see Figure 8.2).

We are seeing these same digital economic trends in other areas, such as Google in mobile advertising where they are partnered with Acxiom Corp., the Epsilon unit of Alliance Data Systems Inc., and Oracle Corp.'s Datalogix.[50] Battling this model is Apple's App ecosystem,[51] which may

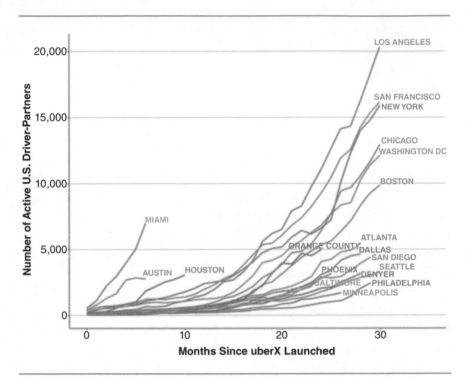

FIGURE 8.2   uberX's U.S. Conquests City by City

Source: An Analysis of the Labor Market for Uber's Driver-Partners in the United States, Professor Alan B. Krueger: https://irs.princeton.edu/sites/irs/files/An%20Analysis%20of%20the%20Labor%20Market%20for%20Uber%E2%80%99s%20Driver-Partners%20in%20the%20United%20States%20587.pdf.

block, subsume, or compete side-by-side as a parallel ecosystem.[52] In either case, the Apple App ecosystem employs more people than all of Hollywood, and, in the United States and Europe, is driving hundreds of thousands of new job creations—more than all the major pharmaceutical companies combined. Neelie Kroes, the European Union Commissioner for the digital agenda, in an interview in 2014 with the *Financial Times*, noted: "The speed of job creation and revenue growth in the app economy is incredible. What other sector grows 25 per cent a year? The ripple effects go far beyond the app makers themselves. Apple and others have started an economic revolution, and I want Europe to be front and center in that action."[53] In this case we have the *zaibatsu* of Apple iOS ecosystem versus the Google search and mobile platform *keiretsu*.[54]

Life science companies will need to clearly define where they are in two critical dimensions: (1) the *digital intensity* [55] in their relationship with customers, and (2) the *digital diversity* reflected in various partners' elements of the operating model and go-to-market capabilities.

Customers and consumers will have different levels of expectation with regard to *digital intensity*. They can be sorted roughly into four categories based on their comfort with digital technologies:

1. *Traditional customers* rely on traditional channels and interactions. Yet, even they leave digital traces.
2. *Experimental customers* selectively engage in digital for the value it delivers. They are discovering how their experiences can improve in the digital world.
3. *Transitional customers* accept that digital is a good thing. They strive to leverage digital more broadly, but may not always be able to do so.
4. *Digital savvy customers,* the most digitally intense group, make digital technology part of all dimensions in their life. Mobile access and engagement is their new frontier.[56]

The more "transitional" or "savvy" customers are (or become), the more collaboration and partnerships with the Health Digitals will prove critical.

Digital diversity will define key elements of the company's operating model and further define areas of partnership and operational alliances building out the digital enterprise and operations. It focuses on (1) *Making Markets*, or the digitalization of commercial support and direct customer interactions; (2) *Sourcing Inputs*, or the digitalization of the supply chain as direct inputs or as coordination; (3) *Running Enterprises*, or digital-enabling the core operating infrastructure of the enterprise; and (4) *Fostering Enablers*, or those aspects of the enterprise culture, talent, and diversity that allow the transition to digital. While a company may choose to engage with Google's cloud services and analytics teams for *Running*, it may further be seeking to accelerate its recruiting of key talent and to create a digital and analytics-driven culture. (See Figure 8.3.)

In 2015, New Health Digitals announced major new investments, initiatives, technologies, and operating realignments to advance in health-care and life sciences. These companies are creating the enabling infra-structure of digital health and digital healthcare. Consequently, the companies that work with them must be clear about the strategies they

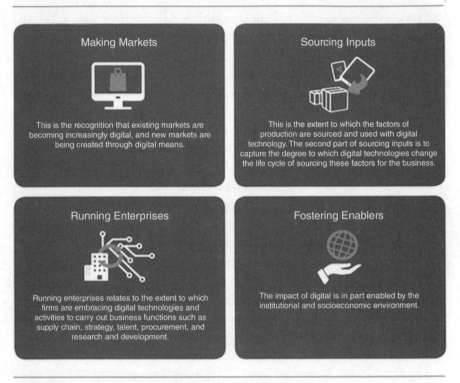

FIGURE 8.3   Defining Digital Diversity
Source: Digital Diversity Index: Guiding Digital Transformation (https://www
.accenture.com/t20150727T213014__w__/us-en/_acnmedia/Accenture/Conversion-
Assets/DotCom/Documents/Global/PDF/Dualpub_9/Accenture-Digital-Density-Index-
Guiding-Digital-Transformation.pdf#zoom=50).

have defined for themselves, and the roles that they will (and won't) take
on. Partnering successfully will require some "strategic wariness," as
portions of solutions are integrated into the apps, clouds, and new vertical
market initiatives emerging from other sources.

COMPETITION: PROTECTING THE BUSINESS

The conundrum of digital ecosystems and cloud technologies is that new
innovations are increasingly accessible. Digital ecosystems have distinct
standards (e.g., Apple's APIs for HealthKit and ResearchKit and development of the Swift programming language[57]). Cloud technologies
achieve global scale by embracing new ideas, requests, standards, and

so on into the environment that is available for all. Imagine the complexity of a single pharmaceutical or device company having to code a unique interface for every health system and electronic record system it encountered—in terms of time to complete, expense to execute, and expense to maintain—this would soon collapse on itself. This universal access to the same capability infrastructure, predictably declining costs, and ever-increasing global scale is why digital is both unavoidable and a catalyst for growth. It is the necessary, but not sufficient, foundation.

Uber went from a shared ride service with different cost tiers into experimenting with package delivery; as we write, there are rumors it may seek autonomous vehicles as another service—essentially competing with the same drivers and car assets that were the foundation to its original business.[58] The company that provided the initial opportunity gains a lens on new sources of growth and large profit pools potentially accessible to them through an adjacent and further disruptive move. That is digital, where the collaborator may become the competitor if it can move more functionality into its digital services model.

Already you can see competing ecosystems evolving. Qualcomm Life, a direct competitor of Philips HealthSuite and consumer-connected devices, is partnered with a leading electronic medical record (EMR) company, Cerner, and health information exchange infrastructure provider, Orion Health.[59] Orion Health in turn is a key partner of Amazon's AWS health cloud services.[60] Qualcomm Life is also a featured connected health partner within the Amazon AWS Partner Network (APN).[61]

Similarly, IBM's Watson Health is partnered with the EMR company Epic,[62] as well as Apple,[63] for advanced analytics and cognitive computing driving disease and population health management approaches. Apple in turn is partnered with Epic for supporting patient access to their health information from Epic EMRs.[64] And so it goes—there are clear sets of highly interdependent digital partners that are also occasional competitors creating the next generation of digital health and healthcare management infrastructure.

So is the solution to pick a confederation, create one, or play across them? The likely answer is a bit of each. Companies will need to create and work across partner networks, keeping in mind the following points:

- *Access to critical real-world data and the technologies to glean insights are baseline requirements.* Value-centric enterprises have significant real-world data requirements and are analytics-driven in decision making and resource allocation. Often the motivation to collaborate or to compete will be driven by this as a primary goal. If data are made fully available, the value of collaboration is higher than competition. If data access is limited, the partner will likely become a future competitor.

- *Relationships will define market capabilities and access.* Not all technology and digital infrastructure companies have the full scope of required services to scale globally. Therefore, a network approach will likely need to be global. This can include customer relationships, technology partners, and go-to-market partners delivering a value service.
- *Point-to-point, therapeutic-to-therapeutic, and device-to-device views of competition may be less important than a network of privileged partnerships.* In devices, sensors, data acquisition, data aggregation, and advanced analytics there are increasingly alternatives. So the network of partners who have a demonstrated ability to play together may be more important than single technology views of collaboration or competition.
- *Digital distributes, democratizes, and pushes capabilities to their limit.* Over time, cloud services and cloud integration will democratize access and costs. The competitors that likely matter most are those able to scale, identify opportunities, and drive costs down faster than a digital competitor.

Digital speed and economics will demand a view on partnerships and collaborations as a set of accessible capabilities that brings the benefit of influence without asset ownership. But the real competitive advantage will be defined by the speed with which value is delivered to the health system and patients, the breadth of the markets and populations reached, and the continuous empowerment of those customers and consumers for better healthcare and health management. The companies and partnerships driving this will be the competitive force to focus on.

CHANGE CATALYZING COLLABORATION CATALYZING CHANGE

This evolving, collaborative era in healthcare is in so many ways a special case of Open Innovation,[65] a topic that is quite mature in management literature. It, too, encompasses the themes of broader and more explicit precompetitive technologies and insights, where the value of collaborative problem solving and effort on difficult issues is higher than exclusivity and the protection of proprietary ideas.

Value innovation requires access to data—real-world data from many disparate sources—and practical insights from those data. While today much of these data come from secondary sources and aggregators (such as United Healthcare's Optum and the Explorys unit of IBM's Watson Health), in the future these data will increasingly be accessed directly from health providers through the data channels going into place that enable the integrated care management models required by healthcare reform legislation.

Value innovation requires remote monitoring and patient-centered services, potentially combined with real-world clinical decision support tools, founded on the principles of precision medicine, that help ensure the highest level of benefit for patients and health providers. These will require a combination of technologies, such as next generation DNA sequencing integrated with physician decision support, or remote-care monitoring sensors in the patient's home. No one entity or company will have the scope of technical knowledge or acumen to define and evolve such a solution on its own, much less tailor it to the requirements of different regions and patient settings. Although we do see intellectual property and specific ways of working being created in these collaborations, we also see that the scope of problems is so broad and the value of new insights so large that the cost of limiting collaboration is greater than the commercial loss from shared intellectual property.

From the perspective of a life sciences company, current customers and suppliers may be the best collaborators. The more critical parties are to each other's success, the broader the basis they may have to collaborate. Our experience suggests that risks are reduced and benefits maximized when collaborations have clear interests in redefining solutions and a history of successfully working together, resolving problems, and putting agreements into place.

Just as change in technological abilities—and in the market's subsequent expectations—is a catalyst for collaborations, collaborations are a catalyst for change. R&D renovation was realized through collaborations across the continuum from earliest concept through to full commercialization; we believe that creating value for patients and healthcare systems will benefit from the same catalyst.

Chapter 9

Talent Strategy for the New Healthcare Ecosystem

People will be the biggest advantage for (or the greatest impediment to) a company's ability to excel in a quickly evolving industry. But recruiting the right mix of new skills and mindsets—and managing performance—won't be easy in this context.

The success of any company's journey to become value-centric rests on its ability to align employee mindsets, norms, behaviors, and empathies to the patient, while compelling them to persistently drive value for the health system overall. Top talent will (1) take the patient's point of view on all issues without negotiation or retreat, (2) accept responsibility for delivering value to the patient and to the health system, (3) seek real-world data and analytics to inform and influence decision making, (4) be collaborative and active managers of the intra- and extra-company partnerships that support the service packages driving value, and (5) transform the company's business model(s) to operate at digital speed, with commensurate economics in mind.

*   *   *

In 2015, Biogen reorganized, placing Adriana "Andi" Karaboutis, formerly of Dell Inc., into a newly created role as executive vice president of technology and business solutions reporting to Biogen's CEO. Biogen's announcement of the move noted, "As the pace of digital innovation accelerates, Andi will play a critical role in our mission to improve human health, and support those who serve patients."[1]

During that same time frame, Sanofi also created a new role—chief patient officer—and appointed clinician Anne Beal, previously deputy executive director at the Patient Centered Outcomes Research Institute (PCORI), to the post.[2] In speaking about her new role, Dr. Beal said, "More important than the bottom line is to bring value to the organization. You bring value to patients by producing more responsive medicines, for payers by helping with patient needs, and for physicians by improving patient outcomes."[3]

We're not here to assess these individuals' performance, nor predict their tenure, success, or level of influence. What's important, in the context of this book, is that both Biogen and Sanofi have recognized the need to create new roles at the senior level. Both positions reflect the kind of organizational transformation we have been describing. Both emphasize the role of digital technologies in changing and improving care for patients, and in adding value to health systems. Both emphasize the need to have value at the forefront. And both indicate an understanding that it will take differentiated talent and new capabilities to excel in the fast-changing world of healthcare.

TRANSFORMING THROUGH TALENT

If there is to be one essential, foundational characteristic of the new value-centric life sciences companies, it is that they will be patient led. All deliberations and strategies will need to place in the foreground the need for patients to be the greatest beneficiaries of a company's therapeutics and also the greatest beneficiaries of health providers' activities. If patients represent the axis around which the company turns, then value creation—for patients and for the health system—should be a natural product.

Ideally, everyone in the company would be aligned around the same axis immediately, but that is impractical in the short term. So what's needed is a plan to build the patient- and value-centered culture, supported by appropriate skills and capabilities, over time. To do that, talent management efforts will need to center around three tasks: (i) ensuring that new talent recruited to the company has the right profile, (ii) ensuring that learning and interaction programs within the company reflect its new axis and goals, and (iii) ensuring that performance ethos and management systems do the same.

To do so, they will rely on broad and real-time data as their essential, foundational tool. Value-centric organizations make decisions based on data and insight and are pervasively patient-centric. While this sounds obvious (why wouldn't all organizations do this?), the reality is that it's usually not the case, particularly with pharmaceutical and bio-pharmaceutical companies that have historically relied on a far more narrow scope of data (clinical trial data), heuristics, and legacy models to inform their decisions.

Patient-journey models within volume-centric organizations, for example, are typically developed by marketing agencies and lack any real-world data-derived insights. In value-centric organizations, however, patient-journey models will reflect a clear view of the standard-of-care, how different approaches might be applied differently to varying patient cohorts, and how a model may be affected by diverse care settings, and the care gaps within formal clinical settings and at home that may gate against full realization of the best possible outcomes. The value-centric approach requires broad access to real-world data, advanced analytics, and talent who can frame the right questions and accurately interpret the output from the analysis. These organizations can't be passive about their use of data—in fact they will be relentless in pursuing the data that support value and the services that ensure it.

That said, most of the business models we've identified—Around-the-Patient, Value Innovators, and the New Health Digitals—require three distinct categories of talent: digital, advanced real-world analytic, and patient centered. Only with these talent categories represented robustly will any businesses using these models be able to build and sustain the capabilities—in these same areas—that they will need to excel.

Digital Talent

Digital talent brings to the table the disruptive influence needed to transform former bricks-and-mortar and "FTE-based"[4] organizations into businesses that are omnipresent, responsive, even anticipatory, and with cost structures that are lower by orders of magnitude with scale. Today, few companies in life sciences and healthcare have that digital expertise or depth; it is mainly found within consumer, media, and entertainment—and in those companies that are purposefully becoming New Health Digitals.

Advanced Real-World-Data Analytic Talent

The value-based world embraces and depends on a wealth of data from electronic medical records, data gathered from personal devices, and social data. And yet, to date, life science and medical device companies don't have the digital infrastructure and talent to use this data well. Individuals who understand how to leverage advanced real-world data analytics come from myriad sources—academic medical centers, health payers, health-focused consulting organizations, and government-funded medical research entities. No organization will be able to align to value, price to value, manage to value, present value to health authorities or risk-bearers, or truly be patient-centric without expertise in this area.

Patient-Centered Talent

It's easy to say that patients are at the center of an organization. It's relatively easy to create PowerPoints and rubrics to guide discussions. But without a real appreciation of what a commitment to patients means in the present —without people who have had working experience with the mindset—a true pivot to the patient will be very difficult to pull off. Assessments will be informed by the "usual suspects" and padded with personal experiences, but they will largely reflect guesswork rather than a full orientation to patient needs. Life science companies have a strong foundational knowledge of the biological processes of disease. They have deep insights into how physicians make treatment decisions. They have developed tools and approaches for understanding different aspects of the patient's journey. But creating a full view of a standard of care, solutions to deficiencies and gaps, and how health outcomes and economics come together requires special skills and capabilities. This comes from clinicians and allied health professionals who have the strategic vantage point, practical experience, and an ability to fully challenge healthcare models.

All of these talents are critical to performance. So how can a biopharma or medical device company build up these critical skills as they transition to a value-centric model? What is the value to the New Health Digitals of partnering with Around-the-Patient and Value Innovators? How do these skills apply to the Lean Innovators?

RECRUITING

Increasingly talent will come from outside the typical sources, which, for all but the most junior and entry-level positions, usually means from other life science companies. And broadening the scope of recruiting may require some changes or expansions in the ranks of your internal and third-party recruiters. Your current team members probably all have backgrounds in life science, biopharmaceutical, pharmaceutical, or traditional consulting organizations, and their personal networks of referrers, LinkedIn contact profiles and so forth are likely all from life science biopharma, pharmaceutical, or traditional consulting organizations as well.

While these sources will continue to yield exceptional talent, companies will also need to attract individuals who actually understand, have experienced, and are connected to the direct delivery of care to patients or for the management of risk associated with this care. This could include individuals with experience in health providers, health insurers, health analytics, healthcare services, or clinicians redirecting their own careers, to name just a few possible sources. And that need may require an organization to augment its recruiting staff.

With regard to the search, it's also important to acknowledge that talent with experience in or sensitivity to healthcare services and patient interactions is necessary *but not sufficient*. Even the world of healthcare providers is struggling to overcome some ingrained habits and perspectives. New talent needs to be able to challenge the status quo, and advance the definition of what's needed to deliver value, while sustaining their empathy and focus on the patient being a beneficiary of all technologies, therapeutics, and services. This, in turn, needs to be strongly and visibly reinforced at the most senior levels of the organization.

Given that healthcare is one of the largest sectors of any developed or developing economy, it makes sense that talent should be recruited from the best universities and academic medical centers, and that the need for constant learning and improvement of skills means the pool of talent is large and has high potential. Still this will require a new network of recruiters, new channels of communications to prospective candidates, new reputation and brand-building, and differentiated interviewing and selection processes.

Most larger companies today use a combination of primary recruiting (at narrow sets of targeted universities and programs within those universities), and experienced hiring at multiple levels (where they use internal and external recruiters, and also post open positions on electronic services such as LinkedIn or Viadeo.com). But there is also a certain efficiency in the marketplace for talent, where candidates are aware of employers that seek their specific profiles of skills and will appreciate specific aspects of their educational and work background. Healthcare providers and payers work in largely the same manner, targeting different institutions and skills needed across their operations. Now, however, we are seeking an increasing need to establish new fundamental profiles of talent, new institutions as sources of talent, and a new group of external recruiters who understand a company's goals and have access to the (new) needed networks. This last aspect may be the most difficult as recruiters tend to specialize in specific types of talent and align to the areas and programs within companies that best fit their talent market access.

Companies need to create efficient external communications that allow individuals to appropriately self-select themselves to the organization overall and specific roles therein. For example, if the biopharmaceutical company is focused on Around-the-Patient digital innovations, there is a need for clinical training that can assess specific care gaps, meaningful solutions to those gaps, and design how they'd best be received by healthcare providers and patients. If patient engagement in the management of their own care is critical to achieving better health outcomes for the patient and value outcomes for the healthcare system, the company may need to have a combination of consumer interaction–focused expertise with incentive and motivational aspects akin to what some health payers deploy to highly targeted patient populations. As analytics focused on real-world outcomes and evidence are increasingly part of risk-bearing health provider and health insurer interactions, there is a higher need for clinical expertise combined with population analytics.

Perhaps most important is defining and building the company's external reputation. Organizations need to establish what is different in their operating model and requirements, and why talent of a specific profile may now want to consider a career with them. For example, physicians and trained clinical talent were hired into pharmaceutical companies in the past in medical affairs, safety and pharmacovigilance, and some R&D positions. Now those companies may need these same skills functioning not only as internal subject matter experts but also as the lead executives overseeing new commercial groups and services, working to create go-to-market strategies, and redefining the structure of risk-bearing contracts in regions with highly consolidated healthcare payers and providers. They will need these individuals to bring together their clinical training and aptitude with an understanding of the new economics of value-based healthcare.

Reputations are not created quickly. It is a result of highly targeted external communications; new relationships with talented key opinion leaders (KOLs) such as leading academics, physician executives, and leading payers; and highly networked new hires and existing employees. The new targeted talent will need to hear the messages of what's really different, see proof in action (for example, through published studies, health provider contracts, acquisitions, joint ventures, etc.), and believe that the growth of the company requires their skills, and emulates their thinking and aspirations before there is a broad willingness to redirect careers.

Even candidate assessment and interviewing processes need to be different than they are today. Many companies now have pre-interview and post-interview assessment tools exploring performance orientation, team or collaborative centricity, and personal values to ensure alignment to and highest success within their cultures. As subtle as it may seem, these activities reflect the current company norms, behaviors, and conceptions of high-potential talent.[5] They now need to be a lens on the future, targeted profiles, mindsets, and behaviors that reshape capabilities and culture in the new directions.[6]

Finally, some markets for talent are tough and constrained. The market for digital skills and data scientists is foremost among these. Here, partnerships may be a critical means of accessing the critical skills. Closely aligned, multiyear partnerships and collaborations may afford rapid access to mature skills, at scale, within a talent management system appropriate for those skills' cultures.[7] This was part of the motivation for several recent collaborations including Medtronic/IBM Watson

Health, Apple/Epic, QualComm Life/Novartis, and Roche/Foundation Medicine. Often these partnerships make the initial hiring process more attractive as the newly hired digital and data scientific talent can better see themselves as part of these forward-looking arrangements.

ONBOARDING

The onboarding and integration process of this talent needs to reflect that same forward-looking mindset to be effective. Otherwise, these new kinds of talent may be viewed as internal subject matter experts rather than as the new primary "drivers." The onboarding process will usually be most successful when a few principles are followed: (1) Maintain new operating capabilities and groups at the core versus the periphery of the organization—they need to be seen as central to new "ways of working" versus an experiment; (2) ensure the new profile and mindsets get to scale quickly—legacy systems and networks are dense and have developed over decades and therefore need to see a scale of new influence that supports meaningful early integration; (3) align leadership models to the new strategies, mindsets, and cultural goals; and (4) align performance management systems to the new goals, while sustaining the performance of the current or legacy model.

The organization's tendencies[8] may be to lag, and remain focused on traditional measures of performance, compensation, and measures of market success. So the core functions and leaders need to be the vanguard of the new ways of working, measuring, and rewarding.[9] How key functions are organized, where they report, the agenda of key governance and decision forums, and core resource allocation processes (e.g., annual strategic and operating planning processes) are all front and center in ensuring that the core goals and capabilities are foregrounded and not marginalized—even unwittingly.

Having a formal lens on the culture is now a necessity. The speed of change in the marketplace and the degree of difference in cultural orientation implied by the transition to value drive to cultural transformation being considered an executive level item and process to oversee. Fortunately, there are now new digital tools that establish a baseline, pace of change, and direction of change.[10] This is not change management in a traditional sense, but cultural and performance management transformation, where the value characteristics are in the profile of talent, in the capabilities they have, embedded as part of the processes of the organization, and directly driving corporate and cascaded goals.

The structure of leadership, key functions, decision forums, and operating groups will validate the intent and priorities of the organization. Senior managers need to ask: Is value reflected in the set-up of the organization (e.g., is digital medicine integrated as a core commercial and medical capability and influencing group, is value-based reimbursement present at a strategic level and enabled outside of traditional market access structures)? Or, how have strategic planning and annual operating planning processes integrated clear and increasing expectations for the proportion of the business driven by value-validated opportunities or value-centered go-to-market approaches. It is clear that the world of healthcare companies is transitioning. Both life science companies and health providers are largely supported by volume business today, but increasingly moving toward value. The imperative for leadership is guiding and pacing this change through these key mechanisms.

A company's performance management systems are the translation of priorities into the explicit goals of functions, business units, key executives, and individuals. The alignment of these systems to the value strategy of the organization is critical. Executives, mid-level managers, and individuals will test the avowed strategy of the organization's advances against the specifics of their performance system. In the journey to value, these changes are not subtle and the need for consistency between strategy and performance management systems is all the more critical.

In an organization focused on volume, for example, the most important goals may be share of voice, market share, and net realized prices. Within a value-centric organization, it will be most critical to have the evidence base in place, be rigorously analytic-led with all decisions, manage downside risks of value contracts, and integrate critical services across partners and functions to ensure population health and health system cost outcomes. So it will be less about quantity than quality, assured mutual outcomes, and operating model performance over time. Whereas the volume companies have emphasized individual performance for market and sales goals, value-centric companies require a coordinated approach that ensures tight accountabilities but more shared objectives.

Without these sorts of tight alignments across functions and processes evolving appropriately over time, the volume organization will miss value.

SKILLS TO CREATE VALUE

To assemble the caliber of team needed, with the right combination of skills, you will need to broaden your sights beyond traditional sources and categories of talent, deepen your talent "bench," and align performance management systems to the two-fold goal of being centered around the patient *and* delivering value to the health system.

Lean Innovators have a strong tilt toward operational, financial, and transaction skills, but now they also need to become innovators and highly focused managers of multiple niche acute and non-acute disease therapeutics. While the revenue model itself is not new, the demands on the more traditional talent, who are accustomed to the more resource-rich, branded product world of large pharma, will be significantly different and greater.

Value-centric organizations need (1) clinical talent with strong problem framing and solving skills; (2) quantitative or data scientists who can advise on data requirements, data stewardship, and advanced analytics; (3) advanced healthcare economics and financial modeling and management skills, (4) digital medicine and services expertise to syndicate solutions around specific populations in differentiated contexts; and (5) business and corporate development expertise that can integrate technologies and services into multiyear relationships with co-investment and co-management of risk.

For companies pursuing the Around-the-Patient and Value Innovator models, some new, required skills will come from the leading academic institutions, but many will come as experienced hires from health providers, health insurers, health economics consulting firms, healthcare services firms, and digital companies moving rapidly into healthcare. Partnerships and collaborations will also prove key to getting to meaningful scale quickly and establishing a culture of data, analytics, and digital speed.

The New Health Digitals will drive their talent acquisition and development initiatives in other directions—seeking key individuals knowledgeable about product-centric life sciences companies, medical devices, and health providers to ensure their ability to translate their capabilities into this sector with accuracy and greater force of effort.

While we have a primary focus on pharmaceutical, biopharmaceutical, medical device, and digital health companies, it is clear that the talent requirements of the health providers, authorities, and payers also looms large. Historically these organizations were skilled at scheduling, coding, creating guidelines for access, evaluating utilization, and treating in highly specialized settings. Now the focus will move toward health, avoiding acute events, moving treatment to low-cost and acuity settings, and having health professionals work to the top of their licensure. Population health management and value-based payments are highly salient and the focus of capability building, new work cultures, and advanced decision support tools. In fact, many of the same skills identified for the value-centric organizations—including digital engagement and digital operations—will apply here. In all, we believe the common skills and the targeted talent will aid acceleration and implementation of new patient- and value-centric business models.

This is a journey that will redefine the enterprise, attract new talent, engage and activate top performers, and transform the value accessible to patients and the healthcare system overall.

LOOKING BACK— LOOKING FORWARD

Chapter 10

A New Age of Healthcare—Placing Patient and Value at the Center

We are at the confluence of enormous change and the emergence of new business models that will disrupt the legacy healthcare institutions, companies, and leaders of the last decades. What will your role be?

Healthcare, the single largest sector in most developed and developing countries, is evolving more quickly every day. Leading companies, startups, and individuals are redefining it to mean something broader than pills, devices, clinical effort, and facilities. This fundamental transformation is being driven by new economic models determining pay for healthcare, new digital operating economics, and broad technology disruption that is changing the characteristics of medicines and the location of services. But there is no map showing where the industry will land. We have the opportunity to shape and guide these changes for the benefit of patients first and foremost, and the healthcare system overall.

The scope and pace of change will be demanding on policy makers, life science company executives, and healthcare leaders. While the disruptions of other sectors presage the scope of business and economic model impact in healthcare, ours is a sector with some fundamental differences from *consumer products, retailing, streaming entertainment, telecommunications, or financial services. In health and healthcare, access for the many is critical, with high levels of public and private corporate investment with the intention of benefiting broad populations. And it is very personal; we care deeply about the end results.*

The ultimate disruption will be catalyzed by three factors: the point at which a critical mass views patient outcomes and value as a requirement, the new economics enabled by digital and precision medicine, and the new, more active roles we are accepting as individuals, patients, leaders, and companies.

Who will be behind the breakout innovations? Is there an asset-light patient care management or value-reimbursement model equivalent to AirBnB for pharma or medtech? The answer is not yet clear, and yet it's certain that those who are not prepared for change will get left behind.

* * *

We are privileged to participate in a field where the primary responsibility is to advance the health of people around the world. As participants and stakeholders, we are constantly striving to ensure that the greatest possible number of people benefit from the best currently available therapies and preventative approaches. Some of us work to address the most devastating diseases with new cures and approaches. Others seek to help individuals better manage chronic conditions. In every case, we know we have peers, colleagues, and supporters on all sides.

Healthcare is actually the largest single sector, when assessed as a percentage of gross domestic product, in almost all developed and developing economies. Governments invest in healthcare, through their respective national health institutes, to ensure ongoing innovation. Individuals and families spend significantly on it.[1] And although there is a perennial debate about how much healthcare spending is productive for economies, companies, or families, the data show that globally we are living longer with higher quality lives than ever before, and our economies are becoming more productive as a consequence.[2] Healthcare is fundamentally important—for us as human beings and for our societies as a whole.

And now we are at an inflection point, with a critical opportunity to redefine and reshape what we consider healthcare to be, how it functions as a market, and what expectations we should have for it as individuals, executives, medical practitioners, companies, private payers, or governments.

Keeping the patient at the center of this redefinition gives us a profound optimism about what these changes can bring in terms of patient and health economic outcomes, truly innovative health and healthcare approaches, and fundamentally improved economics for the healthcare system, companies, families, and individuals.

NEW FUTURE

We can improve, we can reinvent, or we can innovate a new way. For decades we have worked on healthcare cost reductions and initiatives to slow the rate of aggregate spending. Most of these initiatives served to create access limits, price caps, or cost shifting. The past attempts at healthcare reform or cost control made no fundamental progress—absolute spending levels increased without any fundamental change in value realized. This was the dilemma of the "volume" period of healthcare. A focus on capacity building and paying for what was done made sense in the half century where we simply wanted to ensure that all individuals, all citizens, in all regions had basic access and services. However, while we did focus on providing care to patients, it was directed to moments of their greatest need, versus how we keep people healthier all the time, avoiding high-expense interventional procedures, medicines, and devices.

Almost every country in the world now realizes that the structures that built our established systems now create disincentives for true improvements in outcomes and value.

And so things are changing. Realization is followed by action; however haphazard at first, it eventually solidifies into concepts and actions we can discuss, dissect, improve on, upend, and/or reinvent. We are in the midst of a seismic shift where we are resetting our expectations about how we pay for healthcare toward outcomes and value. We are increasingly placing patients at the center of healthcare—focusing on keeping them healthy, engaging them in decisions of how and when to seek care, and creating encouragements for them to manage more of the process themselves.

Healthcare is becoming a real market—we pay when we receive something of value, and we are willing to pay when the value is greater. Think of how financial services, telecommunications, retailing, and other critical aspects of life function today—healthcare is moving the same way. Markets that have mandated these changes will be in place in the next two to five years—in the United States, the United Kingdom, regions in Sweden and Finland, in China—and others that are following quickly thereafter— France, Germany, Japan,[3] and more. While there are clear differences in the policies and approaches in each case, there are also striking common-alities—highly similar themes of focusing on achieving the best possible clinical outcomes with the greatest efficiency and value. Each country or region moving in this direction is focused on transforming a facilities- and talent-centric model into one that leverages data, evidence, and insight to liberate health and healthcare to be in the home, supported by digital infrastructure, engaging the patient-consumer at new levels.

We have the perspective and desire to make it happen; we also have the technology. Digital infrastructures, data and analytic insights, and the growing breadth in therapeutics and remote medical technologies can enable these changes with ever-improving economics and outcomes. In fact, healthcare is going to be a primary beneficiary of the digitalization of everything and the Internet of things—the tools and technologies that deliver our information, allow us to perform our jobs, entertain us, and interlink families and friends. Healthcare is going to have data and insight about what is working, why care fails, and how care and specific thera-peutic approaches can be improved. Healthcare is going to be liberated from physical health facilities and occur in the home or workplace—as effectively as and perhaps more safely than hospitals and clinics.[4] Health-care will be provided by new companies and by companies we've developed relationships with and trust in for other aspects of our lives—companies whose offerings are already in our homes, purses, and pockets.

Healthcare providers will have more influence and control as digital tools, remote consults, and remote monitoring allow them to broaden their relationships with patients and put them back into the business of patient care and relieving them of financial coding and optimization of appointments and schedules. Healthcare is going to be paid for and directed by individuals and their families—we will be buying it selectively, considering what to invest in, what to do ourselves, and planning where to avoid spending. Nothing will remain as it is.

Our research and our work suggest a bold future of beneficial changes:

- *We are redefining where care occurs*—whereas we once struggled to get access to care facilities and practitioners, we are increasingly going to have tools and access from our mobile devices, health wearables, and smart TVs or video "hubs."[5] Healthcare will move to where we are, where we live, and where we work.

- *We are redefining care itself*—we are moving from care interventions at acute moments of need to focusing on health and long-term disease management.
- *We are redefining who is responsible for care*—we are moving from where governments, institutions, and companies were responsible for defining and delivering care, to where we are increasingly responsible for our own health and healthcare decisions. Those institutions and companies delivering this care will see themselves as more responsible to the consumer and patient—relative to those who historically paid or reimbursed them.[6]
- *We are going to be paying for healthcare differently*—increasingly we are not paying for what was done, but for what we get. Healthcare is now a thing of measurable benefit. It can really be thought of as an investment with immediate, near–term, and longer term returns. It is becoming a real market.
- *We are redefining medicines*—expanding the definition beyond chemical or biological therapeutics, and we're also increasingly considering advanced algorithms to define who would benefit most from what treatment and how to ensure that any given therapeutic is delivered in the right way We're using digital technologies and tools to further support the journey to achieve outcomes and value in the use and delivery of medicines.[7]
- *We are redefining the entire value chain of medical innovation*—R&D can now be informed by real-world data available at population scale. Genomics, genetics, pathway biology, and the immunology of our cells are fundamentally changing the outcomes possible, and digital innovation is looking as promising as chemical and biological approaches. While a molecule or therapeutic antibody may be approved and launched as a product, digital R&D does not stop at regulatory approval, as we will demand ever-increasing value and benefit.[8]
- *We are moving toward patient-centric supply chains*—the advent of precision medicine, remote digital monitoring technologies, and digital medical information everywhere allow for a fundamental reconsideration of the supply of medicines, devices, and services to the patient that is at once far more responsive, tailored, and efficient.[9]
- *We are building new companies*—product companies are evolving into services provided to patients and care providers. Health insurers are becoming health providers and analytics companies. Health providers are becoming risk managers and collaboratively building new capabilities. The providers of digital devices and services in our pockets and purses are supporting the management of our health.

As healthcare practitioners, life science companies, biomedical researchers, policy makers, family heads, and individuals, we have the opportunity to shape this future.

Policy makers and governments can create rules of engagement that allow alternative approaches to emerge and innovations to flourish. Individuals, the patients as consumers, can make some determinations of how healthcare is valued. The increasingly risk-bearing healthcare providers can redefine who they work with, how they work, and where they work to achieve outcomes and value.

And others will launch new approaches, products, and services that lead the way to the redefinition of what "health" and "healthcare" mean.

NEW LANGUAGE

Today, when we want to look something up or identify a product for purchase, we can Google it. When we want to go to a physician's office, movie theater, or airport we can Uber. When we want to watch a television show standing in the queue at the airport or chair in our living room we can Hulu. When we want to call our son or daughter at college we can Skype or Facetime. We have taken the services from companies and given them the prominent position of active words in our daily vocabularies. Yet, their sponsoring companies, Uber, Hulu, and so on, have no physical facilities, mall kiosks, or storefronts. Skype owns no cell towers. Hulu has no fixed broadcast or cable channel location. Uber owns no cars.

As disruptive as they have been, these companies recognized a need and initiated an entirely new solution leveraging the growing and ubiquitous digital infrastructure surrounding almost all aspects of our lives. Uber saw that a basic need of people is transportation. Often cabs were hard to come by and not pleasant. Limos were too expensive for most common transportation tasks. At the same time people own cars that they use only a small proportion of the time. Increasingly people are working multiple jobs or roles. The confluence of these forces, the relative accessibility of mobile technologies with highly accurate location awareness, big data technologies, and highly advanced analytics created new business opportunities. In a short period of time, this became one of the highest value companies on the planet—Uber, that also invented a new economic model of the "shared economy."[10]

So what will the healthcare analog be of Google, Uber, Hulu, or Skype? They will appear for sure. There is enormous capacity available in health facilities. We have pharmacies and retail-based clinics appearing in dense and remote areas. Radiologists and other clinicians can already be doing image interpretations and other activities from their homes. We have remote monitoring technologies in the home that can assess our health status on growing dimensions. These new healthcare services companies may be focused on maintaining or improving health, offer new financial models for paying for health and healthcare, or take care of needs once identified.

NEW ECONOMICS

Auto insurance companies use GPS and other tools to offer activity- or use-based policies.[11] Jet aircraft manufacturers now sell "thrust" (power) systems that can be charged by the hour or for the services they deliver.[12] Integrated data, advanced analytics, remote monitoring, and remote sensors all enable new capabilities, economic models, and payment structures. Insurance companies are personalizing premiums to reward healthy behaviors, like UK insurer AXA PPP launching MyActive+ retail platform to sell discounted health technology and wellbeing services to its customers, or Apple Watch and Health Kit being used to reward healthy behaviors with lower premiums.[13]

These new service and outcomes-based models have been proven in even the most demanding and fault-sensitive markets. This is all the equivalent of the Uber model where you pay for a trip based on miles, adjusted for demand at the time of the trip, and then allocated to drivers and passengers based on their quality scores.

Already we are seeing a movement toward outcomes-based reimbursement models for different disease states.[14] As data, analytics, and the new digitally enabled treatment and remote management models also begin to predominate, we are going to see highly innovative payment for service and outcomes models predominate. We are already seeing formal proposals for reimbursement models that can pay for a therapeutic differently in different diseases based on the effectiveness and relative value delivered. Next generation sequencing, integrated with pathway biological insights, evidence from the published literature, and a patient's own medical and family histories are already informing precision medicine approaches in many diseases.[15]

It does not stop there. The same data and information that will be used to set value-based pricing can increase the efficiency of R&D organizations and operations as we focus on the current outcomes from the current standard of care versus that achievable by a novel therapeutic or device with complementary analytics and digitally aligned services. The availability of genomic, lifestyle, and EMR data will allow more "in-silica" research and early stage development where hypotheses and scenarios can be tested on high-speed computers instead of in the traditional laboratories. The availability and ease of remote collection of data will allow the design of trials to change, the size of trials to be reduced, and the value of the pre-approval data enhanced. We will think of R&D and innovation as an ongoing process where insights and digital elements continue to advance around the molecule, antibody, or personalized condition.

Government and selected private sector initiatives are going to be the catalysts for these changes, but the value delivered and even consumer preferences will be the ultimate drivers, with technology and science as the core enablers.

These new strategies and business models are emerging and scaling. Some of the therapeutics innovation leaders are looking at their product as a novel therapeutic combined with remote monitoring and are looking to be reimbursed for the benefit they bring to patients and health systems. Therapeutic medical device companies have declared a transition to a services-based model as underway and growing rapidly in the years to come. The major Digital Gone Healthcare companies are bringing their scale, economics, infrastructure, and technologies to bear on large tracts of the healthcare landscape. In fact, the evolution of different companies' business models we predicted while writing this book were being announced as it was being finalized.[16] Healthcare is now clearly pivoting to the patient and consumer, analytics-driven, digitally enabled, and moving toward new digital economics. This is healthcare disrupted.

YOUR STARTING POINT, YOUR STRATEGIES

Understanding where you are and defining your strategies will require answering the following questions:

- Who are the major disruptors of the future? What sector will they come from and what will be the driver—digital technologies, a scientific breakthrough, real-world data informed insights, human psychology, or behavioral engagement? Or a combination?

- What kind of business will aggregate the distributed parts of the value-chain today in such a way that it's obvious in hindsight, but elusive right now to those entrenched in today's models?
- With patients at the center, how do the other parties—from local provider, to health authorities, to therapeutics and services companies, to remote care management services—line up?
- Is it possible for the leaders of the past 40 years to make the shift to the new or are they destined for ultimate disruption or reduction in their role and influence?
- What are the key attributes of change and new capabilities that will determine a company's ability to survive and thrive?

The current pivots are becoming clear—the shift in focus from volume to science and outcomes, the move to focus on unmet care needs and broad market solutions, the move toward digital health and collaborative care approaches. But will there be more? Will there be a breakthrough model, like Amazon in retailing, that fundamentally disrupts the industry, leaving traditional business models reeling?[17] Is the very fuzzy outline of that model before us now awaiting a leader's name, or a group of names, that will become as familiar as Jobs, Gates, Bezos?

There are many possible areas from which such a giant or team might emerge:

- The health services company that leverages the extraordinary sensors, optics, modems, networking, and processing capabilities of mobile devices, providing expertise comparable to today's leading academic centers to broad populations in underserved parts of the world;
- The "real-world" diagnostics and treatment selection company that integrates home device monitors, wearables, remotely collected clinical diagnostics, social data, and EMR-derived clinical data to select treatments in partnership with providers, persistently assessing effectiveness and value;
- The personalized, "in-silica," science–based companies that enable personalized medicines printed in a home setting using a 3-D printer; and
- The "Uber-like" health coach providing services as needed, where needed, for whoever needs it, redefining how care is paid for and provided with no asset ownership. . . .

There are so many possibilities. The reality is that any legacy player needs to question its optimal role in the shifting landscape. It needs to assess the best path and make the incremental and sometimes fundamental shifts at the right pace to help ensure its longevity and relevancy.

We have asked so many questions, but we will leave you with one more. And if you answer none of the others, answer this for yourself: What is your role in this change and how can you make a difference in this new reality? If you know the answer, then now is the time to take action. If you don't then a steady movement forward is necessary, as the traditional models are already facing obsolescence. Taking no action is not an option.

An exciting era is dawning for those who participate in this new health and healthcare economy—we look forward to the new landscape in this disrupted world of new innovations, vastly improved outcomes for more patients, and greater value for all.

Glossary

Healthcare and life sciences are complex fields to begin with. They reside at the junction of science, medicine, government regulations, and very specific payment or reimbursement models. But recent and continuing changes—advancing healthcare reforms, accelerating new technologies, and emerging operating models—are challenging the knowledge base of even those who have been associated with it for years.

To aid readers of diverse backgrounds, we went through *Healthcare Disrupted* and identified a select set of words, phrases, names, and concepts that we thought would benefit, in particular, from stand-alone explanations. We do define most of the terms where they first appear in the book; this list is meant as an additional reference, a clarifying tool, a way to step back and consider a few key concepts by themselves, and in some cases, this list suggests where readers might find additional information.

Affordable Care Act (ACA): United States legislation, formally the Patient Protection and Affordable Care Act, that has expanded

Medicaid coverage (payment for healthcare for low-income individuals), designed to lower healthcare costs and provide healthcare for more low-income Americans. Informally called "Obamacare."

accountable care organizations (ACOs): These organizations are made up of groups of doctors and other health services providers (hospitals, clinics) that agree to coordinate their efforts in caregiving to ensure that patients receive the quality of care they need at the lowest possible cost. The overarching concept is coordinating care across the continuum, assuring appropriate access, and avoiding treatment at the most expensive facilities if quality and access objective can be realized elsewhere. In the United States, it has evolved as a key element of Medicare reforms.

Agence des Systèmes d'Information Partagés de Santé—ASIP Santé (France): The agency for shared health information systems, ASIP Santé is a Crown agency under the Ministry of Social Affairs and Health, responsible for fostering the broader adoption and use of clinical and health information systems.

biologic: A therapeutic (drug, medicine) made from living biological sources (including microorganisms, living cells or tissues, and proteins, as opposed to chemical synthesis).

biosimilars: Biosimilars (also termed follow-on biologics) are a type of biological product that is FDA approved, and highly similar (in terms of quality, safety, and efficacy) to an already FDA-approved biological product, known as the biological reference product. Biosimilars are not "generics," in that they are not chemically identical. Re-creating biologics is as complex as the innovator therapeutic because the complex proteins are derived from living organisms that are genetically modified. Biosimilar manufacturers do not have access to the reference product manufacturer's molecular clone or original cell bank, nor to their fermentation and purification processes. In contrast, small molecule drugs are made of chemically based entities that can be replicated exactly and at modest expense. Consequently, biosimilars go through a specific and complex approval process design to prove they are identical to the biologic reference product through clinical, animal, and analytical studies.

biotech company: Historically, biotechnology companies were differentiated from pharmaceutical or "large pharma" companies by their work on biologics and rare and specialty diseases. Today all pharmaceutical companies have biologic products and programs, and most biopharmaceutical companies have biologic and small molecule (orally delivered medicines) in the market or R&D pipelines, so the distinctions are more around size, company age, and entrepreneurial operating model.

business model: The design by which a company operates; how it makes money. A "map" or representation of what and why it does what it does. Management guru Peter Drucker articulated five questions, the answers to which frame an organization's business model: (1) What is our mission? (2) Who is our customer? (3) What does the customer value? (4) What are our results? (5) What is our plan?

capacity: The extent to which an organization is doing the most it can with the resources it has, including talent, financial resources, privileged network of partnerships, and so on: working and producing to its fullest potential.

Center for Medicare & Medicaid Innovation (CMMI): CMMI is part of the Centers for Medicare & Medicaid Services, CMS.gov, which in turn is part of the Department of Health and Human Services (HHS) of the United States. The CMMI supports development and testing of new approaches to healthcare delivery and payment. It allows pilot programs to be implemented without specific funding approvals being made by Congress. The center was established to accelerate pilots and generation of evidence around new delivery and payment constructs calling for healthcare reform legislation in the United States, namely patient-centered medical homes, payment reforms, and arrangements that transition from the traditional fee-for-service model to global, bundled, and fixed-fee payments.

comorbidities: When two or more chronic conditions/diseases exist in a patient. One or more may be the result of another, or they can be present independently.

diagnostics company: A research-based health and life sciences company. Diagnostics can be biological, chemical, imaging, genetic, information-based, or combinations thereof. Diagnostics fall into a broad array of types, but the most common are confirmatory (positively or negatively confirms a disease state, genetic mutation, or specific pathogen), prognostic (predictive of the likely outcome of a disease or ailment as the basis for making a treatment decision), or predictive (risk, probability, or predisposition of individual for a particular disease based on family history, genetics, and environment). Most often, diagnostics are used to assess whether a patient has a rare or highly complicated disease state and whether a specific medicine or clinical treatment approach might benefit them. Increasingly health insurers and payers see diagnostics as a means of avoiding very expensive therapies where there will knowingly be no future benefit. Pharmaceutical and biopharmaceutical companies see diagnostics as an assurance that those patients benefiting most from their therapies can be identified and receive treatment with the highest confidence.

diagnosis-related group (DRG): A DRG is a classification system that is focused on in-patient stays and procedures, classifying the patient and received treatments into narrowly defined groups of major body systems and 500 subgroupings used for reimbursement. Examples of DRG codes include "bone marrow transplant" (listed as SURG or surgical) and "neurological eye disorders" (listed as MED or medical). The DRG classification system was developed at Yale in the early 1980s and was financed by the Health Care Financing Authority, the predecessor agency of the Centers for Medicare and Medicaid Services (CMS). DRGs are used in the United States to help government-funded health coverage and other payers monitor the cost of procedures and treatments. Over the years DRG has been revised, refined, and broadened in its use.

disruptive innovation: A term coined by Harvard Business School Professor Clayton Christensen. It has its origins in "creative destruction," popularized in economics by Joseph Alois Schumpeter in the first half of the 1900s, and the S Curve in technology strategy generally attributed to Richard Foster's research at McKinsey & Company in the early 1980s, introduced in his book *Innovation: The Attacker's Advantage*. Disruptive innovation means a product or service that is initially "inferior" starting in a less attractive or demanding market application, but over time creates new markets and new ways of valuing products and services in existing markets. A disruptive innovation upends an existing market, making "current" ways of doing things obsolete, or pushing those ways of doing things aside, often threatening companies that had been leaders and establishing new areas of competition in that existing market.

electronic medical record/electronic health record (EMR/EHR): EMRs have multiple functions. They are specific to individual healthcare providers or healthcare systems—sometimes existing at a national level in certain European and Asian countries. It is an electronic version of a patient's chart, containing the patient's health history as collected and any treatments provided by that healthcare provider. It supports scheduling, coding for reimbursement, and workflow within the healthcare provider. And of increasing importance, it holds the order-sets or specific treatment approaches that a health provider may offer to a patient. With the move to population health management within healthcare reform, EMRs are providing the foundation data for advanced analytics.

French National Health Insurance: Provides for universal coverage and high levels of services to a population that is, on average, older than that of the United States and many Asian economies. Coverage is accomplished through a public–private mix of hospital and ambulatory care and a higher overall volume of service provision than in the United States. It is often used as a reference model of a single payer system that "works" as the health status and patient satisfaction are relatively high and expenditures, as a share of gross domestic product, are lower than in the United States. Agencies such as Caisse nationale de l'assurance maladie des travailleurs salariés, or CNAMTS, are integral to this system with broad and sometimes controversial abilities to seek lower costs on therapeutics and devices. In recent years the French government has anticipated losses in the system and expanded payroll taxes, instituted special taxes, and added a specific tax on the pharmaceutical industry. These announced reforms are designed to bring expenses back in line with overall system revenues.

global healthcare spend: The amount of financial resources spent each year on healthcare, inclusive of clinical treatment in health facilities, therapeutics, devices, and other clinical aspects prescribed but utilized in remote settings. The World Health Organization (WHO) is a good source of information on healthcare spending per country, and overall. The World Bank is also a good source of information on public and private healthcare spending, and on healthcare spending as a percentage of gross domestic product (GDP). It generally does not represent any of the out-of-pocket or opportunity costs of healthcare borne directly by consumers and unreimbursed by any employer, government, or health insurer.

healthcare providers: Individual health facilities or healthcare systems that are part of a single corporate entity providing direct care to patients. This includes hospitals, outpatient facilities, and physician offices.

health services company: A business that facilitates treatment or monitoring of channels of communication between patients and medical professionals and payers. A health services company contributes in some way to the connection between doctors, patients, and payers.

Increasingly, as this book describes, we are seeing technology companies expanding into the health services field.

health technology assessment (HTA): A process by which a healthcare "product" (a therapeutic device, procedure, drug) is measured for efficacy (did it provide a health benefit) and cost-effectiveness, as well as considered from legal, ethical, and societal effect points of view.

healthcare codes: A set of codes by which a healthcare provider can document and classify a patient's condition as the basis for what they will be paid or reimbursed by a public or private health insurer. Healthcare codes are also used to study health trends.

healthcare ecosystem: The network of interdependent relationships involved in healthcare, including all of the players and stakeholders in a healthcare system, from those developing therapeutics (drugs, devices, treatments), to health insurers or payers, to healthcare providers, to those helping patients in their homes, to entities that facilitate interactions between providers and patients, to the patients themselves. In short, it involves people, facilities, technologies, and therapeutics.

healthcare market: The demand for health-related services, goods, and other offerings.

healthcare system: A healthcare system encompasses all the individuals and entities that participate in delivering preventative treatment, diagnoses, treatment, and follow-up care to patients. A healthcare system can be narrowly defined, as it is when we refer to a patient's individual healthcare system: his or her doctors, nurses, and other caregivers (providers). It can also be broadly defined, as when we refer to a country's healthcare system, which would include all of the providers, as well as other players, including companies that produce drugs and devices prescribed for patients.

International Classification of Diseases (ICD): This set of diagnostic codes was developed by the World Health Organization. The most recent revision (ICD-10) was put into effect October 1, 2015. The World Health Organization website explains ICD succinctly, as follows:

> The International Classification of Diseases (ICD) is the standard diagnostic tool for epidemiology, health management, and clinical purposes. This includes the analysis of the general health situation of population groups. It is used to monitor the incidence and prevalence of diseases and other health

problems, proving a picture of the general health situation of countries and populations.

ICD is used by physicians, nurses, other providers, researchers, health information managers and coders, health information technology workers, policy makers, insurers, and patient organizations to classify diseases and other health problems recorded on many types of health and vital records, including death certificates and health records. In addition to enabling the storage and retrieval of diagnostic information for clinical, epidemiological, and quality purposes, these records also provide the basis for the compilation of national mortality and morbidity statistics by WHO Member States. Finally, ICD is used for reimbursement and resource allocation decision making by countries.

life-science company: A broad term usually applied to all manufacturers and service companies providing goods and services to healthcare providers and health payers. It includes pharmaceutical, biopharmaceutical, medical diagnostic, medical device, and related technology companies. Since most of these organizations extend from the research and development phase—often some 10 to 15 years away from being available for patients—through to commercialization, they are referred to as "life science" versus being "healthcare" companies.

lost output: What a company or country (or any entity) could be producing/earning versus what it is producing/earning. Sometimes measured by jobs lost, bankruptcies, and other similar measures. "Output" in the context of a company is a volume measure of goods or services produced or sold.

MAC or "maximum allowable cost": MAC typically refers to a list of off-patent drugs, available from multiple sources, that are subject to capped payment schedules developed or selected by pharmacy benefit managers (PBMs). The payment schedule specifies the maximum unit cost payable by the PBM's client for therapeutics on the MAC list. The MAC list and payment schedules are frequently updated—sometimes as often as every seven days. The following links provide more information:
http://www.managedcaremag.com/archives/0809/0809.maxallowable .html
http://www.amcp.org/WorkArea/DownloadAsset.aspx?id=18734
http://www.ohiopharmacists.org/aws/OPA/asset_manager/get_file/ 99424

http://www.pcmanet.org/research/the-unintended-consequences-of-restrictions-on-the-use-of-maximum-allowable-cost-programs-macs-for-pharmacy-reimbursement

National Health Service (UK): The UK agency, launched in 1948, operating as part of the UK Department of Health, that sees to the provision of publicly funded healthcare for UK citizens (with the exception of some prescription charges and optical and dental services). Funding for the NHS comes directly from taxation.

Since the NHS transformation in 2013, the NHS payment system has become underpinned by legislation. The Health & Social Care Act 2012 moves responsibility for pricing from the Department of Health to a shared responsibility for NHS England and Monitor. For 2015/16, the NHS budget is £115.4 billion. The NHS in England remains free at the point of use for anyone who is a UK resident—currently more than 64.1 million people in the UK alone.

National Institute for Health and Care Excellence (NICE): Provides national guidance, information, and quality standards to improve healthcare, public health, and social services in the UK. NICE is a nondepartmental public body (NDPB); as such, it is independent of government, but accountable to the UK Department of Health. It is known for its assessment of value and quality and outcomes framework (QOF), which has supported decisions to recommend no reimbursement or limited access to medications and devices.

patent cliff: When an innovator therapeutic product company's branded product is no longer protected by a patent or loses exclusivity and can be produced as a generic or biosimilar drug. The pharmaceutical industry as a whole suffered the period of 2009 through 2013 as patents for many key, multibillion dollar blockbuster drugs expired.

health payer: The agency or entity responsible for financing or reimbursing the money spent on formal health services, often called "health benefits" (excluding the cost of over-the-counter medicines and home treatments that individuals may purchase directly). Generally, these are governments, insurance companies, employers, unions, or other entities that cover some or all of the cost of health services for individuals: hospitalizations, surgeries, visits to the doctor, diagnostic services, medicines, devices, and other treatments. "Single-Payer Systems" refers to governments that absorb the cost of formal healthcare for their citizens.

pharmacy benefit management companies (PBMs): These businesses are active intermediaries between pharmaceutical companies and health plan members (insured individuals). Their services are usually contracted for by self-insured employers, health insurers, or government agencies. They provide a range of services that are focused on ensuring that patients receive the right medications and that these are efficiently delivered. Some operate retail or online pharmacies; others work through third-party pharmacies, processing claims and negotiating to reduce or control the cost of prescription medicines for their clients. In recent years their focus has moved from therapeutics for the diseases that affect the largest populations, to specialty therapeutics, to more acute and rare diseases.

population health management: Population health management has the goal of improving the health of patients, lowering costs of care, and helping to ensure the care delivered is efficient and of high quality. It is performed by aggregating patient data from across multiple health information sources and identifying key actions for care providers and coordinators, informed through advanced analytics, that improve both clinical and financial outcomes.

population scale: At the level of an entire state, country, or region—large scale—including everyone, unless otherwise defined. "Treating diabetes at population scale in Massachusetts, or measuring results of a treatment at population scale in Massachusetts" would mean treating everyone in Massachusetts who has diabetes, or measuring the results of a treatment across everyone in Massachusetts who has diabetes. In this book, we refer to pharmaceutical companies taking on responsibility for "increased positive outcomes" at population scale. That phrasing refers to a company taking accountability for, or being assigned accountability for (and being paid by investors or other backers, including governments, on the basis of) improvements in health from a given medicine or treatment—not just in a clinical setting, but also across all the people who are prescribed that medicine or treatment.

provider: Provider(s) can mean hospitals or hospital networks, physicians' groups and networks, nurses' groups and networks, or any combination thereof, as well as individual practitioners who diagnose, treat, prescribe therapeutics, and create treatment plans (including preventative care) for patients, in a variety of locations including private offices, clinics, and hospitals, as well as in patients' homes.

real-world data versus real-world evidence: As regulators, payers, and pharmaceutical companies require more robust evidence around the true effectiveness of new therapeutics and medical devices, they have increasingly relied on real-world data and real-world evidence.

The terms "real-world data" and "real-world evidence" are often used interchangeably. Yet, in reality, they are quite different concepts.

A core aspect of health care involves the fundamental ability to access data that describe the current standard of care, as well as gaps and deficiencies in the care model, and social or patient-reported data, such as patient-reported outcomes. This is where real-world data come from—a myriad of sources that when linked together provide a view of a patient's health history that can be acted on using insights from advanced analytics.

Finding patterns in data: From real-world data, advanced analytics can extract meaningful patterns of information that help clinicians make appropriate treatment decisions. Analytics can be directed to a specific patient population, stage of a disease, or even a group of health providers. Some analytics methods focus on finding patterns that were not previously seen or known—using machine learning and other advanced approaches to let the data itself reveal patterns and relationships that provide new insights.

Real-world data and advanced analytics are changing how clinical trials are designed, how medical affairs experts may identify the "long responders" to specific treatment approaches, and how commercial organizations are evaluating the effectiveness of patient services programs. Increasingly, sources of real-world data provide a focus on the total population within a region or country, encompassing the various questions and insights that distribution data or chart reviews may have provided in the past.

Evidence as key conclusions: Now, the term "evidence" has generally referred to the key conclusions that could be derived from published studies in peer-reviewed journals. For instance, the organ-system focused cancer groups at the American Society of Clinical Oncologists (ASCO) and at the National Comprehensive Cancer Network (NCCN) use published studies to develop their recommendations for new treatment guidelines targeting very narrowly defined patient populations.

The information in these published studies comes from independent and company-sponsored research performed within targeted populations that often range from a few hundred to a few thousand patients. The process usually takes place over years and and encompasses study concept, study funding, study execution, the summarization of results, publication of the information, and the definition of guidelines. All in all, this process takes three to five years, from start to finish.

Traditional evidence has multiple uses today. Leading academic centers harness evidence and their own data to develop specific treatment approaches, pathways, and order sets—standardized lists of treatment steps, diagnostics, and therapeutics for a specific diagnosis—to make consistent and high-quality treatment decisions. Health insurers and payers use guidelines and evidence as the basis for determining whether to support patient access and reimbursement coverage. Pharmaceutical, biopharmaceutical, and medical device companies need to constantly consult these studies to assess and determine their own strategies for undertaking follow-on studies, for creating value dossiers, and for medical communications.

Evidence-generating insights: By contrast, real-world evidence involves using the growing wealth of real-world data, increasingly at the population level, to generate meaningful insights. Real-world evidence essentially is a product of analyzed real-world data. With real-world evidence, the rigor of analysis should be comparable to randomized and controlled clinical studies, be they regulatory or observational. The strength of real-world evidence should be that it's a new form of evidence in itself that complements traditional sources, which holds the promise of bringing more significant patient benefit because of its greater representativeness and timeliness.

Such groups as the Patient-Centered Outcomes Research Institute (PCORI) are advancing novel designs, such as pragmatic studies, that test the effectiveness of a therapeutic in a broad routine clinical practice and bring the rigor of regulatory trials to observational, real-world studies. Companies too are undertaking direct sponsorship of real-work studies and real-world registry-like approaches. Real-world evidence provides the validation between the results seen in regulatory clinical studies that initially support approval and the post-approval validation process, which shows that consistent or improving benefit is being realized.

A *new foundation*: Real-world evidence is now becoming the foundation for new pricing strategies that are more explicitly linked to therapeutic value for patients and health outcome benefits to health systems and risk-bearers. This evidence provides the support and confidence needed to undertake value-based contracting, to deploy patient services, and to run the emerging new patient care management businesses that best manage care processes and resource utilization to optimize value.

Real-world evidence provides a new foundation, or language, for establishing "business to business" relationships or for having leadership conversations between large risk-bearing health systems and increasingly analytic-centric health insurers and payers. Pharmaceutical companies must stay on top of advances in real-world evidence through their own investment and partnerships in real-world data sources and advanced real-world analytics services. They should be reshaping their necessary skill sets to best address the value, market, and financial opportunities that real-world evidence will offer them.

risk: The potential for loss. In *Healthcare Disrupted* we use risk in two respects: (1) risk in a population of patients, where some individuals may be disproportionate consumers of healthcare resources, and (2) risk in the context of new and innovative business and operating models. For example, it may be difficult to tie success to improvements in the health of populations; doing so is a higher-risk proposition than defining success by the volume of sales, as it involves a much more complex equation. So many factors contribute to success when a company is betting on its ability to improve healthcare overall, and doing so, for many companies, means taking on a new kind of risk.

socialized medicine: Using public (government) funds to provide for healthcare for all citizens of a given country with little differentiation in the access provided across regions and income levels.

therapeutic: A medicine or device designed to address an illness, injury, disease, or chronic health condition.

therapeutics reimbursement: medical and pharmacy benefits: Medical versus pharmacy benefit: where therapeutics are administered in specialized health facilities as "infused therapeutics" or "injected" by a health professional (legal requirement), therapeutics are generally reimbursed according to the medical benefit. There are other categories that may also be reimbursed according to the medical benefit, usually where expertise, monitoring, or multi-drug therapeutic approaches are required. Where it is a patient self-administered injection or where it may be an oral therapy, it is generally reimbursed as part of the pharmacy benefit.

Triple Aim framework: Developed by the Institute for Healthcare Improvement (IHI), the IHI Triple Aim framework offers an approach to improving the performance of healthcare systems by improving the experience of care, improving the health of populations, and reducing per capita costs of healthcare. IHI is an independent not-for-profit organization based in Cambridge, Massachusetts.

"value" in therapeutics and medical devices: This is perhaps the single most important term used in *Healthcare Disrupted*. At its core, "value" in healthcare means "benefit" or "gain." But there are many different types of value. A generic drug offers value because it has been proven effective in treating a certain kind of disease or condition, but the value in that sense is passive; it represents potential. The drug only brings a benefit to the company if it is sold, and it only brings a benefit to the patient if it is taken in the appropriate way (dosage, timing, and duration, for example) and has the desired effect.

Recently, the use of the term "value" has taken hold for reimbursement of clinical services to a health provider by a health authority health insurer. This is a transition from fee-for-service (FFS), where payments were made based on what was done, to value-based, where payment is based on the outcomes realized.

Value-based payment contracting is still in its early stages, with different structures being deployed. In the United States most are structured according to shared savings models that incentivize providers to carefully manage spending for a defined patient population through a shared percentage of any net savings realized. The Medicare Shared Savings Program is an example of just such a model.

At present this structure requires health providers to operate in two systems at the same time—FFS and value-based. Under current approaches, Medicare reimburses health systems on a FFS basis; then, at the end of the year, shared savings bonuses are assessed based on benchmarking an individual provider against the rate of increase for the overall FFS population. If a hospital or health system outperforms the FFS population, they get a piece of the savings. So health systems are operating in a FFS world while trying to claim a portion of this value-based incentive.

All in all, these differentiated structures require that payers and patients be tracked in differentiated approaches. For example, a health system has to know all patients in accountable care (ACOs), the services patients are receiving, and the specific costs of those services. This in turn is assessed versus the population goals, and the aggregate costs for specific populations of patients versus those population goals. For most organizations this is requiring a transition from an EMR and cost control orientation to a population and analytics driven one, where outcomes are defined and performance persistently assessed relative to these targets.

Pharmaceutical, biopharmaceutical, and medical device companies are increasingly brought into these value-based constructs as well. For a portion of therapeutics that are infused or injected by health professionals, reimbursement is a part of the "medical benefit" (see definition in this glossary) and therefore subject to many of the same value-based criteria and part of the overall cost of a population of patients. Consequently, these therapeutics are falling under the greatest scrutiny and subject to a growing array of value reimbursement metrics and composite scale (see the following table).

Organization	Components of value
American College of Cardiology (ACC)	Clinical benefit; cost-effectiveness
American Society of Clinical Oncology (ASCO)	Clinical benefit; toxicity; palliation; cost/month
Sloan Kettering Drug Abacus (www.drugabacus.org)	Efficacy; toxicity; novelty; R&D; rarity; population health burden
Institute for Clinical & Economic Review (ICER)	Cost-effectiveness; budget impact
National Comprehensive Cancer Network (NCCN)	Efficacy; safety; evidence quality; evidence consistency; affordability

Source: Accenture analyses, derived from presentations at the Massachusetts Biotechnology Council, Peter Neumann, presenter, "Value Series Part I: The Case for Value," Tufts Center for Evaluation of Value and Risk, October 5, 2015, www.massbio.org/events/calendar/3456-value_series_part_i_the_case_for_value/event_detail.

Other therapeutics fall under the "pharmacy benefit" and are reimbursed according to criteria defined by the payer and the pharmacy benefit manager (e.g., Express-Scripts Holding Company's Express Scripts, CVS Health's CVS Caremark, and UnitedHealth Group's OptumRx) which they or the private employer plan may have contracted with. Here too we are seeing significant use of real-world data and advanced analytics to advance value as a key criterion for providing access and the level of reimbursement within specific diseases.

Overall, value criteria evaluate (i) the clinical outcomes realized versus currently available alternatives and the current standard of care, in part determined by the quantity and quality of published evidence supporting outcomes, (ii) adverse effects or toxicities associated with the therapeutic, (iii) overall cost effectiveness versus alternatives (medical or surgical), and (iv) burden or benefit to the health system overall from the use of the specific therapeutics.

Unfortunately, these scales are not created consistently across sources, they reference different portions of the published literature, and they use different data and measures for economic or financial analyses. This should not dissuade any company from advancing, however, as each contracting health system, payer, or health authority will have its preferred measures and likely be consistent in their use of those. Also, there is a finite number of data sources that can be used and the composite metrics will vary only in the factors they choose to integrate. What it does demand is that companies have access to rich sets of real-world data, evidence-based processes, and analytics-supported strategies.

Most of these value metrics are focused on classically defined clinical evidence from randomized clinical studies and costs of formal clinical care. These miss patient and family outcomes that may be material to an individual's or family's well-being and productivity. They miss the broadening role patients are having in making decisions as to their own care. They do not focus on the economics of the patient's life and the material impact therapeutic and care management processes may have for them. While there is significant progress being made by groups like Patient-Centered Outcomes Research Institute and others, we believe this area could experience the broadest change as device, sensor, and other home hub data become more broadly available, consumer-centric health companies emerge (e.g., Digitals Gone Healthcare), and consumers themselves are more responsible financially and for overall care management.

Notes

INTRODUCTION

1. For a definition of post-approval studies, see: www.fda.gov/MedicalDevices/ DeviceRegulationandGuidance/PostmarketRequirements/PostApprova Studies/ucm135263.htm.
2. Definitions of real-world data and evidence vary. For a discussion, see: http:// social.eyeforpharma.com/column/reality-behind-real-world-data-and- real-world-evidence and https://www.ispor.org/News/articles/Oct07/RLD .asp.
3. As an example, consider Watson Health on the occasion of its acquisition of Emerge (www.radiologybusiness.com/topics/imaging-informatics/q-ibm-s- kyu-rhee-about-watson-merge-healthcare-and-future?nopaging=1) where Kyu Rhee, MD, Watson chief health officer, comments, "The key is to leverage Watson, the cognitive computing system that can see images and can continuously learn and can connect to the evidence that changes every day, because there's always new studies and new journal articles. It's seemingly impossible for any doctor or for any person to go through all of that data and to mine it for those smart insights on their own."

4. As an example of the changes underway, see Novartis's actions in support of its breakthrough heart failure therapy, www.reuters.com/article/2015/06/30/us-novartis-heart-idUSKCN0PA1N720150630 and www.washingtonpost.com/news/to-your-health/wp/2015/07/08/new-once-in-a-decade-novartis-drug-for-heart-failure-approved-by-fda-faq/ where it considers new reimbursement approaches linked to outcomes and deploying remote monitoring.

5. See the seminal article on the difference between payment for services based on a salary (input) versus a piece-rate (output or outcomes) by Edward Lazear, Stanford University, Hoover Institute, *The Journal of Business* 59, no. 3 (July 1986): 405-431; published by The University of Chicago Press; www.jstor.org/stable/2352711; further validated in 2000 in Edward P. Lazear, "Performance Pay and Productivity," *The American Economic Review* 90, no. 5 (December 2000): 134–1361, published by American Economic Association; URL: www.jstor.org/stable/2677854.

6. For an excellent definition of comorbidities and the implications for selection of clinical treatment and care management approaches, see: www.ncbi.nlm.nih.gov/pmc/articles/PMC2713155/.

7. For a model that integrates all therapeutics into individually distributed packets, see: PillPak (www.forbes.com/sites/sarahhedgecock/2015/04/15/this-pharmacy-startup-wants-to-change-the-way-you-take-your-medicine/).

8. Medication errors most often occur because the full set of therapeutics taken are not fully known to an individual prescribing physician and taken into account for a new treatment decision—coordination and information are key to avoiding errors. For background, see: www.ahrq.gov/patients-consumers/care-planning/errors/20tips/index.html and www.mayoclinic.org/healthy-lifestyle/consumer-health/in-depth/medication-errors/art-20048035.

CHAPTER 1: WHY AND HOW THE HEALTHCARE INDUSTRY IS CHANGING SO RAPIDLY

1. www.dailyrecord.com/story/money/business/2014/11/23/health-care-industry-mergers-acquisitions-surge/19446087/.

2. There are significant numbers of private health insurer consolidations underway in the United States: www.wsj.com/articles/doj-girds-for-strict-scrutiny-of-health-insurer-mergers-1435524588?cb=logged0.0906966736074537. For example, Aetna and Humana: www.nytimes.com/2015/07/04/business/dealbook/aetna-agrees-to-acquire-humana-for-37-billion-in-cash-and-stock.html?_r=0; and Centene and HealthNet: www.wsj.com/articles/centene-to-buy-health-net-for-6-3-billion-1435835955.

3. One example of performance-based therapeutics reimbursement in oncology: http://lab.express-scripts.com/insights/drug-options/we-have-to-change-how-we-pay-for-cancer-drugs and www.fiercepharma.com/story/express-scripts-pushes-pay-performance-cut-cancer-drug-prices/2015-05-27.

4. http://medicaleconomics.modernmedicine.com/medical-economics/news/modernmedicine/modern-medicine-feature-articles/payers-buying-practices-what-?page=full.

5. https://developer.apple.com/healthkit/.

6. www.wsj.com/articles/google-abbvie-announce-research-partnership-1409764830.

7. In 2002 and then in subsequent rulings campaign reform was put into place. Originally sponsored by Senators Russell Feingold (D-WI) and John McCain (R-AZ), it revised legal limits of expenditures set in 1974, and prohibited unregulated contributions to national political parties. www.ctn.state.ct.us/civics/campaign_finance/Support%20Materials/CTN%20CFR%20Timeline.pdf.

8. Regarding Dodd-Frank, summaries, discussions, and references on this include: www.banking.senate.gov/public/_files/070110_Dodd_Frank_Wall_Street_Reform_comprehensive_summary_Final.pdf and www.investopedia.com/ask/answers/13/dodd-frank-act-affect-me.asp; Basel II was also adopted at the same time to provide a global, voluntary regulatory framework on bank capital adequacy, stress testing, and market liquidity risk. See: www.bis.org/bcbs/basel3/b3summarytable.pdf.

9. See CPI data from the Bureau of Labor Statistics: www.gpo.gov/fdsys/pkg/ERP-2013/pdf/ERP-2013-table60.pdf. Over the last decade and a half, medical inflation—the cost of inputs and services—trends much higher than general inflation rates and Consumer Price Index net of medical costs: www.cnbc.com/2015/05/22/medical-cost-inflation-highest-level-in-8-years.html; www.bloomberg.com/news/articles/2012-05-21/health care-costs-rise-faster-than-u-s-inflation-rate and www.aon.com/attachments/human-capital-consulting/2015_Global_Medical_Trend_Rate_Survey_Report_2015_01.pdf.

10. For a discussion of the current capacity and the relationships between different fee-for-service reimbursement approaches, see: Laurence Baker, PhD, *The Challenge of Health System Capacity Growth*, Stanford University, National Institute for Health Care Management Foundation: www.nihcm.org/pdf/CapacityBrief-FINAL.pdf; for an assessment of inpatient capacity coming from the former fee-for-service reimbursement in contrast with office and ambulatory facilities required for performance-based agreements, see: www.modernhealthcare.com/article/20120324/MAGAZINE/303249963.

11. Note that in the United States healthcare reform may create a capacity deficit in future years. There are some forecasts that family practice, pediatrics, internal medicine, geriatric psychiatrists, and women's health may be in short supply. There is also a view that the retirement of significant numbers of physicians in other subspecialties, such as oncology, may create new shortages in future years. In contrast, some studies show that new healthcare management and staff models (e.g., remote monitoring) will change the profile of requirements and demand, for example: https://iom.nationalacademies.org/~/media/Files/Activity%20Files/Workforce/Nursing/Health%20Care%20System%20Reform%20and%20the%20Nursing%20Workforce.pdf.

12. Guide to NHS waiting times: www.nhs.uk/choiceinthenhs/rightsandpledges/waitingtimes/pages/guidepercent20topercent20waitingpercent20times.aspx.

13. WHO Guide to Drugs and Therapeutics Committees: http://apps.who.int/medicinedocs/pdf/s4882e/s4882e.pdf; see also Spanish PTC: www.ncbi.nlm.nih.gov/pmc/articles/PMC4096492/.

14. O. Shavit, "Utilization of Health Technologies—Do Not Look Where There Is a Light; Shine Your Light Where There Is a Need to Look! Relating National Health Goals with Resource Allocation Decision-Making; Illustration through Examining the Israeli Healthcare System," *Health Policy*, 92, nos. 2–3 (2009): 268–275.

15. Review of the Health Technology Assessment program in the United Kingdom for *The Lancet*: www.thelancet.com/journals/lancet/article/PIIS0140-6736(13)61724-9/abstract.

16. Discussion of positives and negatives of past healthcare reimbursement models covering the features of capitated models of reimbursement in detail. For a survey, see: www.ncbi.nlm.nih.gov/pmc/articles/PMC1495203/; http://content.healthaffairs.org/content/29/9/1661.full; and www.hcfe.research.va.gov/docs/2012_frakt_capitation_ha.pdf.

17. Examples include: www.cdc.gov/nchs/data_access/ftp_data.htm; www.data.gov/health/; http://ec.europa.eu/health/indicators/echi/index_en.htm; http://data.worldbank.org/topic/health; https://www.nlm.nih.gov/hsrinfo/datasites.html.

18. https://www.cms.gov/Regulations-and-guidance/legislation/EHRIncentivePrograms/DataAndReports.html.

19. See the Health and Human Services publication of the ACA: www.hhs.gov/healthcare/rights/law/index.html and the *New England Journal of Medicine* "Progress Report" on the same: www.nejm.org/doi/full/10.1056/NEJMhpr1405667.

20. www.washingtonpost.com/news/to-your-health/wp/2015/04/23/surgeon-general-vivek-murthy-wants-to-move-u-s-health-care-toward-a-prevention-based-society/.

21. http://healthaffairs.org/blog/2015/05/05/the-health-reform-landscape-medicare-payment-scorecard/.

22. J. M. McWilliams, "Performance Differences in Year 1 of Pioneer Accountable Care Organizations": www.nejm.org/doi/full/10.1056/NEJMsa1414929; www.hhs.gov/news/press/2015pres/05/20150504a.html; and D. J. Nyweide, W. Lee, T. T. Cuerdon, et al., "Association of Pioneer Accountable Care Organizations vs. Traditional Medicare Fee for Service with Spending, Utilization, and Patient Experience," *JAMA* 313, no. 21 (2015): 2152–2161. DOI:10.1001/jama.2015.4930.

23. See the IHI's concept design document: www.ihi.org/Engage/Initiatives/TripleAim/Documents/ConceptDesign.pdf.

24. www.washingtonpost.com/news/to-your-health/wp/2015/04/23/surgeongeneral-vivek-murthy-wants-to-move-u-s-health-care-toward-a-preventionbased-society/.

25. The United Kingdom is advancing rapidly in their healthcare reforms: www.careukhealthcare.com/our-services/clinical-assessment-and-treatment-services-cats.

www.hsj.co.uk/comment/the-independent-sector-can-help-the-nhs-invest-in-new-care-models/5083093.article#.VV8nC8t0yM8.

www.hsj.co.uk/comment/the-independent-sector-can-help-the-nhs-invest-in-new-care-models/5083093.article#.VV8nC8t0yM8.

www.theguardian.com/society/2014/nov/19/private-firms-nhs-contracts-circle-healthcare-bupa-virgin-care-care-uk.

www.theguardian.com/society/2015/apr/25/far-more-nhs-contracts-going-to-private-firms-than-ministers-admit-privatisation.

www.bbc.com/news/election-2015-32538789.

www.careukhealthcare.com/our-services/clinical-assessment-and-treatment-services-cats.

www.theguardian.com/uk-news/2014/jul/02/cancer-care-nhs-outsourcing-ccgs-unison-virgin.

www.hsj.co.uk/home/commissioning/exclusive-new-nhs-company-reveals-outcomes-based-targets/5084915.article.

www.nationalhealthexecutive.com/Inspection-and-Regulation/monitor-launches-investigation-into-trust-finances.

www.hah.co.uk/.

www.medtechcentre.co.uk/news/.

www.abpi.org.uk/our-work/library/guidelines/Documents/joint_working_with_the_pharmaceutical_industry.pdf.

www.healthimpact.org.uk/content/resources/z154_modelling_the_burden_of_cv_disease.pdf.

www.hqip.org.uk/assets/NCAPOP-Library/NCAPOP-2013-14/UCL-HF-2013-Report-2013-ONLINE-v2.pdf/.

www.england.nhs.uk/wp-content/uploads/2014/10/5yfv-web.pdf.

www.gponline.com/nhs-branded-drug-spend-capped-deal/article/1219825.

26. Again see: www.ncbi.nlm.nih.gov/pmc/articles/PMC3243126/pdf/1347_amia_2011_proc.pdf and http://esante.gouv.fr/en/asip-sante.

27. For a summary of reforms in France, see:

Health Systems in Transition (HiT) profile of France, European Observatory on Health Systems & Policies (www.hspm.org/countries/france25062012/countrypage.aspx).

"Managing Chronic Conditions: Experience in 8 Countries," European Observatory on Health Systems & Policies, 2008: (www.euro.who.int/__data/assets/pdf_file/0008/98414/E92058.pdf).

Healthways Awarded Contract to Expand National Chronic Disease Management Program in France and France's Overseas Territories, *Reuters*, April 7, 2011: www.reuters.com/article/2011/04/07/idUS226778+07-Apr-2011+BW20110407.

T. Saudubray, C. Saudubray, C. Vibaud, G. Jondeau, A. J. Valleron, A. Flahault, and T. Hanslik, "Prevalence and Management of Heart Failure in France: National Study among General Practitioners of the Sentinelles Network," *Rev Med Interne* 26, no. 11 (2005): 845–850.

D. Malaquin and C. Tribouilloy, "Epidemiology of Heart Failure," *Rev Prat*, 60, no. 7 (2010): 911–915.

Referentiel de couts, Donnees 2009, Classification V11c. (www.atih.sante.fr/openfile.php?id=3389).

"A New Era of Reimbursement in France," Eyeforpharma, March 19, 2014, http://social.eyeforpharma.com/market-access/new-era-reimbursement-france.

28. For Spain please reference:

Rafael Vázquez García (coordinator) et al., *Insuficiencia cardiaca [Recurso electrónico]: proceso asistencial integrado.* 2ª ed. Sevilla: Consejería de Salud y Bienestar Social, 2012.

J. F. Delgado et al., *Rev Esp Cardiol.* 67, no. 8 (2014): 643–650.

www.simon-kucher.com/sites/default/files/simon-kucher_partners_healthcare_insights_2013-1.pdf.

www.farmaindustria.es/idc/groups/public/documents/publicaciones/farma_119462.pdf.

www.biomedcentral.com/1472-6963/10/153.

M. I. Anguita Sánchez, M. G. Crespo Leiro, E. de Teresa Galván, M. Jiménez Navarro, L. Alonso-Pulpón, and J. Muñiz García, "Prevalence of Heart Failure in the Spanish General Population Aged over 45 Years. The PRICE Study." *Rev Esp Cardiol* 61, no. 10 (2008): 1041–1049 (www.ncbi.nlm.nih.gov/pubmed/18817680).

H. Mendoza, M. Jesus Martín, A. García, F. Aros, F. Aizpuru, J. Regalado De Los Cobos, M. Concepción Belló, P. Lopetegui, and J. M. Cia, "'Hospital at Home' Care Model as an Effective Alternative in the Management of Decompensated Chronic Heart Failure," *European Journal of Heart Failure* 11 (2009): 1208–1213, doi:10.1093/eurjhf/hfp143.

29. See: www.irekia.euskadi.eus/en/news/2366-sarean-osakidetza-basque-health-service-channels-the-multi-channel-health-services-centre-unveiled, www.osasun.ejgv.euskadi.net/, and www.nll.se/publika/lg/kom/Evenemang/ALEC/Presentations%20Speakers/Jesus%20Maria%20Fernandez_ALEC%202014.pdf.

30. For a full explanation of the power and value of registries with population-scale electronic medical record data and in support of population analytics, see: T. A. Workman, *Engaging Patients in Information Sharing and Data Collection: The Role of Patient-Powered Registries and Research Networks* [Internet]. Rockville, MD: Agency for Healthcare Research and Quality (US), September 2013. Available from: www.ncbi.nlm.nih.gov/books/NBK164513/.

31. For a range of models and reforms emerging in Sweden, see:

www.hjart-lungfonden.se/Sjukdomar/Hjartsjukdomar/Hjartsvikt/&prev=search.

http://ki.se/en/lime/value-based-health-care.

www.dssnet.dk/f/f1/Value-based-reimbursement-and-experiences-from-Sweden.-Jonas-Wolin.pdf.

www.ehma.org/files/17.00%20Birger%20Carl%20Forsberg%200068.ppt.

Numbers estimated from data obtained from A. Barasa, M. Schaufelberger, G. Lappas, K. Swedberg, M. Dellborg, and A. Rosengren, "Heart Failure in Young Adults: 20-Year Trends in Hospitalization, Aetiology, and Case Fatality in Sweden," *European Heart Journal* 35, no. 1 (2014). Data obtained from B. Agvall, T. Paulsson, M. Foldevi, U. Dahlström, and U. Alehagen, "Resource Use and Cost Implications of Implementing a Heart Failure Program for Patients with Systolic Heart Failure in Swedish Primary Health Care," *International Journal of Cardiology* 176, no. 3 (2014): 731–738. Estimates based on B. Agvall, L. Borgquist, M. Foldevi, and U. Dahlstrüm, "Cost of Heart Failure in Swedish Primary Healthcare," *Scandinavian Journal of Primary Health Care* 23, no. 4 (2005): 227–232.

www.stockholm-network.org/downloads/publications/Capturing_Value.pdf.

https://www.postkodlotteriet.se/Formanstagare/Vara-formanstagare/ Formanstagarorganisation/HjartLungfonden.htm&prev=search.

www.wsj.com/articles/ SB10001424052702303603904579491971221879580.

https://www.bcg.com/documents/file64538.pdf.

www.medtecheurope.org/newsletternews/339/86.

www.ucr.uu.se/rikssvikt-en/index.php/regarding-s-hfr/7-about-the-swedish-heart-failure-registry.

32. See: www.hbs.edu/faculty/Publication%20Files/20100604RandSIFINAL_ b4e1d82c-1410-4152-bea6-d5d17a112fcb.pdf; http://effectivehealthcare .ahrq.gov/ index.cfm/search-for-guides-reviews-and reports/?pageaction= displayproduct&productid=1234; and Accenture research.

33. See King v. Burwell; Supreme Court of the United States, King et al. v. Burwell, Secretary of Health & Human Services, et al.; Certiorari to the United States Court of Appeals for the Fourth Circuit; No. 14–114; argued March 4, 2015—decided June 25, 2015.

34. For more details on recent progress and the impact of electronic medical records and Health Information Exchanges in practice, see: https://www .accenture.com/t20150523T024232__w__/us-en/_acnmedia/Accenture/ Conversion-Assets/DotCom/Documents/Global/PDF/Dualpub_14/ Accenture-Doctors-Survey-2015-US-Infographic.pdf.

35. A full summary of the status of these programs' market penetration can be read with data files accessed at: https://www.cms.gov/Regulations-and-guidance/legislation/EHRIncentivePrograms/DataAndReports.html.

CHAPTER 2: STRATEGIC CHOICES NO HEALTHCARE COMPANY CAN AVOID

1. Value dossiers can come in different forms but typically provide an integrated information resource of evidence of the clinical, economic, and patient-reported outcomes value for a new therapeutic, device, or intervention relative to the absolute cost and illness burden of that disease.

2. See the collaboration agreement between Merck & Co. and Maccabi Health System as one example: www.mercknewsroom.com/news-release/maccabi/merck-and-israels-maccabi-healthcare-leverage-unique-real-world-database-inform and www.informationweek.com/healthcare/clinical-information-systems/big-data-better-health-tracking/d/d-id/1111839?; another example involves a medical device manufacturer, Boston Scientific, and the real-world health data analytic subsidiary of United Healthcare in an initiative focused on heart failure patients: www.massdevice.com/boston-scientific-seeks-heart-failure-innovation-partnership-with-optum-labs/.

3. One example of such an initiative is Novartis International AG and Qualcomm Life, Inc., which together are exploring how these technologies can change clinical trial design and make the trials more comparable to real-world settings: www.xconomy.com/san-diego/2015/01/15/qualcomm-novartis-deal-portends-wave-of-clinical-trial-innovation/.

4. http://techcrunch.com/2015/06/23/googles-new-health-wearable-delivers-constant-patient-monitoring/.

5. See: https://www.cerner.com/Solutions/Research/Personalized_Health/; and www.geneinsight.com/background for two examples of initiatives from an Electronic Medical Record application and solutions provider and healthcare delivery system respectively. See an integrated and collaborative model for healthcare professions to manage the transition of patients from acute to non-acute and home settings: www.healthcare.philips.com/main/about/news/articles/2014/salesforce.wpd.

6. For example, a back-office process and data management integration between a large healthcare provider system and health insurer: www.unitedhealthgroup.com/newsroom/articles/feed/optum/2013/1014optum360launch.aspx?sc_lang =en. In another example, these same organizations created a value-analysis and procurement organization called SharedClarity: www.modernhealthcare.com/article/20121013/MAGAZINE/310139972.

7. A summary of these expectations is in recent Accenture patient survey research: www.accenture.com/us-en/insight-great-expectations-why-pharma-companies-cant-ignore-patient-services-survey.aspx, https://www.accenture.com/us-en/insight-accenture-consumer-survey-patient-engagement-summary.aspx, and https://www.accenture.com/us-en/insight-patient-services-survey-unmet-needs.

8. For many common procedures, such as a coronary artery bypass graft (or CABG) or total hip and knee replacement, reimbursement is at a fixed rate to the healthcare provider. The same is true of childbirth, where a normal vaginal delivery is a fixed reimbursement in most U.S. states. Costs of therapeutics and medical/surgical consumables used are borne under this single rate.

9. Increasingly value-based reimbursement contracts require healthcare providers to evaluate what specific services are provided to which patients to achieve population health quality, outcomes, and financial goals. Rarely is this specific to an individual patient but increasingly this is assigned to a population. This means that economics and medical decisions increasingly come together—providers have to ensure that the allocation of resources across a population is efficient and most appropriate for the whole *and* the individual.

10. For a recent summary of financial incentive impacts on hospital acquired infections, see: www.medscape.com/viewarticle/847199; older analyses corroborate this: https://www.cms.gov/mmrr/Downloads/MMRR2013_003_03_a08 .pdf and http://dx.doi.org/10.5600/mmrr.003.03.a08.

11. This is a very carefully balanced process. The goal is to ensure that the patient is provided the anti-infective combination at the right time to control and resolve the infection while staying within the goals of avoiding broad use that may contribute to resistant bacteria. See: www.tha.org/HealthCareProviders/ AboutTHA/PressRoom/InfectionRateDropHi0967/index.asp; and http:// journals.plos.org/plosone/article?id=10.1371/journal.pone.0023137.

12. There is emerging work in applying predictive analytics to the challenge of hospital infections and infection control: https://www.healthcatalyst.com/ using_healthcare_data_to_optimize_clinician_time/.

13. The following section is derived from a detailed Accenture Strategy study completed in June 2015 entitled "Value Creation through Digitization in the Pharmaceutical Industry" led by Jan Ising, Clemens Oertel, Christine Knackfuss, and Isabelle Heiber.

CHAPTER 3: OLD MODELS AND NEW

1. www.forbes.com/sites/brookecrothers/2015/07/13/tesla-most-popular-u-s-electric-vehicle in-q1-while-norway-leads-globally-says-ihs/; www.cheatsheet .com/automobiles/will-tesla-break-the-electric-vehicle-sales-record-in-2015 .html/?a=viewall; and http://cleantechnica.com/2015/04/06/us-electric-car-sales-no-surprises-tesla-model-s-nissan-leaf-bmw-i3-on-top-again/.

2. Historically the industry focused on a concept of the "blockbuster" or "super blockbuster," generally viewed as a therapeutic with over $1 billion in annual revenues, increasing through the years to being more than $2.5 billion in annual revenues. While these began as largely low-molecular weight or "chemical entities," they soon became biotechnology-based and incorporated biologics. During much of the 1990s and early 2000s the second or third entry into a "blockbuster" therapeutic category with a modest positive differentiation generated the highest performance. These strategies were based on the reimbursement and payment mechanisms at that time and predicated on operating models that emphasized commercial scale and scope as key performance enablers. See "Quest for the Best," *Nature Reviews Drug Discovery* 2 (October 2003): 838–841. doi:10.1038/nrd1203. Also, see: Bruce L. Booth Jr., Maria A. Gordian, Jeb E. Keiper, and Rodney W. Zemmel, "The Right Dose of Risk, Pharma Companies Focus Too Much on the Highly Risky Development of Novel Drugs," *The McKinsey Quarterly* 2, no. 4 (2002).

3. Over-the-counter therapeutics were typically those that once were prescribed, reached or approached patent expiry, and then were offered as a branded, consumer-accessible therapeutic that did not require a prescription.

Examples of these include Nexium® for gastric distress and Allegra® for allergy management.

4. WellDoc BlueStar® Diabetes management application is prescribed by a health provider and reimbursed by selected health insurers. It is available on the Google and Apple app stores in assurance of wide accessibility. See: www.welldoc.com.

5. Reimbursement approaches are becoming far more complicated with specialty therapeutics and increased use of biologics administered in physician offices or ambulatory sites. An excellent summary is P.M. Danzon, "Pricing and Reimbursement of Biopharmaceuticals and Medical Devices in the USA," *Encyclopedia of Health Economics*, Volume 3, Philadelphia, PA: University of Pennsylvania, 2014. doi:10.1016/B978-0-12-375678-7.01209-8.

6. For example, value-contracting, performance contracting, outcomes contracting, and so on.

7. Formally known as the National Institute for Health and Care Excellence. See: www.nice.org.uk/.

8. Center for Medicare & Medicaid Innovation (the Innovation Center). See: www.innovation.cms.gov/.

9. https://www.accenture.com/us-en/insight-patient-services-survey-unmet-needs.aspx.

10. For an early but still relevant and provocative overview of value and population health, see: Michael E. Porter, PhD, "What Is Value in Health Care?" *N Engl J Med* 363 (December 23, 2010): 2477–2481. doi:10.1056/NEJMp1011024; a more contemporary presentation is at William J. Kassler, MD, MPH, Naomi Tomoyasu, PhD, and Patrick H. Conway, MD, "Beyond a Traditional Payer — CMS's Role in Improving Population Health," *N Engl J Med* 372 (January 8, 2015): 109-111. doi:10.1056/NEJMp1406838.

11. In mid-2015, ExpressScripts announced its plans to differentiate reimbursement for the same therapeutic in different diseases based on the results realized: www.wsj.com/articles/new-push-ties-cost-of-drugs-to-how-well-they-work-1432684755.

12. See Accenture Higher Performance Business studies, 2012 and 2013: https://www.accenture.com/t20150523T061911__w__/us-en/_acnmedia/Accenture/Conversion-Assets/Microsites/Documents3/Accenture-Life-Sciences-Beyond-The-Patent-Cliff-Signs-Of-Recovery-in-Biopharmas-New-Normal.pdf; https://www.accenture.com/us-en/blogs/blogs-accenture-biopharma-high-performance-business-research-key-finding-1.aspx.

13. All of our Around-the-Patient Innovators are highly ranked within the American Association for the Advancement of Science employers survey: http://sciencecareers.sciencemag.org/career_magazine/previous_issues/articles/2014_10_17/science.opms.r1400147.

14. For examples, see: www.healthcare.philips.com/main/about/news/articles/2014/salesforce.wpd; http://newsroom.gehealthcare.com/precision-medicine-makes-the-presidential-primetime/; and www.gereports.com/post/115324685665/shooting-disease-with-silver-bullets-ge-ventures.

15. For example, the highest value corporation in the world is Apple, coming from their advanced and pervasive platforms and ecosystem of content, applications, and devices.

16. For example, in the New England region of the United States, Partners HealthCare has an operating unit know as Neighborhood Health Plan that offers Medicaid and private insurance products on the Massachusetts insurance exchange or "Connector." Similarly, large regional systems such as University of Pittsburgh Medical Center (UPMC) offer coverage for the region in which they offer services. There are, of course, legacy models such as Kaiser and Geisinger.

CHAPTER 4: LEAN INNOVATORS

1. *British Journal of Clinical Pharmacology* 70 (September 2010), no. 3: 335–341. doi:10.1111/j.1365-2125.2010.03718.x; www.ncbi.nlm.nih.gov/pmc/articles/PMC2949903/ and www.imshealth.com/imshealth/Global/Content/Document/Market_Measurement_TL/Generic_Medicines_GA.pdf.

2. Each year, more than 2.6 billion prescriptions are filled in the United States using generic drugs. Compare that amount with approximately 1.2 billion brand-name prescriptions dispensed each year. www.fda.gov/downloads/AboutFDA/Transparency/Basics/UCM226568.pdf.

3. In the 1930s, Salomon, Levin, and Elstein opened a small pharmaceutical plant called Assia (Aramaic for doctor) in Petah Tikva; Zori (Hebrew for health) was founded in Tel Aviv; and Teva was established by Dr. Gunter Friedlander in Jerusalem. See history at: www.tevapharm.com/about/history/.

4. These are generally "low-molecular-weight therapeutics," as they are usually less than 900 daltons; as such, they are also called "small molecule" medicines. Formulated in most cases as an oral therapy, in pills, they are designed to regulate or stimulate a normal biological process.

5. Health systems also experienced an enormous benefit due to the range of highly efficacious therapeutics hitting patent expiry or failing patent challenges and thereby going generic. This benefit took the form of an increased ability to make needed therapies available to a wide range of patients at a more affordable cost.

6. The drugs that were easily replicated as generics are known as "low-molecular-weight therapeutics." They are generally less than 900 daltons and are referred to as "small molecule" medicines. Biologics are not low-molecular-weight therapeutics and do not play to the manufacturing and commercial capabilities of the classic generics company.

7. The same practices apply to other common categories such as routine antibiotics and anti-infectives. For the trends in this area, see: www.forbes.com/sites/greatspeculations/2014/05/29/with-the-highest-generic-purchasing-power-walgreen-to-benefit-from-rising-generic-sales/, www.imshealth.com/imshealth/Global/Content/Corporate/IMS%20Health%20Institute/Insights/Understanding_Pharmaceutical_Value_Chain.pdf,

http://medcitynews.com/2011/04/generic-wave-to-drive-cardinal-healths-profitability-in-coming-years/, https://www.ftc.gov/system/files/attachments/us-submissions-oecd-other-international-competition-fora/pharmaceuticals_us_oecd.pdf, and http://blueshiftideas.com/reports/051401GenericDrugJointPurchasingWillSqueezeManufacturers.pdf.

8. ExpressScripts Drug Trend Report 2015: http://lab.express-scripts.com/drug-trend-report/.

9. http://fortune.com/2015/10/25/valeant-bill-ackman-hedge-funds-losses/

10. Sources: www.cnbc.com/2015/10/26/valeant-we-are-in-full-compliance-committee-to-review-allegations.html; www.reuters.com/article/2015/10/26/us-valeant-pharmacies-idUSKCN0SK1FZ20151026; www.bloomberg.com/news/articles/2015-10-26/valeant-ceo-s-outsider-roots-spun-market-gold-until-they-didn-t.

11. Source: www.wsj.com/articles/valeant-raises-full-year-guidance-after-topping-third-quarter-projections-1445250887.

12. A *Forbes* article from February 27, 2015 notes that an Elsevier research report sampled 4421 drug groups, of which 222 drug groups increased in price by 100 percent or more (between November 2013 and November 2014). There were outlier cases (17 drug groups) where price increases of more than 1000% were noted. One example was the commonly prescribed therapeutic bacterial infective, tetracycline, where the per-tablet price increased from $0.0345 to $2.3632, or 67-fold, over the same one-year time period. See: www.forbes.com/sites/greatspeculations/2015/02/27/why-are-generic-drug-prices-shooting-up/; www.drugchannels.net/2014/08/retail-generic-drug-inflation-reaches.html.

13. For full coverage of an audit of a PBM contract done by Pharmacy Outcomes Specialists, which represents companies, managed care organizations, unions, and government agencies, see: http://www.usatoday.com/story/money/personalfinance/2014/03/03/pharmacy-benefit-managers-healthcare-costs-savings/5495317/.

14. For an overview, see the *Wall Street Journal*, November 6, 2015: www.wsj.com/articles/lilly-merck-receive-inquiries-from-justice-dept-over-drug-pricing-1446828214. Additionally, see: http://fortune.com/2015/11/20/merck-ceo-drug-prices-turing/.

15. For more details on the acquisition and pricing see: www.nytimes.com/2015/09/21/business/a-huge-overnight-increase-in-a-drugs-price-raises-protests.html?_r=0 and www.forbes.com/sites/luketimmerman/2015/09/23/a-timeline-of-the-turing-pharma-controversy/. For more detail on Turing, see: http//www.cnbc.com/2015/12/23/turing-pharma-seeks-ceo-to-replace-martin-shkreli-plans-job-cuts.html and http://www.nytimes.com/2015/12/18/business/shkreli-fraud-charges.html?_r=0.

16. Coverage of the U.S. Senate Special Committee is available at: www.dailymail.co.uk/wires/ap/article-3303726/Senate-panel-seeks-information-4-drug-companies.html.

17. For the full results of the Kasier health poll from October 28, 2015, see: http://kff.org/health-costs/poll-finding/kaiser-health-tracking-poll-october-

2015/ and http://files.kff.org/attachment/topline-methodology-kaiser-health-tracking-poll-october-2015.

18. Source: www.wsj.com/articles/actavis-changes-name-to-allergan-after-deal-for-botox-maker-1434370774.

19. Source: www.cnbc.com/2015/07/27/israels-teva-pharmaceutical-to-buy-allergans-generic-pharmaceuticals-business.html. Pfizer and Allergan announced in November 2015 that the companies will combine in a stock transaction valued at $363.63 per Allergan share, for a total enterprise value of approximately $160 billion. See: http://fortune.com/2015/11/23/pfizer-allergan-merger/.

20. See: http://social.eyeforpharma.com/commercial/top-five-pharma-stories-2015-0, http://www.wsj.com/articles/pfizer-allergan-on-cusp-of-merger-deal-1448217490, http://www.forbes.com/sites/antoinegara/2015/11/23/pfizer-and-allergan-merger-ranks-as-biggest-ever-pharmaceutical-deal/, and http://www.newyorker.com/news/john-cassidy/the-pfizer-allergan-merger-is-a-disgrace. (Pfizer, as this book went to press, was pursuing a merger with Allergan/Actavis to leverage its portfolio and management team, and pursue tax inversion benefits.)

21. Their growth is in part aided by the circumstances of current financial markets, that is, the accessibility of capital, the relative low cost of debt, and the geographies that allow them low effective tax rates. Stated differently, current financial market and tax strategies are allowing them a cost of capital that aids their acquisition and integration strategies. Changing circumstances or policies could turn that advantage into a source of vulnerability—but for the present these companies have optimized their location and financing approaches to the context and options available. www.bloomberg.com/politics/articles/2015-07-30/tax-savings-drove-valeant-burger-king-deals-senate-report-says, www.bloomberg.com/news/articles/2013-05-21/actavis-lowers-tax-rate-to-17-after-warner-chilcott-deal, and www.investorsalley.com/top-3-ways-to-profit-from-the-tax-inversion-craze/.

22. Already there are early moves by the Lean Innovators to overhaul their operating infrastructure and capabilities through critical partnerships. A leading early example is Teva and IBM's Watson Health (www.genengnews.com/gen-news-highlights/ibm-watson-health-opens-hq-launches-partnerships/81251718/ and https://www-03.ibm.com/press/us/en/pressrelease/47632.wss), where Teva is working with IBM Watson Health Cloud to use real-world data and advanced analytics to understand complex and chronic conditions such as asthma, pain, migraine, and neurodegenerative diseases. In addition, a joint Teva–IBM Research team will deploy Big Data and machine learning technology to create disease models and advanced therapeutic solutions. "Teva is actively exploring the e-health evolution with a strong focus on fulfilling unmet and emerging patients' needs," said Guy Hadari, SVP and CIO for Teva Pharmaceutical Industries Ltd., on September 10, 2015, in a joint IBM and Teva statement (https://www-03.ibm.com/press/us/en/pressrelease/47632.wss) looking to "put the best information and insights in the hands of physicians, care teams and patients, to empower treatment optimization for individuals and populations across the spectrum of acute and chronic conditions."

23. http://ir.valeant.com/investor-relations/events-and-presentations/Event-Details/2015/JP-Morgan-2015-Healthcare-Conference/default.aspx.

24. Biosimilars are officially defined as a type of biological product that is approved by the FDA because it is highly similar to an already FDA-approved biological product, known as the biological reference product (reference product), and has been shown to have no clinically meaningful differences from the reference product. See: www.fda.gov/Drugs/DevelopmentApprovalProcess/HowDrugsareDevelopedand Approved/ApprovalApplications/TherapeuticBiologicApplications/Biosimilars/ucm241718.htm.

25. http://news.yahoo.com/novartis-test-pricing-model-heart-failure-drug-131144702--finance.html.

26. http://surescripts.com/about-us/what-we-do.

27. For background, see earlier references and a review of the U.S. market in: http://lab.express-scripts.com/drug-trend-report/.

28. See "Trends in Prescription Drug Use among Adults in the United States from 1999–2012," *JAMA* 314, no. 7 (2015): 1818–1830. doi:10.1001/jama.2015.13766 or http://jama.jamanetwork.com/article.aspx?articleid=2467552. In 2012, 59 percent of Americans 20 years of age and older took at least one prescription therapeutic per day and 15 percent were taking five or more therapeutics. These figures are almost double those from two years prior, in 2000.

29. Topical therapeutics such as Denavir® (Penciclovir) are used for Herpes labialis, costing close to $700 without pharmaceutical benefit payment, with many PBMs suggesting physician prescribe generic valacyclovir or famciclovir.

CHAPTER 5: AROUND-THE-PATIENT INNOVATORS

1. Clay Christensen, Scott Cook, and Taddy Hall, "Marketing Malpractice: The Cause and the Cure," *Harvard Business Review*, December 2005: https://hbr.org/2005/12/marketing-malpractice-the-cause-and-the-cure.

2. http://social.eyeforpharma.com/column/value-innovation-realized-through-services.

3. A good clinical overview of this new breakthrough therapeutic: www.forbes.com/sites/larryhusten/2015/07/07/novartis-heart-failure-drug-gains-speedy-fda-approval/.

4. An excellent summary of heart failure treatment guidelines may be referenced at: www.heart.org/idc/groups/heart-public/@wcm/@hcm/@gwtg/documents/downloadable/ucm_456868.pdf.

5. www.reuters.com/article/2015/06/30/us-novartis-heart-idUSKCN0PA1N720150630.

6. See the full interview with Reuters at: www.reuters.com/article/2015/06/30/us-novartis-heart-idUSKCN0PA1N720150630.

7. The full interview can be read at: www.wsj.com/articles/novartis-looking-at-ways-to-win-over-cost-concerned-health-insurers-1436522314.

8. Also at www.wsj.com/articles/novartis-looking-at-ways-to-win-over-cost-concerned-health-insurers-1436522314.

9. www.forbes.com/sites/matthewherper/2015/04/13/ibm-announces-deals-with-apple-johnson-johnson-and-medtronic-in-bid-to-transform-health-care, www-03.ibm.com/press/us/en/pressrelease/46582.wss.

10. www.bizjournals.com/boston/blog/health-care/2015/04/study-by-biogen-patientslikeme-suggests-wearables.html; www.betaboston.com/news/2015/04/15/biogen-patients-like-me-study-suggests-fitness-trackers-can-help-people-with-multiple-sclerosis/.

11. www.fiercepharmamarketing.com/story/astrazeneca-ponies-heart-attack-patients-new-vida-health-app/2015-07-20.

12. Definitions and policies of secondary versus primary use of clinical data: www.ncbi.nlm.nih.gov/pubmed/20543306; www.healthit.gov/policy-researchers-implementers/secondary-use-ehr-data; https://www.academyhealth.org/files/publications/HIT4AKLegalandPolicy.pdf; and http://skynet.ohsu.edu/~hersh/secondary-use-pr.pdf.

13. Two recent examples of major financial investments by Around-the-Patient Innovators include Roche with Foundation Medicine: www.forbes.com/sites/matthewherper/2015/01/12/roche-spends-1-03-billion-for-majority-stake-in-cancer-genomics-firm/; and Merck and Company's Global Health Innovation Fund's majority investment in Preventice and eCardio: http://mobihealthnews.com/36397/ecardio-preventice-merge-merck-ghi-fund-majority-stakeholder/.

CHAPTER 6: VALUE INNOVATORS

1. Whereas an absence of disease is known a health state, the persistent presence of clinical signs of a specific disease activity with clear underlying biological and symptomatic basis, with or without treatment, is considered a disease state.

2. *Coding* is the formal term for Current Procedural Terminology (CPT). Diagnosis Related Groups are organizations that determine the level of payment that a health provider may receive from an insurance provider for performing a specific activity. See: https://www.cms.gov/Research-Statistics-Data-and-Systems/Statistics-Trends-and-Reports/MedicareFeeforSvcPartsAB/downloads/DRGdesc08.pdf.

3. www.ncbi.nlm.nih.gov/pmc/articles/PMC1487507/; www.cigna.com/healthcare-professionals/resources-for-health-care-professionals/clinical-payment-and-reimbursement-policies/medical-necessity-definitions; www.euro.who.int/__data/assets/pdf_file/0011/119936/E70446.pdf; www.fda.gov/NewsEvents/PublicHealthFocus/ExpandedAccessCompassionateUse/default.htm; and http://iom.nationalacademies.org/~/media/Files/Report%20Files/2011/Clinical-Practice-Guidelines-We-Can-Trust/Clinical%20Practice%20Guidelines%202011%20Insert.pdf.

4. www.tirebusiness.com/article/20120705/NEWS/307059994; www.exhibitoronline.com/corpevent/article.asp?id=1034.

5. A leading provider definition of population health management can be found at: www.partners.org/innovation-and-leadership/population-health-management/;

other relevant coming from healthcare reform at: http://healthaffairs.org/blog/ 2015/04/06/what-are-we-talking-about-when-we-talk-about-population-health/ and https://www.cms.gov/Newsroom/MediaReleaseDatabase/Fact-sheets/2015-Fact-sheets-items/2015-01-26-3.html.

6. Sources:

K. K. Ho, J. L. Pinsky, W. B. Kannel, and D. Levy., "The Epidemiology of Heart Failure: The Framingham Study," *J Am Coll Cardiol* 22 (1993): 6A.

M. R. Cowie, A. Mosterd, D. A. Wood, et al., "The Epidemiology of Heart Failure," *Eur Heart J* 18 (1997): 208.

A. W. Hoes, A. Mosterd, and D. E. Grobbee, "An Epidemic of Heart Failure? Recent Evidence from Europe," *Eur Heart J* 19, Suppl L(1998): L2.

L. Bonneux, J. J. Barendregt, K. Meeter, et al., "Estimating Clinical Morbidity Due to Ischemic Heart Disease and Congestive Heart Failure: The Future Rise of Heart Failure," *Am J Public Health* 84 (1994): 20.

A. Mosterd, J. W. Deckers, A. W. Hoes, et al., "Classification of Heart Failure in Population Based Research: An Assessment of Six Heart Failure Scores, *Eur J Epidemiol* 13 (1997): 491.

V. L. Roger, "The Heart Failure Epidemic," *Int J Environ Res Public Health* 7 (2010): 1807.

A. S. Go, D. Mozaffarian, V. L. Roger, et al., "Heart Disease and Stroke Statistics—2013 Update: A Report from the American Heart Association," *Circulation* 127 (2013): e6.

J. J. McMurray, M. C. Petrie, D. R. Murdoch, and A. P. Davie, "Clinical Epidemiology of Heart Failure: Public and Private Health Burden," *Eur Heart J* 19 Suppl P (1998): P9.

R. S. Vasan, E. J. Benjamin, and D. Levy, "Prevalence, Clinical Features and Prognosis of Diastolic Heart Failure: An Epidemiologic Perspective," *J Am Coll Cardiol* 26 (1995): 1565.

M. M. Redfield, S. J. Jacobsen, J. C. Burnett Jr., et al., "Burden of Systolic and Diastolic Ventricular Dysfunction in the Community: Appreciating the Scope of the Heart Failure Epidemic. *JAMA* 289 (2003): 194.

T. A. McDonagh, C. E. Morrison, A. Lawrence, et al., "Symptomatic and Asymptomatic Left-Ventricular Systolic Dysfunction in an Urban Population," *Lancet* 350 (1997): 829.

J. M. Gardin, D. Siscovick, H. Anton-Culver, et al., "Sex, Age, and Disease Affect Echocardiographic Left Ventricular Mass and Systolic Function in the Free-Living Elderly. The Cardiovascular Health Study," *Circulation* 91 (1995): 1739.

M. S. Lauer, J. C. Evans, and D. Levy, "Prognostic Implications of Subclinical Left Ventricular Dilatation and Systolic Dysfunction in Men Free of Overt Cardiovascular Disease (The Framingham Heart Study)," *Am J Cardiol* 70 (1992): 1180.

G. S. Bleumink, A. M. Knetsch, M. C. Sturkenboom, et al., "Quantifying the Heart Failure Epidemic: Prevalence, Incidence Rate, Lifetime Risk and Prognosis of Heart Failure: The Rotterdam Study," *Eur Heart J* 25 (2004): 1614.

P. A. McCullough, E. F. Philbin, J. A. Spertus, et al., "Confirmation of a Heart Failure Epidemic: Findings from the Resource Utilization Among Congestive Heart Failure (REACH) Study," *J Am Coll Cardiol* 39 (2002): 60.

Writing Group Members, D. Lloyd-Jones, R.J. Adams, et al., "Heart Disease and Stroke Statistics—2010 Update: A Report from the American Heart Association," *Circulation* 121 (2010): e46.

T. E. Owan and M. M. Redfield, "Epidemiology of Diastolic Heart Failure," *Prog Cardiovasc Dis* 47 (2005): 320.

A. M. Brown and J. G. Cleland, "Influence of Concomitant Disease on Patterns of Hospitalization in Patients with Heart Failure Discharged from Scottish Hospitals in 1995," *Eur Heart J* 19 (1998): 1063.

M. Jessup and S. Brozena, "Heart Failure," *N Engl J Med* 348 (2003):2007.

E. J. Topol, T. A. Traill, and N. J. Fortuin, "Hypertensive Hypertrophic Cardiomyopathy of the Elderly," *N Engl J Med* 312 (1985): 277.

W. H. Gaasch, "Diagnosis and Treatment of Heart Failure Based on Left Ventricular Systolic or Diastolic Dysfunction," *JAMA* 271 (1994): 1276.

A. A. Elesber and M. M. Redfield, "Approach to Patients with Heart Failure and Normal Ejection Fraction," *Mayo Clin Proc* 76 (2001): 1047.

R. S. Vasan, M. G. Larson, E. J. Benjamin, et al., "Congestive Heart Failure in Subjects with Normal versus Reduced Left Ventricular Ejection Fraction: Prevalence and Mortality in a Population-Based Cohort," *J Am Coll Cardiol* 33 (1999). 1948.

J. S. Gottdiener, R.L. McClelland, R. Marshall, et al., "Outcome of Congestive Heart Failure in Elderly Persons: Influence of Left Ventricular Systolic Function. The Cardiovascular Health Study," *Ann Intern Med* 137 (2002): 631.

F. Bursi, S. A. Weston, M. M. Redfield, et al., "Systolic and Diastolic Heart Failure in the Community," *JAMA* 296 (2006): 2209.

M. R. Zile and D. L. Brutsaert, "New Concepts in Diastolic Dysfunction and Diastolic Heart Failure: Part I: Diagnosis, Prognosis, and Measurements of Diastolic Function," *Circulation* 105 (2002): 1387.

E. P. Havranek, F. A. Masoudi, K. A. Westfall, et al., "Spectrum of Heart Failure in Older Patients: Results from the National Heart Failure Project," *Am Heart J* 143 (2002): 412.

F. A. Masoudi, E. P. Havranek, G. Smith, et al., "Gender, Age, and Heart Failure with Preserved Left Ventricular Systolic Function," *J Am Coll Cardiol* 41 (2003): 217.

T. E. Owan, D. O. Hodge, R. M. Herges, et al., "Trends in Prevalence and Outcome of Heart Failure with Preserved Ejection Fraction," *N Engl J Med* 355 (2006): 251.

D. M. Lloyd-Jones, M. G. Larson, E. P. Leip, et al., "Lifetime Risk for Developing Congestive Heart Failure: The Framingham Heart Study," *Circulation* 106 (2002): 3068.

F. P. Brouwers, R. A. de Boer, P. van der Harst, et al., "Incidence and Epidemiology of New Onset Heart Failure with Preserved vs. Reduced Ejection Fraction in a Community-Based Cohort: 11-Year Follow-Up of PREVEND," *Eur Heart J* 34 (2013): 1424.

D. Levy, S. Kenchaiah, M. G. Larson, et al., "Long-Term Trends in the Incidence of and Survival with Heart Failure," *N Engl J Med* 347 (2002): 1397.

V. L. Roger, S. A. Weston, M. M. Redfield, et al., "Trends in Heart Failure Incidence and Survival in a Community-Based Population," *JAMA* 292 (2004): 344.

W. H. Barker, J. P. Mullooly, and W. Getchell, "Changing Incidence and Survival for Heart Failure in a Well-Defined Older Population, 1970–1974 and 1990–1994," *Circulation* 113 (2006): 799.

L. H. Curtis, D. J. Whellan, B. G. Hammill, et al., "Incidence and Prevalence of Heart Failure in Elderly Persons, 1994–2003," *Arch Intern Med* 168 (2008): 418.

K. Bibbins-Domingo, M. J. Pletcher, F. Lin, et al., "Racial Differences in Incident Heart Failure among Young Adults," *N Engl J Med* 360 (2009): 1179.

C. M. Wong, N. M. Hawkins, P. S. Jhund, et al., "Clinical Characteristics and Outcomes of Young and Very Young Adults with Heart Failure: The CHARM Programme (Candesartan in Heart Failure Assessment of Reduction in Mortality and Morbidity)," *J Am Coll Cardiol* 62 (2013): 1845.

L. Djoussé, J. A. Driver, and J. M. Gaziano, "Relation between Modifiable Lifestyle Factors and Lifetime Risk of Heart Failure," *JAMA* 302 (2009): 394.

National Heart Lung and Blood Institute, *Morbidity and Mortality Chartbook on Cardiovascular, Lung and Blood Diseases* (Bethesda, MD: NIH, 1996).

P. S. Jhund, K. Macintyre, C. R. Simpson, et al., "Long-Term Trends in First Hospitalization for Heart Failure and Subsequent Survival between 1986 and 2003: A Population Study of 5.1 Million People," *Circulation* 119 (2009): 515.

C. S. Lam, E. Donal, E. Kraigher-Krainer, and R. S. Vasan, "Epidemiology and Clinical Course of Heart Failure with Preserved Ejection Fraction, *Eur J Heart Fail* 13 (2011): 18.

Meta-Analysis Global Group in Chronic Heart Failure (MAGGIC). "The Survival of Patients with Heart Failure with Preserved or Reduced Left Ventricular Ejection Fraction: An Individual Patient Data Meta-Analysis," *Eur Heart J* 33 (2012): 1750.

D. Levy, M. G. Larson, R. S. Vasan, et al., "The Progression from Hypertension to Congestive Heart Failure," *JAMA* 275 (1996): 1557.

W. B. Kannel, K. Ho, and T. Thom, "Changing Epidemiological Features of Cardiac Failure," *Br Heart J* 72 (1994): S3.

J. He, L. G. Ogden, L. A. Bazzano, et al., "Risk Factors for Congestive Heart Failure in U.S. Men and Women: NHANES I Epidemiologic Follow-Up Study," *Arch Intern Med* 161 (2001): 996.

M. Gheorghiade, R. O. Bonow, "Chronic Heart Failure in the United States: A Manifestation of Coronary Artery Disease," *Circulation* 97 (1998): 282.

B. M. Massie and N. B. Shah, "Evolving Trends in the Epidemiologic Factors of Heart Failure: Rationale for Preventive Strategies and Comprehensive Disease Management," *Am Heart J* 133 (1997): 703.

S. Kenchaiah, J. C. Evans, D. Levy, et al., "Obesity and the Risk of Heart Failure," *N Engl J Med* 347 (2002): 305.

S. H. Rahimtoola, M. D. Cheitlin, and A. M. Hutter Jr., "Cardiovascular Disease in the Elderly: Valvular and Congenital Heart Disease," *J Am Coll Cardiol* 10 (1987): 60A.

A. Kalogeropoulos, V. Georgiopoulou, S. B. Kritchevsky, et al., "Epidemiology of Incident Heart Failure in a Contemporary Elderly Cohort: The Health, Aging, and Body Composition Study," *Arch Intern Med* 169 (2009): 708.

S. Baldasseroni, C. Opasich, M. Gorini, et al., "Left Bundle-Branch Block Is Associated with Increased One-Year Sudden and Total Mortality Rate in 5517 Outpatients with Congestive Heart Failure: A Report from the Italian Network on Congestive Heart Failure," *Am Heart J* 143 (2002): 398.

G. M. Felker, R. E. Thompson, J. M. Hare, et al., "Underlying Causes and Long-Term Survival in Patients with Initially Unexplained Cardiomyopathy," *N Engl J Med* 342 (2000): 1077.

K. Sliwa, A. Damasceno, and B.M. Mayosi. "Epidemiology and Etiology of Cardiomyopathy in Africa," *Circulation* 112 (2005): 3577.

S. Stewart, D. Wilkinson, C. Hansen, et al., "Predominance of Heart Failure in the Heart of Soweto Study Cohort: Emerging Challenges for Urban African Communities." *Circulation* 118 (2008): 2360.

G. M. Felker, L. K. Shaw, and C. M. O'Connor, "A Standardized Definition of Ischemic Cardiomyopathy for Use in Clinical Research," *J Am Coll Cardiol* 39 (2002): 210.

A. W. Haider, M. G. Larson, S. S. Franklin, et al., "Systolic Blood Pressure, Diastolic Blood Pressure, and Pulse Pressure as Predictors of Risk for Congestive Heart Failure in the Framingham Heart Study," *Ann Intern Med* 138 (2003): 10.

A. M. Richards, M. G. Nicholls, R. W. Troughton, et al., "Antecedent Hypertension and Heart Failure after Myocardial Infarction," *J Am Coll Cardiol* 39 (2002): 1182.

J. P. Hellermann, T. Y. Goraya, S. J. Jacobsen, et al., "Incidence of Heart Failure after Myocardial Infarction: Is It Changing over Time?" *Am J Epidemiol* 157 (2003): 1101.

R. S. Velagaleti, M. J. Pencina, J. M. Murabito, et al., "Long-Term Trends in the Incidence of Heart Failure after Myocardial Infarction," *Circulation* 118 (2008): 2057.

T. Fall, S. Hägg, R. Mägi, et al., "The Role of Adiposity in Cardiometabolic Traits: A Mendelian Randomization Analysis," *PLoS Med* 10 (2013): e1001474.

C. W. Yancy, M. Jessup, B. Bozkurt, et al., "2013 ACCF/AHA Guideline for the Management of Heart Failure: Executive Summary: A Report of the American College of Cardiology Foundation/American Heart Association Task Force on Practice Guidelines," *Circulation* 128 (2013): 1810.

F. Gueyffier, C. Bulpitt, J. P. Boissel, et al., "Antihypertensive Drugs in Very Old People: A Subgroup Meta-Analysis of Randomised Controlled Trials: INDANA Group," *Lancet* 353 (1999): 793.

The SOLVD Investigators, "Effect of Enalapril on Mortality and the Development of Heart Failure in Asymptomatic Patients with Reduced Left Ventricular Ejection Fractions," *N Engl J Med* 327 (1992): 685.

R. Garg and S. Yusuf, "Overview of Randomized Trials of Angiotensin-Converting Enzyme Inhibitors on Mortality and Morbidity in Patients with Heart Failure: Collaborative Group on ACE Inhibitor Trials," *JAMA* 273 (1995): 1450.

7. "Epidemiology and Risk Profile of Heart Failure," *Nat Rev Cardiol* 8, no. 1 (January 2011): 30–41. Published online November 9, 2010. doi:10.1038/nrcardio.2010.165; www.ncbi.nlm.nih.gov/pmc/articles/PMC3033496/.

8. Heart failure patients are one of the leading groups in acute chronic diseases, 21% of inpatient and 55% of outpatient spend overall: www.imshealth.com/deployedfiles/ims/Global/Content/Insights/IMS%20Institute%20for%20Healthcare%20Informatics/Healthcare%20Spending/Insurance_Report_Brief.pdf and www.commonwealthfund.org/~/media/files/publications/issue-brief/2014/aug/1764_hong_caring_for_high_need_high_cost_patients_ccm_ib.pdf.

9. Sources:
http://circoutcomes.ahajournals.org/content/4/1/68.abstract; http://circoutcomes.ahajournals.org/content/4/2/143.extract; and http://circoutcomes.ahajournals.org/content/8/Suppl_2/A250.abstract.

Also, in particular: Circulation: Cardiovascular Quality and Outcomes. 2011; 4: 143-145. doi: 10.1161/CIRCOUTCOMES.111.960641; and European Society of Cardiology: "What Are the Costs of Heart Failure," *Europace* 13 (2001): ii13–ii17. doi: 10.1093/europace/eur081, European Society of Cardiology.

www.ncbi.nlm.nih.gov/pmc/articles/PMC3682396/ as well as: "Heart Failure Epidemiology: European Perspective," *Curr Cardiol Rev* 9, no. 2 (May 2013): 123–127.

Published online 2013 May. doi: 10.2174/1573403X11309020005, http://intl-europace.oxfordjournals.org/content/europace/13/suppl_2/ii13.full.pdf, and Internal Accenture Analysis.

10. The pharmaceutical industry has a code of conduct that addresses these issues directly: www.phrma.org/sites/default/files/pdf/phrma_marketing_code_2008-1.pdf; these exist in every developed economy, for example in the United Kingdom: www.pmcpa.org.uk/thecode/InteractiveCode2015/Pages/clause18

.aspx; and example of comparable legislation versus self-regulation in Australia: www.austlii.edu.au/au/legis/cth/bill_em/tgatb2013540/memo_0.html.

11. Results of the pilot study can be found at: "Heart Failure Care Delivery Models (HFCDM) – En lösning för förbättrad och effektivare vård för hjärtsviktspatienter vid Karolinska Universitetssjukhuset."

12. 2011 Statistics Sweden: www.visitstockholm.com/Global/About%20Us/ Publikationer/Facts%20about%20business%20in%20Stockholm%202012 %20%281%29.pdf.

13. www.advisory.com/daily-briefing/2013/08/12/medtronic-branches-into-chronic-condition-management.

14. http://newsroom.medtronic.com/phoenix.zhtml?c=251324&p=irol-newsArticle&ID=1961261   and   http://newsroom.medtronic.com/ phoenix.zhtml?c=251324&p=irol-newsArticle&id=1851106.
www.forbes.com/sites/theapothecary/2013/08/24/medtronic-is-changing-its-business-will-the-system-let-it/; www.advisory.com/daily-briefing/2013/ 08/12/medtronic-branches-into-chronic-condition-management.

15. http://newsroom.medtronic.com/phoenix.zhtml?c=251324&p=irol-news Article&ID=1961261 and http://newsroom.medtronic.com/phoenix .zhtml?c=251324&p=irol-newsArticle&id=1851106.
www.forbes.com/sites/theapothecary/2013/08/24/medtronic-is-changing-its-business-will-the-system-let-it/.

16. www.hhs.gov/ocr/privacy/hipaa/understanding/coveredentities/De-identification/guidance.html and "Strategies for De-Identification and Anonymization of Electronic Health Record Data for Use in Multicenter Research Studies," *Med Care* 50 Suppl (July 2012): S82-S101. doi:10.1097/ MLR.0b013e3182585355; also found at: www.ncbi.nlm.nih.gov/pubmed/ 22692265.

17. An example of this is the United HealthCare and provider system-backed entity, SharedClarity: http://sharedclarity.net; www.modernhealthcare .com/article/20140303/NEWS/302259955; www.mddionline.com/article/ boston-scientific-loses-out-medtronic-and-abbott-sharedclarity-stent-contracts.

18. A major financial investment by Around-the-Patient Innovators Roche with Foundation Medicine: www.forbes.com/sites/matthewherper/2015/ 01/12/roche-spends-1-03-billion-for-majority-stake-in-cancer-genomics-firm/.

19. A classic view of the power of product adjacencies aligned to current customers appeared in *Harvard Business Review*, December 2003, "Growth Outside the Core" by Chris Zook and James Allen: https://hbr.org/2003/12/ growth-outside-the-core.

20. See Medtronic 2015 JP Morgan Healthcare Conference public announcement and presentation: http://investorrelations.medtronic.com/phoenix .zhtml?c=76126&p=irol-calendarpast.

CHAPTER 7: THE NEW HEALTH DIGITALS

1. Doctors Survey 2015 Six-Country Full Detail Report; summary may be seen at: https://www.accenture.com/no-en/insight-accenture-doctors-survey-2015-healthcare-it-pain-progress.aspx.

2. http://data.worldbank.org/indicator/SH.XPD.TOTL.ZS/countries?display =default.

3. For a summary of Apple R&D spend, see: www.aboveavalon.com/notes/2015/5/3/significant-rd-increase-suggests-apple-is-working-on-something-big.

4. http://fortune.com/2014/11/17/top-10-research-development/; www .engadget.com/2014/10/16/google-randd-growth/; and http://ycharts.com/companies/GOOG/r_and_d_expense.

5. For R&D budgets of major pharmaceutical companies: http://fortune.com/2014/11/17/top-10-research-development/.

6. This is changing with the new Alphabet parent entity of Google (www.abc .xyz)—but not reported as of the writing of this book.

7. Google 2014 10-k: www.sec.gov/Archives/edgar/data/1288776/000128877615000008/goog2014123110-k.htm.

8. www.gv.com/2014/.

9. Discussions of the Epic and Apple HealthKit initiative: www.medical newstoday.com/articles/295230.php; www.informationweek.com/healthcare/mobile-and-wireless/apple-partners-with-epic-mayo-clinic-for-healthkit/d/d-id/1269371.

10. There are numerous discussions of clinician's preference for iOS and iPhone and its relative share of 85 percent: www.forbes.com/sites/dandiamond/2014/09/12/iphone-6-one-third-of-doctors-might-buy-it-by-thanksgiving/; http://mobihealthnews.com/32232/in-depth-mobile-adoption-among-us-physicians/; www.engadget.com/2013/06/04/physicians-who-use-mobile-apps-prefer-iphones-and-ipads/.

11. https://itunes.apple.com/us/app/mychart/id382952264?mt=8; www. modernhealthcare.com/article/20150205/NEWS/302059938; http://mobihealthnews.com/34568/apple-picks-13-apps-for-people-with-diabetes/; https://support.apple.com/en-us/HT203037.

12. See https://aws.amazon.com/health/providers-and-insurers/; and https://aws .amazon.com/health/providers-and-insurers/partners/.

13. A overview of these trends was featured in a PBS documentary: www.pbs .org/program/rx-quiet-revolution/.

14. http://mobihealthnews.com/46764/philips-dutch-medical-center-salesforce-announce-diabetes-monitoring-app/

15. www.careinnovations.com/about/.

16. http://news.careinnovations.com/press-releases/intel-ge-care-innovations-partners-with-the-front-porch-center-for-innovation-and-wellbeing-to-test-telehealth-with-senior-living-residents.

17. Formal announcement of scope of J&J and IBM Watson Health collaboration: www-03.ibm.com/press/us/en/pressrelease/46582.wss#release.

18. With a focus on clinical outcomes, precision medicine, and individualization of care and "value" to the health systems: http://newsroom.medtronic.com/phoenix .zhtml?c=251324&p=irol-newsArticle&ID=2034597; www.forbes.com/sites/ matthewherper/2015/04/13/ibm-announces-deals-with-apple-johnson-johnson-and-medtronic-in-bid-to-transform-health-care/.

19. https://www.epocrates.com/who/media/news/press-releases/athenahealth-completes-acquisition-epocrates.

20. Qualcomm Life creates sets of technologies that enable integrated solutions across partnered technology companies and their customers: www .qualcommlife.com/ecosystem; https://www.qualcomm.com/news/releases/ 2015/01/05/qualcomm-announces-new-connected-health-collaboration-walgreens.

21. http://mobihealthnews.com/22092/qualcomm-life-acquires-healthycircles-former-microsoft-health-execs-startup/.

22. www.qualcommlife.com/qualcomm-acquires-capsule-technologie and http:// mobihealthnews.com/46734/qualcomm-life-acquires-capsule-moving-it-into-in-hospital-medical-device-connectivity/

23. www.prnewswire.com/news-releases/qualcomm-life-announces-new-connected-health-collaborations-at-connect-2015-300134862.html.

24. See: http://news.bostonscientific.com/2015-08-03-Boston-Scientific-Announces-Equity-Investment-And-Sales Cooperation-Agreement-With-Preventice-Solutions; and www.preventice.com/about-us/overview/.

25. For a recent discussion of past, current, and alternative economics of digitals within the app stores and streaming businesses, see a recent article in *The Financial Times*: www.ft.com/intl/cms/s/0/01a151fc-0b8b-11e5-8937-00144feabdc0.html#slide0.

26. Patient advocacy and peer sites where treatment strategies and experiences are shared have become a more important part of the consumer/patients' life and infrastructure for managing their disease: www.healthline.com/health-news/social-media-connects-patients-021314#1; https://www.patientslikeme .com.

27. The mobile app for physicians, Doximity, is increasingly working to integrate across care teams and allow for physicians to get peer consults on specific patient cases: www.news-medical.net/news/20150618/Doximity-Society-of-Hospital-Medicine-team-up-to-better-serve-US-hospitalists.aspx.

28. Healthcare will be one of the applications that will accelerate value in the Internet of things (IoT): www.forbes.com/sites/tjmccue/2015/04/22/117-billion-market-for-internet-of-things-in-healthcare-by-2020/; www.himss .org/News/NewsDetail.aspx?ItemNumber=40536; www.aging.scnate.gov/ imo/media/doc/Intel%20-%20IoT-Healthcare%20Policy%20Principles %20FINAL%207-25-14%20%20(3).pdf; Big Data at Center of Disruptive Technologies, McKinsey Global Institute (May 2013): www.mckinsey .com/insights/business_technology/disruptive_technologies.

29. For example, Qualcomm Life and Roche partnered for remote monitoring: www.meddeviceonline.com/doc/qualcomm-roche-ink-remote-patient-monitoring-partnership-0001.

30. Most long-term planning is focused on new markets or new platforms—for example, will Apple be offering a new generation AppleTV as a subscription and gaming platform, autonomous vehicles, and HomeKit as platforms.

31. www.pewinternet.org/2015/04/01/us-smartphone-use-in-2015/.

32. https://fiber.google.com/newcities/.

33. Google X has advanced a smart contact lens with Novartis, advanced diabetes management analytics, and tools and diagnostics with Sanofi and Joslyn Diabetes Center, Boston. www.firstwordpharma.com/node/1311128#axzz3kZd9n1CB.

34. http://www.fastcompany.com/3054352/elasticity/google-life-sciences-rebrands-as-verily-uses-big-data-to-figure-out-why-we-get-si. (As this book went to press, Google Life Sciences had rebranded as Verily, emphasizing its focus on understanding "health" to its fullest possible extent.)

35. See Google's "Ten Things We Know to Be True." www.google.com/about/company/philosophy/.

36. www.businessinsider.com/apple-suppliers-trading-strategy-2013-11; http://money.cnn.com/2015/05/29/investing/apple-suppliers-stocks/.

37. A *zaibatsu* versus a *keiretsu* because of tight control coming back to a single point versus a confederated approach.

38. https://www.aprecia.com/zipdose-platform/zipdose-technology.php and www.sciencealert.com/the-fda-has-just-approved-the-first-3d-printed-drug.

39. www.sciencealert.com/the-fda-has-just-approved-the-first-3d-printed-drug.

CHAPTER 8: TOWARD A NEW MODEL OF COLLABORATION AND COMPETITION

1. For examples of these criteria, see United States at: www.phrma.org/sites/default/files/pdf/phrma_marketing_code_2008-1.pdf and http://oig.hhs.gov/fraud/docs/complianceguidance/042803pharmacymfgnonfr.pdf; and United Kingdom at http://efpia.eu/calendar/113/22/Pharma-Compliance-2014 and www.abpi.org.uk/our-work/library/guidelines/Pages/default.aspx.

2. Examples of health payers acquiring or exclusively partnered with clinical practices are increasing: www.modernhealthcare.com/article/20120102/MAGAZINE/301029918; in addition there are health providers that are acquiring payer entities: https://www.nhp.org/pressreleases1/NHP-Partners MediaFactsheet.pdf.

3. The historical challenges of R&D productivity are well covered in the management literature of the pharmaceutical and biopharmaceutical industry. Recent summaries include: Fabio Pammolli, "The Productivity Crisis in Pharmaceutical R&D," *Nature Reviews Drug Discovery* 10 (June 2011): 428–438. doi:10.1038/nrd3405, and www.nature.com/nrd/journal/v14/n7/full/nrd4650.html.

4. For a full development and overview of the functioning of one such ecosystem cluster, see: www.massbio.org/writable/editor_files/impact_2020_full_report_04032014_email.pdf (link as of July 29, 2015).

5. Recent analyses and commentary point to the increase in specialty therapeutics driving up aggregate costs under both the pharmacy and medical benefit portions of reimbursement payments (U.S. model referenced here), see: https://www.imshealth.com/deployedfiles/imshealth/Global/North%20America/United%20States/Managed%20Markets/5-29-14%20Specialty_Drug_Trend_Whitepaper_Hi-Res.pdf and http://lab.express-scripts.com/drug-trend-report/.

6. The legal aspects of healthcare collaborations can be very complex. The authors encourage readers considering collaborations between health providers, life science companies, and health payers to consult legal counsel knowledgeable about the institutions and regions in consideration. For relationships between pharmaceutical companies and health providers it is common that the collaboration be submitted to a "fair market value assessment (FMV)" that evaluates the value of technologies or services exchanged and investments made to ensure that it avoids being considered an "inducement" where the exchange may influence product selections, volume purchase, or relative market share. See "OIG Compliance Program Guidance for Pharmaceutical Manufacturers": http://oig.hhs.gov/authorities/docs/03/050503FRCPGPharmac.pdf

   For a health provider perspective, see: www.modernhealthcare.com/article/20130921/MAGAZINE/309219995.

7. Details of the joint Novartis/NHS-Wales joint lung cancer and heart failure program, announced on August 24, 2015, can be found at: www.wales.nhs.uk/sitesplus/888/page/83025.

8. http://hitconsultant.net/2015/06/16/philips-wmchealth-announce-500m-partnership-transform-patient-care/.

9. www.businesscloudnews.com/2015/06/04/philips-health-cloud-lead-privacy-compliance-upgradability-shaping-iot-architecture/.

10. For quote from WBCHealth president and CEO Michael Israel, see: www.healthcare-informatics.com/news-item/philips-wmchealth-partner-500m-deal.

11. https://www.regenstrief.org/cbmi/areas-excellence/drug-safety/merck-partnership/.

12. www.jpost.com/Health-and-Science/Maccabi-Health-Services-shares-database-with-Merck-325676.

13. Intel formed a multicenter collaboration for interpreting molecular data from cancer and other complex diseases: https://www.genomeweb.com/informatics/ohsu-intel-collaborate-cancer-and-complex-disease-research; www.bio-itworld.com/2015/9/2/intel-joins-cancer-centers-build-secure-networks-patient-data-sharing.html; and http://fortune.com/2015/08/19/intel-details-cancer-cloud/.

14. Refers to Health Insurance Portability and Accountability Act that was passed by Congress in 1996, which provided for specific protections of personal health data.

15. Z. D. Stephens, S. Y. Lee, F. Faghri, R. H. Campbell, C. Zhai, et al., "Big Data: Astronomical or Genomical?" *PLoS Biol,* 13, no. 7(2015): e1002195. doi:10.1371/journal.pbio.1002195   http://journals.plos.org/plosbiology/article?id=10.1371/journal.pbio.1002195.

16. www.fiercebigdata.com/story/accenture-duke-university-partner-advanced-analytics-development/2015-08-17,   andhttps://newsroom.accenture.com/news/accenture-and-duke-university-collaborate-on-analytics-research.htm.

17. http://trinetx.com.

18. i2b2, Informatics for Integrating Biology and the Bedside, is an NIH-funded National Center for Biomedical Computing based at Partners HealthCare System (https://www.i2b2.org).

19. A brilliant example of this is the Multiple Myeloma Research Consortium: http://themmrc.org/about/the-mmrc-model. It runs a technology platform that integrates all data and supports intra-consortium collaborations:

    Overarching Model: http://themmrc.org/about/the-mmrc-model/.

    Board: http://themmrc.org/about/leadership/board-of-directors/.

    www.themmrf.org/about-mmrf/.

    https://research.themmrf.org.

    Trials Model: www.themmrf.org/research-partners/the-commpass-study/.

    Tissue Banking: http://themmrc.org/drug-development-efforts/myeloma-tissue-bank/.

    Project review committee: http://themmrc.org/about/leadership/project-review-committee/.

    Others examples include the NY Genome Center: www.nygenome.org/; Pfizer-funded Insulin Resistance Pathway consortium: ww.pfizer.com/news/press-release/press-release-detail/pfizer_enters_into_research_consortium_-to_expand_understanding_of_diabetes_and_obesity_pathobiology; and the CLL Research Consortium: http://cll.ucsd.edu/.

20. We are now seeing this change as the American Society of Clinical Oncologists (ASCO) initiate their CancerLinQ program for advancing insights and new treatment approaches for the most devastating cancers or health provider and venture funded start-ups such as Health Catalyst.

21. For one example, see the joint entity created by United HealthCare, Dignity Health, and others called SharedClarity: http://sharedclarity.net/studies/.

22. Network design in the era of digital operations and businesses is becoming an important specialization. Classically, hub-and-spoke networks were the dominant design—one major node and many different branches. If the hub fails, accidently or intentionally, the entire network can be compromised or collapsed. By contrast, mesh networks are self-healing, with another node taking the place of a failed one. There is valuable and secure anonymity in that nodes can come and go, assume roles, and relegate roles as they like. They have the quality of pervasiveness in that the network routes around

dead nodes or other blocks. They are also highly efficient, simple, and inexpensive. See: www.technologyreview.com/fromtheeditor/404601/from-the-editor-mesh-networking-matters/; www.wired.com/2014/01/its-time-to-take-mesh-networks-seriously-and-not-just-for-the-reasons-you-think/; and www.economist.com/node/1176136.

23. Pathway biological systems are foundations to human biology, protection of health, and for intervening on diseases. For more, see: *Nature Reviews Genetics* 5 (November 2004): 826–837. doi:10.1038/nrg1471; *Genome Inform* 16, no. 1(2005): 192–202; and https://www.genome.gov/27530687.

24. https://www.qualcomm.com/news/releases/2015/08/31/qualcomm-life-announces-new-connected-health-collaborations-connect-2015.

25. www.eweek.com/small-business/qualcomm-life-partners-with-davita-healthcare-p2link.html and https://www.qualcomm.com/news/releases/2015/08/31/qualcomm-life-announces-new-connected-health-collaborations-connect-2015.

26. https://www.qualcomm.com/news/releases/2015/01/29/roche-and-qualcomm-collaborate-innovate-remote-patient-monitoring.

27. www.drxcapital.com.

28. https://qualcommventures.com/blog/catalyzing-digital-medicine-introducing-drx-capital-a-joint-novartis-and-qualcomm-investment-company/ and www.fiercebiotechit.com/story/novartis-teams-qualcomm-100m-digital-health-fund/2015-01-19.

29. www.fiercecro.com/story/novartis-adds-qualcomm-its-list-trial-partners/2015-01-12 and www.fiercemedicaldevices.com/story/novartis-ppd-conduct-clinical-pilot-study-using-medical-device-connectivity/2015-07-16.

30. http://investors.foundationmedicine.com/releasedetail.cfm?ReleaseID=905240.

31. For another Novartis and Qualcomm joint venture example, see: www.fiercebiotechit.com/node/16781/print

32. See Accenture's research on patient-centric supply chains, *Push to Pull: From Supply Chains to Patient-Centric Value Networks*, 2015: https://www.accenture.com/t20150626T013813__w__/us-en/_acnmedia/Accenture/Conversion-Assets/DotCom/Documents/Global/PDF/Indurties_17/Accenture-Life-Sciences-Push-to-Pull.pdf.

33. www.research.ibm.com/cognitive-computing/watson/watsonpaths.shtml#fbid=Bg4SvM632Ne and https://www-03.ibm.com/press/us/en/pressrelease/46768.wss.

34. www.forbes.com/sites/brucejapsen/2015/07/30/cvs-and-ibms-watson-partner-to-predict-patient-health-needs/.

35. http://newsroom.medtronic.com/phoenix.zhtml?c=251324&p=irol-newsArticle&ID=2034597.

36. www.forbes.com/sites/matthewherper/2015/04/13/ibm-announces-deals-with-apple-johnson-johnson-and-medtronic-in-bid-to-transform-health-care/.

37. www.investor.jnj.com/releasedetail.cfm?ReleaseID=913244.

38. http://fortune.com/2015/09/02/salesforce-health-cloud-healthcare/.

39. https://newsroom.accenture.com/news/accenture-helps-life-sciences-companies-improve-patient-support-with-launch-of-the-accenture-intelligent-patient-platform.htm.

40. www.businesscloudnews.com/2015/06/04/philips-health-cloud-lead-privacy-compliance-upgradability-shaping-iot-architecture/.

41. The Philips consumer offering was announced but not launched as of this writing, and was scheduled for October in Germany at the Internationale Funkausstellung and then other international markets in 2016. www.firstwordpharma.com/node/1312781#axzz3l3RXjJMS.

42. http://appleinsider.com/articles/15/06/25/with-iphone-apple-watch-apple-playing-a-key-role-in-consumerization-of-healthcare.

43. https://aws.amazon.com/economics/, www.forbes.com/sites/ciocentral/2015/06/10/the-economics-of-cloud-computing-are-in-a-word-confusing/2/.

44. https://www.accenture.com/ke-en/insight-digital-supply-network-modern-supply-chain-management.aspx.

45. See Digital Operating Model, Accenture research: https://www.accenture.com/ke-en/insight-digital-operating-model-summary.

46. For a detailed vignette on across-regional and within-regional growth of Uber, see: www.theatlantic.com/business/archive/2015/01/is-uber-a-middle-class-job-creator-or-not/384763/; and http://talkingpointsmemo.com/edblog/understanding-the-economics-of-uber.

47. For an excellent overview of Uber economics and disruption of markets, see: http://bruegel.org/2014/09/the-economics-of-uber/.

48. www.economist.com/news/business/21654068-taxi-hailing-company-likely-disrupt-delivery-business-driving-hard.

49. Uber actively recruits advanced data scientists to its dynamic pricing engine: identifying and predicting city specific traffic, travel, and demand patterns; optimizing the assignment process of matching/dispatching drivers to riders; and matching multiple riders to a driver. It is an entirely digital operating model. https://www.uber.com/jobs/45370.

50. www.wsj.com/articles/google-touts-mobile-ad-technology-1432220552.

51. www.wired.com/2015/06/apples-support-ad-blocking-will-upend-web-works/.

52. www.theatlantic.com/technology/archive/2015/01/the-app-economy-is-now-bigger-than-hollywood/384842/; and www.ft.com/cms/s/0/d3aacf38-1cb8-11e4-88c3-00144feabdc0.html#axzz3kzaAPFwE.

53. Interview in FT.com, August 6, 2014: www.ft.com/cms/s/0/d3aacf38-1cb8-11e4-88c3-00144feabdc0.html#ixzz3kzbGD8wv.

54. Some readers may not be familiar with the terms *zaibatsu* and *keiretsu*. For that reason, we provide a brief definition: *Zaibatsu* is a large conglomeration of companies with interlocking ownership with a single entity or family at the center. The *keiretsu* is an informal vertical monopoly, where the company in control may not own the other companies—rather there are likely highly interdependent suppliers. *Zaibatsu* were highly coordinated and created high

value for the whole. The *keiretsu* had far less economically beneficial relationships but greater independence and operating autonomy.

55. Source: Multiple Accenture research studies: *Your Customers, Your Compass*, Accenture, 2015; *B2B Customer Experience: Start Playing to Win and Stop Playing Not to Lose*, Accenture, 2014; and *Customer 2020: Are You Future-Ready or Reliving the Past?* Accenture, 2015.

56. Source: Accenture Research; "Your Customers, Your Compass," Accenture, 2015; "B2B Customer Experience: Start Playing to Win and Stop Playing Not to Lose," Accenture, 2014; and "Customer 2020: Are You Future-Ready or Reliving the Past?" Accenture, 2015.

57. https://developer.apple.com/library/ios/documentation/Swift/Conceptual/Swift_Programming_Language/.

58. Early rumors indicated an interest by Uber in certain cities for autonomous vehicles, see: www.theguardian.com/technology/2015/sep/17/uber-well-ease-the-transition-to-self-driving-cars; http://techcrunch.com/2015/09/18/autonomous-cars-break-uber/#.pzlxqs:YqB1; and www.govtech.com/fs/perspectives/Ubers-Plan-for-Self-Driving-Cars-Bigger-Than-Its-Taxi-Disruption.html. The corresponding rumors also appeared that Tesla with their autonomous cars could see Uber's high-end business as available to them; see: www.cnbc.com/2015/08/17/is-elon-musk-going-to-turn-tesla-into-the-next-uber.html.

59. www.cerner.com/cerner_and_qualcomm_collaborate/ and https://www.orionhealth.com/media-center/news/news/201502182563.

60. https://aws.amazon.com/solutions/case-studies/orion-health/.

61. https://aws.amazon.com/blogs/apn/visit-the-aws-pop-up-loft-for-aws-healthtech-day-thursday-jan-29th/.

62. https://www-03.ibm.com/press/us/en/pressrelease/46768.wss.

63. www.informationweek.com/big-data/big-data-analytics/apple-ibm-partner-for-healthcare-analytics/d/d-id/1319959; and www.forbes.com/sites/matthewherper/2015/04/30/five-big-questions-about-apple-and-ibms-japanese-ipad-giveaway/.

64. http://venturebeat.com/2014/09/17/ehr-giant-epic-explains-how-it-will-bring-apple-healthkit-data-to-doctors/; www.forbes.com/sites/zinamoukheiber/2014/06/04/behind-epic-systems-alliance-with-apple/; and www.modern healthcare.com/article/20150205/NEWS/302059938.

65. "Open Innovation" was a term popularized by Henry Chesbrough, adjunct faculty member at the University of California, Berkeley, Haas School of Business, in *Open Innovation: The New Imperative for Creating and Profiting from Technology* (Cambridge, MA: Harvard Business School Press, 2003); and then subsequently in *Open Business Models: How to Thrive in the New Innovation Landscape* (Cambridge, MA: Harvard Business School Press, 2006); and *Open Services Innovation: Rethinking Your Business to Grow and Compete in a New Era* (San Francisco: Jossey-Bass, January 2011). Also see: http://openinnovation.net/category/henry-chesbrough/.

CHAPTER 9: TALENT STRATEGY FOR THE NEW HEALTHCARE ECOSYSTEM

1. http://blogs.wsj.com/cio/2014/08/21/dell-cio-andi-karaboutis-leaving-for-biotech-firm-biogen/.

2. www.fiercepharmamarketing.com/story/sanofi-aims-outcomes-brand-new-chief-patient-officer/2014-03-31.

3. Source: http://social.eyeforpharma.com/column/soldier-patients-will.

4. FTE is the abbreviation for Full-Time Equivalent: a standard measure for number of employees required to complete a certain task or type of work.

5. For a detailed overview of hiring at Google, as one example, see: www.wired.com/2015/04/hire-like-google/.

6. For a discussion of the need for a new profile of talent within the Australian healthcare and public service sectors, see: https://www.accenture.com/t20150527T210433__w__/au-en/_acnmedia/Accenture/Conversion-Assets/DotCom/Documents/Local/en-gb/PDF/Accenture-Now-Hiring-Public-Entrepreneurs.pdf#zoom=50.

7. Attracting and retaining data scientists in particular requires having an "analytics" and "data stewardship" emphasis in decision making, business processes, and technology tools. For a description of this, see: www.fastcompany.com/3050005/the-coming-war-for-data-scientists-and-how-to-win-it and www.cio.com/article http://bits.blogs.nytimes.com/2013/11/12/program-seeks-to-nurture-data-science-culture-at-universities/?_r=0/2971624/it-strategy/an-analytics-culture-change-needs-strong-data-stewards.html. For a comparable view on digital talent, see: www.mckinsey.com/insights/strategy/raising_your_digital_quotient, www.talentculture.com/workplace-culture-and-innovation/bottom-up-leadership-and-digital-skills-training/, www.egonzehnder.com/leadership-insights/destination-digital-finding-and-building-the-talent-to-get-there.html, and www.forbes.com/sites/homaycotte/2015/04/07/cdo-you-say-chief-digital-officer-i-say-chief-data-officer/.

8. For a classical development of this, see: *Levers of Control: How Managers Use Innovative Control Systems to Drive . . .* by Robert Simons (Cambridge, MA: Harvard Business Press, 1995); work by Chris Argyris, one example being "Teaching Smart People How to Learn," *Harvard Business Review*, May–June 1991; and C. Argyris and D. A. Schön, *Organizational Learning: A Theory of Action Perspective* (Reading, MA: Addison-Wesley, 1978).

9. The Swiss pharmaceutical company Novartis provides numerous examples of this. In one such case Joe Jimenez, Novartis CEO, is quoted within a healthcare provider publication on their goal of enabling new ways of working and value-based reimbursement: www.beckershospitalreview.com/healthcare-information-technology/novartis-ag-uses-tech-to-rebrand-itself.html; Novartis Pharma head David Epstein further notes this with respect to the pending launch of their new heart failure therapeutic: www.reuters.com/article/2015/06/30/us-novartis-heart-idUSKCN0PA1N720150630.

10. For a formal development of one methodology now, see ChangeTracker in Christina Kirsch, John Chelliah, and Warren Parry, "Drivers of Change: A Contemporary Model," *Journal of Business Strategy* 32, no. 2 (2011): 13–20; and https://www.accenture.com/us-en/service-accenture-change-tracking-overview.aspx.

CHAPTER 10: A NEW AGE OF HEALTHCARE—PLACING PATIENT AND VALUE AT THE CENTER

1. There are two ways to look at spending—the proportion of total household spending on healthcare and the proportion of total healthcare spending (16 to 18 percent of GDP made by households versus governments and private payers). Household spending: www.bls.gov/news.release/cesan.nr0.htm; total proportion of spending by households: in 2013, households accounted for the largest share of spending (28 percent), followed by the federal government (26 percent), private businesses (21 percent), and state and local governments (17 percent). https://www.cms.gov/research-statistics-data-and-systems/statistics-trends-and-reports/nationalhealthexpenddata/downloads/highlights.pdf.

2. The productivity or losses from high healthcare spending is a persistent topic of research and debate. One recent overview that surveys multiple public sources is: http://aspe.hhs.gov/health/reports/08/healthcarecost/report.pdf. As an illustration of the range of discussions prompted by recent American Hospital Association reports, see: www.modernhealthcare.com/article/20150413/news/304139979.

3. We covered U.S. and European health reform changes in detail in Chapter 2 and throughout this book. Recent reforms in Japan that look to improve coverage and value can be found at: www.japantimes.co.jp/news/2015/06/02/national/science-health/experts-doubt-shift-generic-drugs-best-prescription-health-care-system/#.VfSmZbRbv6Q; www.mofa.go.jp/policy/page3e_000089.html; www.japantoday.com/category/politics/view/abe-pledges-to-carry-out-sweeping-reforms; and McKinsey Global Institute, *The Future of Japan: Reigniting Productivity and Growth*, March 2015, 13–14.

4. With rates of hospital-acquired infections remaining at 1 in 25 across settings, there is an increased emphasis of avoiding or minimizing exposure. See http://health.gov/hcq/prevent-hai.asp; www.ncbi.nlm.nih.gov/books/NBK2683/; www.ncbi.nlm.nih.gov/pmc/articles/PMC3963198/; and the debate in http://articles.mercola.com/sites/articles/archive/2014/04/09/hospital-acquired-infections.aspx.

5. See converging technologies for healthcare providers and patients: www.healthcareitnews.com/news/apple-injects-health-features-watch; www.cnet.com/news/health-care-app-uses-apple-watch-to-id-doctors-follow-privacy-law/; https://www.klick.com/health/news/blog/strategy/will-apple-tv-become-the-next-web-browser/; and http://appleinsider.com/articles/15/04/01/apple-

and-ibm-unveil-8-new-mobilefirst-ios-apps-new-healthcare-and-industrial-products-categories.

6. www.healthit.gov/providers-professionals/patient-participation; www.healthit .gov/patients-families; www.ahrq.gov/sites/default/files/wysiwyg/research/ findings/factsheets/patient-centered/ria-issue5/ria-issue6.pdf; and www .healthaffairs.org/healthpolicybriefs/brief.php?brief_id=86.

7. The concept of digital medicines is advancing and getting increasingly better definition: www.businesswire.com/news/home/20150910005497/ en/U.S.-FDA-Accepts-Digital-Medicine-Drug-Application#.VfWU2LRbv6Q; www.cnbc.com/2014/10/20/digital-medicine-high-tech-health-care-on-the-way.html; D. Steinberg, "Building a Business Model in Digital Medicine," *Nature Biotechnology* 33 (2015): 910–920. doi:10.1038/nbt.3339, published online September 8, 2015; and www.wsj.com/articles/ SB10001424052702303973704579351080028045594.

8. The value of big and real-world data in R&D is an emerging area of focus and early impact. For more, see: www.mckinsey.com/insights/ health_systems_and_services/how_big_data_can_revolutionize_ pharmaceutical_r_and_d; www.strategyand.pwc.com/media/file/ Revitalizing-pharmaceutical-RD.pdf; and Peter Tormay, "Big Data in Pharmaceutical R&D: Creating a Sustainable R&D Engine," *Pharm Med* 29 (2015): 87–92. doi:10.1007/s40290-015-0090-x.

9. See "From Push to Pull: From Supply Chains to Patient-Centric Value Networks," Accenture Research 2015: https://www.accenture.com/ t20150626T013813__w__/us-en/_acnmedia/Accenture/Conversion-Assets/ DotCom/Documents/Global/PDF/Indurties_17/Accenture-Life-Sciences-Push-to-Pull.pdf.

10. See: http://fortune.com/2015/07/31/uber-valuation-funding-round/ and www.wsj.com/articles/uber-valued-at-more-than-50-billion-1438367457. For the Shared or Share Economy listen to and read: www.forbes.com/ pictures/eeji45emgkh/airbnb-snapgoods-and-12-more-pioneers-of-the-share-economy/; and www.economist.com/news/leaders/21573104-internet-everything-hire-rise-sharing-economy.

11. For a summary, see: www.naic.org/cipr_topics/topic_usage_based_insurance .htm.

12. For discussions of the transition from product to service, see: www.economist. com/node/1288736; www.som.cranfield.ac.uk/som/dinamic-content/media/ Executive%20Briefing%206%20-%20RR%20Totalcare%20-%20Mtg% 20the%20Needs%20of%20Key%20Customers%20%20-%208%20Mar %2010%20v9.pdf; and www.pwc.ca/en/service-support/general-aviation-pay-by-the-hour.

13. Full details are available at: www.computerweekly.com/news/4500253423/ Why-insurer-Axa-is-entering-the-retail-e-commerce-market and http://articles .philly.com/2015-05-02/business/61727626_1_life-insurance-fitbit-term-life.

14. The U.S. government's programs in this area are cited: https://www.medicare .gov/hospitalcompare/linking-quality-to-payment.html and https://www.cms .gov/Medicare/Medicare-Fee-for-Service-Payment/PhysicianFeedbackProgram/

valuebasedpaymentmodifier.html#What%20is%20the%20Value-Based %20Payment%20Modifier%20(Value%20Modifier); in Europe, a 2015 summary from the U.K. parallels the same trends: www.nao.org.uk/wp-content/ uploads/2015/06/Outcome-based-payment-schemes-governments-use-of-payment-by-results.pdf; and a recent overview of the value accessible through outcomes-based payment approaches: http://healthcare.mckinsey.com/sites/default/files/the-trillion-dollar-prize.pdf.

15. See Frampton, et al., "Development and Validation of a Clinical Cancer Genomic Profiling Test Based on Massively Parallel DNA Sequencing," *Nat Biotechnol* 31, no. 11 (November, 2013): 1023-31. doi:10.1038/nbt.2696. Epub 2013 Oct 20., www.ncbi.nlm.nih.gov/pubmed/24142049, and www.foundationmedicine.com/wp-content/uploads/2014/05/Final-FoundationOne-Br.pdf.

16. The Healthcare-Gone-Digital company Philips was moving into consumer-grade health and healthcare personal technologies (https://www.wareable.com/health-and-wellbeing/philips-announces-health-watch-and-other-wellness-gadgets-1624) and the Digital-Gone-Healthcare company, Qualcomm Life, the division of the mobile technologies leader Qualcomm, is moving into hospital and services extension of acute facilities (www.qualcommlife.com/images/pdf/press/HCP_P2link_QCL%20Connect%202015%20Press%20Release_8%2031%2015_FinalPDF.pdf and www.qualcommlife.com/images/pdf/press/NAH_FINAL_Press%20Note_US_Care%20Beyond%20Walls%20and%20Wires%20Expansion%20FINAL.pdf).

17. www.retail-week.com/technology/how-amazon-changed-retailing/5037276.article.

GLOSSARY

1. A excellent recent overview of business model definitions can be found in the *Harvard Business Review* at https://hbr.org/2015/01/what-is-a-business-model.

2. The concept was first introduced in a Harvard Business School working paper: Clayton M. Christensen, Richard Bohmer, John Kenagy, and Jeffrey Elton, "Managing the Disruption of Healthcare," Harvard Business School Working Paper, No. 00-085, June 2000; published in *Harvard Business Review*, September-October 2000, https://hbr.org/2000/09/will-disruptive-innovations-cure-health-care.

3. See V.G. Rodwin, "The Health Care System under French National Health Insurance: Lessons for Health Reform in the United States," *American Journal of Public Health* 93, no. 1 (2003): 31–37, www.npr.org/templates/story/story.php?storyId= 92419273.

4. See www.thelocal.fr/20150331/five-things-to-know-about-frances-healthcare-law, and http://uk.reuters.com/article/2015/03/15/uk-france-reforms-healthcare-idUKKBN0MB0PL20150315.

5. www.nice.org.uk/standards-and-indicators.

6. www.managedcaremag.com/archives/2015/1/should-specialty-drugs-be-shifted-medical-pharmacy-benefit.

7. http://library.ahima.org/xpedio/groups/public/documents/ahima/bok1_049797.hcsp?dDocName=bok1_049797.

8. https://www.cms.gov/outreach-and-education/outreach/partnerships/downloads/11315-p.pdf.

9. www.ihi.org/Topics/TripleAim/Pages/default.aspx.

10. https://www.cms.gov/Medicare/Medicare-Fee-for-Service-Payment/sharedsavingsprogram/index.html?redirect=/sharedsavingsprogram.

11. http://lab.express-scripts.com/insights/drug-options/we-have-to-change-how-we-pay-for-cancer-drugs; www.wsj.com/articles/new-push-ties-cost-of-drugs-to-how-well-they-work-1432684755; and www.fiercepharma.com/story/express-scripts-pushes-pay-performance-cut-cancer-drug-prices/2015-05-27.

12. The area we defined and developed in a groundbreaking research study: Committee on Quality of Health Care in America, Institute of Medicine, *Crossing the Quality Chasm: A New Health System for the 21st Century* (Washington, D.C.: National Academies Press, 2001), ISBN: 0-309-51193-3, 364 pages, 6 x 9; an illustration of these principles can be seen in a study of diabetes management by patients at www.ncbi.nlm.nih.gov/pubmed/15623407; and for an important overview of patient engagement, see www.healthaffairs.org/healthpolicybriefs/brief.php?brief_id=86.

13. www.pcori.org.

About the Authors

Jeff Elton, Ph.D., is a Managing Director in Accenture Strategy, and Global Lead of Accenture Predictive Health Intelligence and Accenture Intelligent Patient Solutions, which are focused on advancing real-world analytics and the next generation of business models for healthcare organizations and companies.

Currently a board member of the Massachusetts Biotechnology Council, Jeff has more than 25 years of experience as a global executive and consultant in the healthcare and life sciences field. Prior to Accenture, Jeff was Senior Vice President of Strategy and Global Chief Operating Officer at Novartis Institutes of BioMedical Research, Inc., founding CEO of an oncology molecular diagnostics and therapeutic pathways company, and founding board member and senior advisor to several early-stage biotechnology companies focused on curing a single disease or on platform technologies focused on curing or facilitating treatment of diseases including Parkinson's, diabetes, and various forms of cancer.

He has also been a partner with McKinsey & Company and adjunct faculty in health sector management at Boston University's Questrom School of Business. Jeff has a Ph.D. and an MBA from The University of Chicago, Booth School of Business.

Anne O'Riordan is the Global Industry Senior Managing Director of Accenture Life Sciences. Based in China since 2007, she has worked throughout Europe, the United States, and Asia for the past 25 years, helping pharmaceutical, medical technology, and consumer health companies rethink, reshape, and restructure their businesses to deliver better patient outcomes. Specifically, her work has included the transformation of both front and back offices including business and IT strategy, sales and marketing optimization, manufacturing and laboratory process, organization and systems change, R&D transformation, business process outsourcing, application outsourcing, and infrastructure transformation on a global, regional, and local level. Over the past 15-plus years she has published numerous articles on business transformation in the life sciences industry.

Anne has been the global lead of Accenture's Life Sciences business since March 2012. From 2009 to 2012, she led the Life Sciences practice for Accenture in Asia. Before and during that period, from 2006 to 2012, she was the global growth and strategy lead for Accenture's Products Operating Group, a role that involved setting the business strategy, executing mergers and acquisitions, and setting up an internal innovation capability to incubate new business services. Prior to living in Asia, Anne was based in London for nine years and led Accenture's European Health and Life Sciences practice. Anne also spent eight years working with pharmaceutical companies in the U.S. marketplace. She has been a member of the Products Operating Group board since 2006.

Anne has a BSc in Biotechnology as well as a postgraduate degree in financial accounting and management information systems (MIS).

Index